MEMO TO THE
PRESIDENT ELECT

Also by Madeleine Albright

Madam Secretary: A Memoir

The Mighty and the Almighty: Reflections on America, God, and World Affairs

Memo to the President Elect

How We Can Restore America's
Reputation and Leadership

Madeleine Albright

with Bill Woodward

HARPER

An Imprint of HarperCollins*Publishers*
www.harpercollins.com

HarperCollins books may be purchased for educational, business, or sales promotional use. For information, please write: Special Markets Department, HarperCollins Publishers, 10 East 53rd Street, New York, NY 10022.

FIRST EDITION

Library of Congress Cataloging-in-Publication Data
    Albright, Madeleine Korbel.
        Memo to the President elect : how we can restore America's reputation and leadership / Madeleine Albright with Bill Woodward. — 1st ed.
            p.   cm.
        Includes bibliographical references and index
        ISBN: 978-0-06-135180-8
        1. United States—Foreign relations—2001–   2. Political leadership.   I. Woodward, William, 1951–   II. Title.
    JZ1480.A955   2008
    327.73—dc22   2007041322

08 09 10 11 12   ov/rrd   10 9 8 7 6 5 4 3 2 1

Dedicated to America's presidents, both good and not-so-good, whose labors on behalf of our country have endowed the office with its rich history, and to the candidates for the White House in 2008, whose willingness to place their records and reputations on the line reflect what leadership demands and democracy is all about

Contents

Prologue

For Americans, the death of a president is traumatic. We mourn together the passing of a man and a piece of our history. In meeting halls across the land, the squalls of partisanship are calmed. Mortality softens our view of one another. Whether in person or vicariously, we file by the casket.

The death of a president led to this book, for it was on January 2, 2007, at a funeral service for Gerald Ford, that I conceived it. The setting was Washington's majestic National Cathedral where, counting Ford, five presidents—members of an exclusive club—were gathered. Also present were six first ladies, members of another exclusive club, which included for the first time an aspirant to membership in both.

Ford is the only president to take the oath without having had his name on a national ballot. He was an unlikely chief executive, known less for his accomplishments than his kindly temperament. He was the kind of politician who might show up for dinner without feeling he had to be the center of attention, the archetypical Middle American, made extraordinary by the office he held.

On this bleak midwinter morning, Ford had no way to avoid the spotlight: newspapers ran stories about his life, cable stations recycled documentaries, former colleagues searched for the right adjectives to sum him up. In the cathedral, the presidents sat in the front pews—Carter, Bush, Clinton, Bush. I wondered if they were thinking of the day when the nation would put aside all else to remember them; it is how our minds work, to think such thoughts at a funeral, whether one has been president or not.

Mindful of the security, I had arrived early. Waiting for the service to begin, I recalled my experience with the future presidents' club. As a student, I had interviewed John Kennedy—then still a senator—for my college newspaper. The only question I remember asking was whether he would give me his autograph; he was happy to oblige. As an adult, I had the privilege of advising a number of Democratic candidates for national office—including Geraldine Ferraro, the first woman to run on the ticket of a major party. All the candidates I counseled were people whom I admired, but even so all but one of them lost, the exception being Bill Clinton, who invited me to serve as secretary of state, the best job I could imagine.

President Ford's memorial service could not have been more traditional—grand old Protestant hymns, fluttering flags, declarations of pride in America, and confidence in that promise of promises: "Whosoever liveth and believeth in me shall never die." It is with words of this nature that we both accept our ending and peer beyond it, acknowledging mortality but preparing for what comes next. Americans especially are in the habit of looking forward. That has certainly been my reflex, which is why the idea came to me even while saying goodbye to an old president that I might compose a memo to a new one.

Motivational speakers tell us that we should learn how to brief the boss in the time it takes to ride an elevator from the tenth floor to the first. A useful skill, but when the boss is about to assume the American presidency, we need more space. A candidate may be able to campaign on a slogan, but a president must govern. You don't learn that on an elevator.

As this is written, we can only guess which candidate will prevail in the 2008 balloting. I write now because we should be considering now, before we vote, the national security puzzles the next president will have to solve. I write as well because I cannot contain my dismay at the direction our current leaders have taken us. It is said that, in his later years, Mark Twain wrote with a pen warmed up in hell; I have noticed steam coming from the keyboard of my laptop. Because I have been trained as a diplomat, my words are usually understated; because I am by nature blunt, my anger at the Bush administration's misreading of America and the world will occasionally burn its way to the surface. More than anger, though, I feel sadness—as do many Americans, regardless of political affiliation—that we have strayed so far from the broad avenues of common sense. That sadness is not confined to us; I was told by one friendly European (and there still are some), "We need for America—the real America—to be back." The next president will determine whether that happens and, if so, what it will mean.

My primary goal in this memo is not to look behind us, but to explore the daunting lineup of challenges that fall under the heading "What is to be done?" On one hand, the president elect will benefit from a nearly universal desire to see someone new in the White House. On the other, he will face a Herculean task in trying to remedy the harm that has been caused to America's well-being and good name.

Before proceeding, a word about gender. When I was in college, books analyzing the executive branch assumed that the president and, for that matter, the secretary of state would be male—presumptions that have become obsolete. Regardless of how this election turns out, a woman president is in our future. In writing prospectively, I had to choose between either the masculine or feminine pronoun in referring to the next president; or, alternatively, I could have used both, as in, "The next president, when in front of photographers, should never lift his or her beagle by the ears." I thought it would be more charitable to the reader to refer to the occupants of high offices by the gender of the incumbent—thus the president is referred to as "he" and the secretary of state as "she." An imperfect solution, but I hope acceptable.

The most common type of memo, at least in Washington, is internal and administrative—outlining, for example, a federal agency's new policy on font preferences or the retention of e-mails. My own interest, however, has been captured by meatier memos, those that seek to explain or persuade and that address issues of weight: war, peace, prosperity, and justice. While UN ambassador, I wrote memos to President Clinton when I thought that the normal decision-making process needed a jolt. The papers were returned with Clinton's comments scribbled on the side of the pages; at times, I felt as if I were back in school when I looked to see what the president had to say. Often, I didn't learn much because Clinton's writing is so tricky to decipher. At least he didn't correct misspellings, as Jimmy Carter meticulously did.

As secretary of state, I occasionally sent highly confidential "night notes," so called because they were transmitted to the White House at the end of the day and retained outside the normal record-keeping system. I ask you to conceive of this book as an extended variation of such a memo, though it is self-evidently not exactly what it purports to be. An actual memo to a president elect would assume that the recipient has a more intimate knowledge of government and history than this does; it would also, in fact, be confidential. The fun is imagining what such a memo would be like, if written free from the fear that it might become public. Thus, if you are offended by the analysis found in the following pages, please play along and pretend you were never allowed to read it in the first place.

The approach I have taken, as you will see, is to tackle the subject of the next presidency in two parts: the first analyzes the various national security tools that will be available to our forty-fourth president—a kind of user's guide to the White House; the second discusses how these instruments might be applied to meet twenty-first-century problems.

Throughout, I stress international policies, not domestic; after all, this is the arena I know. I make no apologies, moreover, for believing that the international aspect of a president's work is the most exciting. This is where the commander in chief has the opportunity to alter history's course and make the leap from national leader to global, from politician to statesperson. It is the international responsibilities of the president that cause people across the globe to follow American elections with more interest, I regret to say, than that shown by some of our own citizens.

Due to the interval between my writing and when the next president takes office, I have had to guess what will happen between the fall of 2007 and the end of 2008. This is nerve-racking because so little can be ruled out—including sudden changes in the leadership of key countries, economic disruptions, flu pandemics, natural disasters, and so on. I am naturally upbeat so I am willing to predict that American democracy will survive the sillier aspects of the campaign—and unwilling to assume another 9/11 or catastrophe of comparable scope. I expect the debate over U.S. policy in Iraq will continue with intensity and that the president will announce troop reductions and mission adjustments, but no definitive end point to our deployments there or in Afghanistan. I believe the Middle East will remain turbulent (the safest of bets) and that Al Qaeda will extend its reach further into Africa and Asia. Energy and environmental security will (properly) dominate discussion of global challenges while Iran's nuclear program though still worrisome will not, as yet, have led to war. Here at home, when U.S. policies go astray, Congress and the White House will blame each other, as will civilians and the military, as will Bush administration officials and former Bush administration officials. The arguments will continue until, finally, everyone agrees to blame the CIA.

In the months that have passed since President Ford's funeral, I have asked friends, colleagues, students, and even a group of former foreign ministers (known as "Madeleine and her exes") what advice they would give to the next president. I did this both in fun and in hopes of hearing ideas good enough to steal. As I found when I was in government, the problem with most advice is that it is better on the "what" than on the "how." We can all look under the hood of a sputtering car and wish that it were repaired, but we do not all know how to take the components apart and reassemble them without creating an even bigger mess. Presidents appreciate being told what they might do, but they need people around them who can show them how to do it.

A second problem with soliciting advice is that it can lead to a too-long list of priorities. At the beginning of each semester, I ask my students at Georgetown to list what they consider to be the most important issues. The classroom blackboard soon bears witness to tribulations ranging from bioterror and cyber-sabotage to infant mortality and the many regional flavors of interreligious strife. The students are instructed to make their own charts in pencil and to follow actual events closely. By the end of the semester their priorities have either been pared down or reversed. Presidents go through the same process. In the beginning, it is hard to rule out any problem-solving initiative; presidents want to do so much. In the end, they hope to be remembered for a few projects that propel events in the right direction.

When I arrived in America, at age eleven, Harry Truman was president. When the next occupant of that office is sworn in, I will be seventy-one. As a girl, I would never have thought to question what Truman said. The president spoke for the USA, the USA stood for truth. I have learned to be more critical, as have Americans generally, some even to the point of becoming disrespectful. Though I don't subscribe to sugarcoating, I do believe we should bear in mind the immense difficulty of the president's job—and the storied history of the office itself. We should understand what we too often forget: presidents are not superhuman but much the same as us—capable of grand gestures and noble aspirations, but also pettiness and preoccupation with self. While not anticipating miracles, I nevertheless hope that the new chief executive will be someone for whom I voted and in whom I can place confidence. I will be primed to cheer on Election Night, wave banners and whoop as if I still were eleven. Whether I am delighted or disappointed by the outcome, however, is irrelevant to this memo, for I know that in any case I will pray for the next president to be as equal to the job as anyone can be. I will want that president to make wise decisions—for my sake and that of my children and grandchildren, for our country and the world.

PART ONE

CHAPTER I

A MANDATE TO LEAD

MEMORANDUM (personal and confidential)

To: The President Elect
From: Madeleine K. Albright
Date: Election Night, 2008

Congratulations on your success. Well done! You have won a great victory. But with that victory comes the responsibility to lead a divided nation in a world riven by conflict and inequity, wounded by hate, bewildered by change, and made anxious by the renewed specter of nuclear Armageddon. In days to come, leaders you've never heard of, from countries you can barely locate, will assure you of their friendship and offer you assistance. My advice is to accept, for you will need help. We Americans like to think of ourselves as exemplars of generosity and virtue, but to many people in many places, we are selfish, imperious, and violent. The voters will want you to transform this perception while also protecting us, defeating our enemies, and securing our economic future—in other words, to do as promised during your campaign.

The president of the United States has been compared to the ruler of the universe, a helmsman on a great sailing ship, the *Mikado*'s Grand Poo-bah, a lonely figure immersed in "splendid misery" (Jefferson's description), and "the personal embodiment [of the] . . . dignity and majesty of the American people" (William Howard Taft's). Students of the office have identified an array of presidential roles: commander in chief, master diplomat, national spokesperson, head administrator, top legislator, party leader, patron of the arts, congratulator of athletic teams, and surrogate parent. Your political advisors will want you to focus on activities that will keep your poll numbers high and get you reelected. I urge you to concentrate on duties that will restore our country's reputation and keep us safe.

On January 20, 2009, you will place your hand on the Bible and, prompted by Chief Justice Roberts, swear in front of three hundred million Americans and six billion people worldwide to "preserve, protect and defend the Constitution of the United States." Following George Washington's example, you will add a heartfelt "so help me God." The oath completed, you will become the world's most powerful person. It will no longer be happenstance when you enter a room and the band strikes up "Hail to the Chief." You have attained our nation's highest office; the question, not yet answered, is whether you have what it takes to excel in the job.

• • •

Eight years ago, as the second millennium drew to a close, the outlook for America could not have been brighter. The world was at peace, the global economy healthy, and the position of the United States unparalleled. The platform on which George W. Bush ran for president in 2000 referred to the era as "a remarkable time in the life of our country." Colin Powell, the incoming secretary of state, told Congress, "We will need to work well together because we have a great challenge before us. But it is not a challenge of survival. It is a challenge of leadership. For it is not a dark and dangerous ideological foe we confront, but the overwhelming power of millions of people who have tasted freedom. It is our own incredible success that we face."

Like any inheritance, incredible success can be invested productively or not. Tragically, America's political capital has been squandered. When comparing notes with former cabinet members—Democrat and Republican alike—I have seen people shake their heads in disbelief at the manner in which presidential power has been misused. The consensus question: What could they have been thinking? From day one, the wrong people were in top positions. The decision-making process was distorted or bypassed. Ideological conformity was valued over professionalism, and falsehoods were allowed to masquerade as truth. Principles that are central to America's identity were labeled obsolete, and historic errors were made without accountability. Important national security tools, including diplomacy, were set aside. I had hoped that President Bush would salvage his administration during its final years, but the gains made were both belated and marginal. Sad to say, you will enter office with respect for American leadership lower than it has been in the memory of any living person.

As a child in Europe, I hid in bomb shelters while Nazi planes flew overhead. Listening to the radio, I exulted at the voice of Churchill and the wondrous news that American troops were crossing the Atlantic. I was seven years old when Allied forces hit the beaches at Normandy and later repelled Hitler's army at the Battle of the Bulge. By the time the war was won I was eight, anxious to discover what peace might be like, and already in love with Americans in uniform.

To Abraham Lincoln, the United States was "the last best hope of Earth." To me, it will always be the land of opportunity. I could not imagine wanting to live anywhere else, nor conceive what the twentieth century would have been like without my adopted country. That is why it is so disturbing to learn of reports that most people in most countries now believe that America "provokes more conflicts than it prevents" and that we have a "mainly negative" influence in the world.

The tragic blunder of Iraq stands out, but there have been others—neglect of our allies, overreliance on the military, allowing the likes of Dick Cheney and Donald Rumsfeld to be the face of America. Yes, we have an excuse: the world is different now, but that is all the more reason to be mindful of proven strengths. The terrorist outrage of 9/11 was shocking, but we have lived for decades with the knowledge that death could arrive from across the sea. The attacks were cause for grief and anger, and for reassessing our institutions and strategies; they were not good reason for panic or for abandoning our principles when we needed them most.

After 9/11, the Bush administration started well but soon forgot who our country's most serious enemies were. Many

Americans were convinced that we had invaded Iraq because Saddam Hussein was responsible for 9/11. Thus a majority felt that confronting Hussein would strike a blow against Al Qaeda. Many agreed with the president that the world could be divided neatly into those aligned with the United States and those cheering on the terrorists. Many admired the president's certainty even as we came to have doubts about what he seemed most certain about.

I am an optimist who worries a lot. The reasons for worry surround us, some hidden, others visible daily on CNN, Fox News, and Al-Jazeera. The turbulence and vitriol may seem overwhelming. The poison of hate is in the air. Still, my overriding message to you as you prepare to assume the presidency is to have confidence in who we are and what we believe, for, even in my lifetime, we have faced graver risks, kept our nerve, and overcome.

We might assume that a memo such as this, if written half a century ago, would have painted a picture of a safe and strong America. After all, Osama bin Laden was, at that time, still an infant. Al Qaeda did not exist, and international terrorism was not a major concern. The United States was the unchallenged leader of the free world. The globe, itself, was less complicated and slower paced. Yet in the 1950s, George Kennan wrote that "Our national consciousness is dominated at present by a sense of insecurity." Walter Lippmann worried that "We are living in an age of disorder and upheaval. Though the United States has grown powerful and rich, we know in our hearts that we have become . . . insecure and anxious. . . . For we are not sure whether our responsibilities are not greater than our wisdom."

Even my favorite college text concluded gloomily that "Only the most stubborn and obtuse would venture optimistic predictions for the future . . . men everywhere are gripped by fear . . . man's technical knowledge and capacity have outstripped his moral capacity."

This foreboding was traceable not to human failures but to human ingenuity. The advance from the conventional to the nuclear bomb was of a magnitude greater than any since the first short-tempered man picked up a piece of wood and used it as a club. From Hiroshima on, the possibility of immediate, collective extinction became a part of our lives. We worried that the knowledge and means to build nuclear weapons would spread rapidly; some felt it a sign from God that the end of the world was at hand.

We were anxious, as well, that the American dream was not living up to its billing. While a comic book Superman fought for "truth, justice and the American way," our international adversaries labeled us as greedy and racist. We didn't wholly disagree. "The superiority of our way of life," the political theorist Hans Morgenthau wrote fifty years ago, "is no longer as obvious either to us or to the rest of the world as it used to be. To hundreds of millions of people, the communist way of life appears to be more attractive than ours."

At home, congressional committees competed to root out communist sympathizers in the State Department and army, quarreling over who was responsible for putting the red in Red China. Soviet leaders boasted of their economic and industrial prowess, predicted that they would bury us, and triumphantly launched into space the first satellite (Sputnik), first dog (Laika), and first man (Yuri Gagarin). Ninety miles from Florida, a communist dictator established a revolutionary beachhead, and threatened to create others throughout the hemisphere. The superpowers were in a race to build and test ever more destructive warheads. Schoolchildren practiced hiding under desks; community planners stocked underground shelters with Spam and chicken noodle soup. Then, as now, America yearned for fresh leadership.

In 1960, America elected a new president. John Kennedy brought with him a tonic he called "vigah" and a dynamic way of looking at the world. His inaugural is well remembered for his brash pledge to "pay any price, bear any burden . . . in order to assure the survival and the success of liberty." He also spoke of "a long twilight struggle . . . against the common enemies of man: tyranny, poverty, disease, and war itself." This broad focus reflected Kennedy's belief that the West could not compete against communism through military might alone. We had to gain the allegiance of marginalized populations for, while America claimed to have a unique and all-encompassing vision, so did the communists. To win converts, we had to explain our ideas to people who had no experience with freedom and only hostile encounters with the West. We had to convince the widest possible audience that we were on their side.

Kennedy's inaugural responded to this challenge by speaking in turn "to those old allies whose cultural and spiritual origins we share," then to "those new states whom we welcome to the ranks of the free," to "those peoples in huts and villages across the globe striving to break the bonds of mass misery," to "our sister republics south of the border," to "the United Nations," and "finally, to those nations who would make themselves our adversary."

In the months that followed, Kennedy honed America's image by creating the Alliance for Progress, the Peace Corps, and the Agency for International Development; declaring a moratorium on atmospheric nuclear tests; and conveying his desire for "genuine peace, the kind of peace that makes life on earth worth living . . . not merely peace for Americans but peace for all men and women—not merely peace in our time but peace for all time."

John Kennedy understood that Americans must practice effective diplomacy on every continent. An early supporter of independence for colonies in Africa and Asia, he was considered a hero in such places as Algeria, Kenya, and Indonesia. The picture of our first Catholic president hung on the walls of huts and haciendas throughout Latin America. JFK won over French speakers by referring to himself jauntily as "the man who accompanied Jacqueline Kennedy to Paris." When the Berlin Wall went up, he asked the people of West Berlin "to lift your eyes beyond the dangers of today, to the hopes of tomorrow, beyond the freedom merely of this city of Berlin . . . to the advance of freedom everywhere, beyond the wall to the day of peace with justice, beyond yourselves and ourselves to all mankind." Kennedy's eloquence seemed to exemplify an America sure of its direction and skilled in the art of bringing others along.

An assassin's bullet brought a shocking end to JFK's presidency, but not to the demand for global diplomacy at which he had excelled. Lyndon Johnson, though burdened by the albatross of Vietnam, enhanced America's international standing through his fight against poverty and support for civil rights. Richard Nixon eased anxieties by pursuing détente with the Soviet Union and an opening to communist China. Gerald Ford engineered approval of a means for monitoring and reporting on the status of freedom behind the Iron Curtain—the

Helsinki Final Act. Jimmy Carter elevated human rights to the center of U.S. foreign policy, declared America's opposition to apartheid, and brokered a historic peace between Israel and Egypt. Ronald Reagan emphasized U.S. support for democracy and pushed against the shaky underpinnings of the Soviet empire. The senior President Bush supported German unification and forged a broad coalition to roll back Iraq's invasion of Kuwait.

As decade gave way to decade, presidents from both parties created a clear role for America as leader of the international system—as a defender of law and builder of global institutions, a country whose influence was felt in all regions and whose views were widely respected. Though far from unblemished, theirs was a record of profound achievement. The nuclear weapons we so much feared were not again used, and the number of declared nuclear powers paused at five. The division of Europe ended. The Soviet Union broke up. Democracy spread. Old enemies became friends. Civilization itself seemed to be on the move, taking the stairs two steps at a time.

And yet, in the years immediately following the cold war, I surprised my students by saying that I thought the world would grow more perilous. We had become accustomed to the risks of superpower rivalry and had painstakingly developed the means to contain them. The new era, though freer, would also prove less predictable. Nations and people redefined their interests; old grievances resurfaced. We would have to exert ourselves to keep from slipping back.

Thus, in the 1990s, Bill Clinton brought Kennedy-style zest to the task of governing in a time of change—expanding and reforming NATO, supporting debt relief for the poorest countries, promoting democracy without trying to impose it, pursuing peace, and doing more than any other leader to rally the world against international terror.

On the eve of NATO's intervention to prevent mass killing in Kosovo, Clinton called me at the time he usually did, the middle of the night, because he rarely slept and didn't think anyone else might need to. Together, we reviewed the steps we had taken to find a diplomatic solution to the crisis. Prior to the fighting, Clinton had pushed us for every scrap of information. Sitting at his desk, trying to ward off a headache by pressing a can of Diet Coke to his temple, he questioned everything—the history, personalities, social and cultural factors, risks to our troops, potential cost to civilians, and whether our post-conflict plans were realistic. He was determined to do the mission right because he knew he could be wrong. He was thorough; that was his style on Kosovo and on every issue that mattered.

To his secretary of state, Clinton's approach was a precious asset. It was not hard for me to convince people overseas that the United States understood and cared. They already knew, because they had been listening for years to a president who had taken the time to learn about them, who had shown that he was concerned about their futures and who wanted to help if he could.

In his second inaugural address, Bill Clinton referred to our country as "the indispensable nation." I liked the phrase so much I borrowed it until it became associated with me. Some thought the term arrogant, but that is not how I meant it. Rather, I felt it captured the reality that most large-scale initiatives required at least some input from the United States. I also hoped the phrase would create a sense of pride among Americans, so we would be more willing to invest in overseas projects and less reluctant to take on tough assignments.

Although our country has much in common with others, it has no current competitor in power and reach. This creates opportunities but also temptations. For better or worse, American actions serve as an example. If we attempt to put ourselves outside the law, we invite others to do the same. That is when our moral bearings are lost and the foundation of our leadership becomes suspect. I have always believed America is an exceptional country, but that is because we have led in creating standards that work for everyone, not because we are an exception to the rules.

Today, as you prepare to assume the presidency, the preeminence of American power remains among the major facts of twenty-first-century life, but our ability to control events through the use of that power has eroded. This, too, is among the major facts of twenty-first-century life.

The reasons are well known. We have made a muddle of fighting terror—lacking a coherent strategy and failing to establish a clear connection between the steps we take and the results we desire. Our promotion of democracy has caused unease even among those advocating democratic reforms in their countries—because when we speak of democracy, many people think of Iraq, nobody's desired model. With our attention focused on the Persian Gulf, we have lacked effective policies toward transcendent challenges such as energy and the environment. We have responded slowly and with an unsteady hand to emerging problems in Asia, Latin America, and Africa. Once the premier practitioners of global diplomacy, we have behaved as amateurs.

Even the most basic building blocks of U.S. power appear

chipped and worn. Our military has been deployed to the point of exhaustion, including our National Guard and Reserves. Our international economic leadership has been hurt by an inconsistent approach to trade and by budget policies that have spun the gold of surpluses into the straw of record deficits. Our alliances in Europe and the Asian Pacific have been strained. And on nuclear weapons, human rights, and the rule of law, we are thought to be hypocrites.

Your job as president will be to recapture what has been lost and to proceed from there. You must begin with the understanding that our right to lead is no longer widely accepted. We have lost moral legitimacy. If we fail to comprehend this, we will not know how to formulate a successful strategy. We will be like a lawyer who assumes that, because of past triumphs, she has the jury in her pocket when she hasn't, precisely because the jury resents being taken for granted.

In Kennedy's time, the memory of World War II was part of every adult's consciousness; so, too, was America's role in rebuilding Western Europe and helping Japan to become a democracy. The rehabilitation of former Axis powers was seen as a luminous accomplishment. America's leadership was still disputed, but its credentials were acknowledged. The country that had stood up to Hitler, Mussolini, and Tojo had earned, at a minimum, a respectful hearing from people everywhere.

We can no longer assume that our understanding of our own history is widely shared. Relatively few hear the word "America" and think first of the Battle of Lexington or the landings at Omaha Beach. To those under the age of twenty—the majority in many countries—the cold war confrontation between freedom and communism means little. To many, the Statue of Liberty has been replaced in the mind's eye by a hooded figure with electrodes. In marketing terms, the American brand needs a makeover.

Amid the swirl of events these past fifteen years, four trends pose a clear and present danger to American interests—first, terror and the rise of anti-Americanism in the Arab and Muslim worlds; second, the erosion of international consensus on nuclear proliferation; third, growing doubts about the value of democracy; and fourth, the gathering backlash against globalization due primarily to the widening split between rich and poor.

There is a fifth potential danger that could exacerbate the other four. Historically, America has responded to periods of deep involvement overseas by trying to withdraw. This was true after World War I, after Vietnam, and again following the cold war. As secretary of state, I devoted much of my energy striving to convince Americans that history had not ended when the Berlin Wall came down. Contrary to present perceptions overseas, the American people would much prefer to concentrate on problems at home than throw our weight around internationally. This is particularly the case when our efforts abroad go unappreciated. After Iraq, Americans will be reluctant to take risks. And so we should be, but not so reluctant that new threats are allowed to grow.

We are in a cantankerous mood. We were reminded by Hurricane Katrina that the fight against poverty and injustice in our own society remains unfinished. We worry that our jobs are being exported and our borders overrun. There is much going on in the world that we don't understand and feel increasingly disinclined to try. A recent poll found that 42 percent of Americans say the United States should "mind its own business inter-

nationally and let other countries get along the best they can."
Tending to one's own affairs is a virtue in America, and not
much is expected of foreigners in any case. Why not disengage?
Why shouldn't we let others take the lead?

As president, it will be your responsibility to answer these
questions. It is essential that you restate the case for, and re-
define the content of, American leadership. This is not 1808 or
1908. If the tools of American power are allowed to rust, alternative powers will fill the void. Some will do no harm; others
will do no good. The time will arrive when we must awaken
again, and there is a risk that we will respond too late. Far better
to remain vigilant. We have unique capabilities; we must use
them for the right purposes.

We should be reassured by the fact that the American people
are viewed more favorably than our policies and that many
people who are angry at some of what we do nevertheless want
us to succeed overall. The same polls that show a decline in our
popularity also suggest that the globe is not eager for a superpower rival to emerge—China's military ambitions are viewed
with suspicion; Russian leaders are distrusted; Iran's president is
positively disliked. The disappointment with us arises when we
are thought to act without regard to the interests and concerns
of others: when, for example, we dismiss the advice of Arabs
and Turks before invading a country in their neighborhood;
when we oppose a treaty on climate change or an international
criminal court, instead of working with others to improve those
arrangements; or when we make a political football out of immigration policy while simultaneously demanding that Mexico
give top priority to the fight against illegal drugs.

You get inaugurated for the first time just once, so make the
most of it. As soon as you begin to speak, America's voice will

change. Around the globe, ears that have closed will open at least for a moment; so, too, will minds. Be certain of the signature phrase you want. With FDR, it was "All we have to fear is fear itself." With JFK it was "Ask not." With George H. W. Bush, it was something about a "fresh breeze." Clinton talked about change ("We force the spring") and our forty-third president—remember this?—pledged that America would "show purpose without arrogance."

Aim high, but keep your words down to Earth. It is in the nature of presidential candidates to paint a rosy picture of what the world would be like in the event they are elected, as if the skies would open so that justice and righteousness might flow down. Expect no such gift. You are about to inherit a peck of troubles with no power over the heavens and little enough here below.

CHAPTER 2

What Kind of President?

A president knows that his name will be the label for a whole era," wrote Ted Sorensen. "Textbooks yet unwritten and schoolchildren yet unborn will hold him responsible for all that happens." Hmm.

Perhaps, like George Washington, you will one day be described by your biographer as pious, patriotic, just, temperate, impartial, modest, prudent, "undaunted as Hannibal," and "as respectful of the laws as Socrates." It is an exhilarating thought—until one recalls that Hannibal was crushed by the Romans and Socrates made to drink hemlock.

Presidents enter office expecting to succeed; many do not, at least in the manner anticipated. Abraham Lincoln's goal was to save the union, not end slavery. Woodrow Wilson wanted to revive a lagging domestic economy, not create a new international role for the United States. FDR campaigned against the Depression and stayed to defeat fascism. Presidents find themselves judged by the surprise tests sprung upon them by history.

That is when, for better or worse, the full measure of your own character will be exposed—and your place along the spectrum between Franklin Pierce and Mount Rushmore determined.

A presidential transition embodies change in more than one sense. Yes, you will alter the tone and substance of American policy, but you will also undergo a personal transfiguration. As a campaigner, you spoke for your party, directed an army of volunteers, and told crowds what would make them cheer. As president, you must speak for our nation, command the world's mightiest military, and tell us what we need to know.

Do not doubt that the job for which you have sacrificed so much will prove unimaginably hard. Your powers will appear far more impressive to others than they will seem to you. Many who flatter you to obtain favors will, when your back is turned, complain about not getting even more. You will seldom feel in control of your own life. Scrutiny will be intense and continual; no conversation will be fully private. You will grow older quickly, and be reminded constantly that a halo need fall only a short distance before it begins to feel like a noose.

With the campaign so recently completed, you will be eager to fulfill the many promises made. Unfortunately, some ideas that seemed clever before audiences in Atlanta or Cleveland will appear less so when revisited from the White House. Good rhetoric does not always translate into sound policy.

While courting voters in 1992, Bill Clinton vowed to end the practice of forcibly repatriating Haitian migrants picked up at sea. The promise was popular with liberals and refugee advocates, but also unwise. Although sending the migrants home seemed to be inhumane, it was less so than giving Haitians an incentive to trade their meager life savings for seats on over-crowded sailboats that all too often capsized. Clinton, when president elect, realized that honoring his pledge might prompt an exodus from Haiti of as many as one hundred thousand people. Prudently, he retreated.

By all means, live up to your promises if you can. If that proves impractical, you will be in good company. When, in 1916, Woodrow Wilson campaigned for reelection, he did so on the slogan "He kept us out of war." In 1940, Franklin Roosevelt promised that "Your boys are not going to be sent into any foreign wars." In 1964, Lyndon Johnson declared that "We are not about to send American boys 10,000 miles . . . to do what Asian boys ought to be doing for themselves." Three winning campaigns; three broken commitments—it may seem cynical to say so, but losing candidates can't keep any commitments at all.

The men who wrote the Constitution did remarkably well, considering the absence of female guidance. The establishment of the presidential office was one of their more farsighted—and controversial—accomplishments. The proponents of a unitary chief executive had to beat back objections from those who argued that a president would too closely resemble a king. The outcome might have been different if the deliberations had been presided over by someone less revered than George Washington. The founders were confident that at least the first president would be worthy of trust.

Once in office, Washington insisted that he be treated formally but not royally. He rented fine houses, hosted elaborate dinners, and rode about in a fancy coach with liveried footmen. There was, however, no kneeling or ring-kissing in his presence, no "your majesty" demanded in salutations, and no crown (or even a powdered wig) atop his head. After two terms, he set a precedent by retiring to his farm, the most prominent political figure to yield power voluntarily since Cincinnatus returned to the plow after defeating the enemies of ancient Rome.

Washington's moderation concerning the ceremonial aspects of his office did not translate into reticence about exercising power. By assuming for himself the right to recognize foreign governments, greet and dismiss ambassadors, and negotiate treaties, he established the primacy of the president in the conduct of international affairs. He rejected a demand by Congress that it be shown copies of correspondence received from foreign governments and he made clear that the president alone had the power to commit the nation to a specific action. U.S. Representative John Marshall, later chief justice of the Supreme Court, declared that the president was "the sole organ of the nation in its external relations, and its sole representative with foreign nations."

Washington's example leaves no doubt that, as president, you will be in charge. The question is: What kind of leader do you intend to be?

A president elected in the twenty-first century cannot reasonably be expected to emulate a chief executive who served when our country was young. Thomas Jefferson had a library of six thousand books, wrote more than twenty thousand letters, played the violin, designed Monticello, founded the University of Virginia, compiled his own version of the New Testament, introduced the swivel chair to America, and grew nineteen varieties of the English pea. Like Jefferson, John Tyler played the violin; as for other activities, he had fifteen children. James Garfield could write in Greek with one hand and in Latin with the other simultaneously. It is amazing what some of these gentlemen found the time and opportunity to do. Of course, unlike us, they did not have all their waking hours consumed by time-saving devices.

Perhaps it would be better to search for a model among modern presidents. You will likely think first of the two most currently in fashion: Harry Truman and Ronald Reagan.

In his time, Truman suffered in comparison to Franklin Roosevelt, his beloved predecessor. Unlike the aristocratic FDR, Truman lacked grace. He climbed the political ladder with help from the Missouri Democratic machine and was thought a small man, unequal to the demands of the White House. I recall my father being amazed that America was such a free country that a music critic could ridicule a vocal recital given by Truman's daughter and when the president threatened to break the critic's nose, people laughed—at the president.

Truman is a hero now to Republicans and Democrats alike, for he is associated, in retrospect, with the golden age of postwar American leadership. His character and style are as admired as his creation of NATO and his other accomplishments. He was plainspoken, decisive, and took full responsibility. Wrote Dean Acheson of his boss: "The 'little touch of Harry,' which kept us all going, came from an inexhaustible supply of vitality and good spirits. He could, and did, outwork us all, with no need for papers predigested into one-page pellets of pablum. When things went wrong, he took the blame . . . when things went right, he . . . [gave] one of his lieutenants the credit. . . . These are qualities of a leader who builds esprit de corps. He expected, and received, the loyalty he gave."

Truman was relentlessly upbeat about what America could

achieve, yet he was far from starry-eyed about human character. A few weeks after Hitler's surrender, he warned that "it is
easier to remove tyrants and concentration camps than it is to
kill the ideas which gave them birth." It is intriguing to imagine
how the man known as "Give 'em Hell Harry" might have dealt
with Al Qaeda.

Truman's standing has grown over time; Ronald Reagan
became an icon while still president. To some (including me),
this was hard to comprehend. Reagan's authorized biographer,
Edmund Morris, admits that he couldn't figure his subject out.
Wrote Henry Kissinger:

> Reagan's was an astonishing performance—and, to aca-
> demic observers, nearly incomprehensible. Reagan knew
> next to no history, and the little he did know he tailored to
> support his firmly held preconceptions. He treated bibli-
> cal references to Armageddon as operational predictions.
> Many of the historical anecdotes he was so fond of recount-
> ing had no basis in fact. . . . The details of foreign policy
> bored Reagan. He had absorbed a few basic ideas about the
> dangers of appeasement, the evils of communism, and the
> greatness of his own country, but analysis of substantive
> issues was not his forte.

As a manager of foreign policy, Reagan's simplistic approach
and lack of knowledge led to confusion. In eight years, he ran
through six national security advisors and, according to his own
secretary of state, "the CIA and [its director] Bill Casey were as
independent as a hog on ice and could be as confident as they
were wrong." Reagan also presided over a disastrous military
intervention in Lebanon and the Iran-Contra scandal.

Notwithstanding all this, George W. Bush reportedly told John McCain, "I don't want to be like my father. I want to be like Ronald Reagan." A June 2005 survey conducted by the Discovery channel selected Reagan as the greatest person in American history ahead of Lincoln, Washington, and Martin Luther King, Jr.

Reagan may not have known all the facts a president should grasp, but he did understand how to talk to the American people. Faced by hostile questions from reporters, he amiably repeated themes he knew would strike a chord on Main Street. Reagan had a sure sense of when to shrug, give a little chuckle, or raise an eyebrow. After watching LBJ agonize over Vietnam, Nixon resign over Watergate, and Carter bemoan the nation's "crisis of spirit," Americans responded well to a president who spoke of rising suns, a shining city on a hill, and a country "too great for small dreams."

This is not the place to argue whether Reagan won the cold war or, alternatively, like the rooster who claimed credit for the sunrise, he just happened to be around when the USSR lost it. The former actor was favorably cast opposite a succession of aged Soviet leaders, three of whom grew ill and died by the middle of Reagan's tenure. Still, our fortieth president deserves credit for drawing a clear moral distinction between the West and East at a time when others were either blurring that distinction or reconciling themselves to a permanent division of Europe. Reagan gave full support to Poland's Solidarity movement and created the National Endowment for Democracy—a means for promoting democratic institutions that continues to give dictators headaches. He also knew the power of words: "Mr. Gorbachev, tear down this wall!" was a statement so blunt no other president would have thought to utter it. National leaders are supposed to be sophisticated; Reagan at his best exhibited the quiet genius of common sense.

Though he is revered by conservatives for his devotion to principle, Reagan was a more flexible politician than is commonly remembered. A partisan, he worked well with congressional Democrats; an opponent of foreign aid, he increased it; staunchly anticommunist, he actively pursued arms limitation agreements with the Soviets; a supporter of Israel, he put forward a peace proposal denounced by the Israeli government. Like most presidents, he wanted to be seen as a man of peace, even telling friends that he suspected God had spared him from the assassin's bullet for this purpose. His proposal to create a missile-proof shield over America, called Star Wars, was thought a fantasy by his own military advisors; still, it reflected Reagan's sincere desire to protect humankind from nuclear annihilation.

Truman laid the groundwork for the West's cold war success; Reagan was present at the culmination. Good results translate into good reputations. Emerson advised, "Insist on yourself, never imitate." Fair enough, but knowing the qualities that sustained past presidents is invaluable. America's premier expert on the presidency, Richard Neustadt, determined that the modern White House demands "experienced politicians of extraordinary temperament." He cited as elements of proper temperament FDR's obvious relish for the job, Truman's "unselfconscious rootedness," Eisenhower's lack of pretension, and JFK's humor. Clinton, too, loved the presidency and invited Neustadt to dinner to talk about it. He also hosted Newt Gingrich, who, like Clinton, seemed to know the story behind every stick of White House furniture. It is not for me to judge whether your own temperament is extraordinary, but you will not be fit for the office if you fail to appreciate the contrast between the smallness of the building and the largeness of the history that has been made within its walls.

"I can understand the theory of wanting to free people," said Gerald Ford in an interview two years before his death. But "I just don't think we should go hellfire damnation around the globe freeing people, unless it is directly related to our own national security." Ford's comment illustrates a basic point: the kind of president you will strive to be reflects the kind of country you believe America should be. This question has been mulled over by presidents for more than two hundred years: What is our republic's rightful role? Should the United States be content to serve as a model for others or seek actively to spread freedom? Should our presidents be guided by narrow considerations of national self-interest or by our zeal to lift lives and solve global problems?

Historians in search of thematic clarity have traditionally used these questions to divide U.S. leaders into realists and idealists, with Theodore Roosevelt the model for the former and Woodrow Wilson the epitome of the latter. Roosevelt presided over America's emergence as a world power, sent the U.S. fleet to circumnavigate the globe, rejoiced in our conquest of the Philippines, and blustered his way past local opposition to build the Panama Canal. Roosevelt was ambitious for America and not shy about claiming credit for himself. Wilson, however, had ambitions of an even more exalted sort. Following the allied victory in World War I, he astonished hard-boiled European politicians by inquiring: "Why has Jesus Christ so far not succeeded in inducing the world to follow His teachings in these matters?

It is because He taught the ideal without devising any practical means of attaining it. That is why I am proposing a practical means to carry out His aims."

Wilson was referring to the League of Nations, but he brought a similar mind-set to all his diplomacy. He believed that America should be above European intrigues, that all governments should be transparent in their dealings, that every country should be a democracy, and that the world need only settle on a few universal rules to achieve lasting peace. "There is coming a time, unless I am very much mistaken," declared Wilson, "when nations shall agree with nation that the rights of humanity are greater than the rights of sovereignty."

Such sentiments, and the policies that flowed from them, caused Henry Kissinger to complain that "no other nation has rested its claim to international leadership on its altruism." Like others who consider themselves realists, Kissinger believes that countries respond far more to strategic interests than to high-minded appeals. For them, U.S. actions taken in the name of morality will not be moral at all unless tied to political facts, for they will not otherwise produce moral outcomes. The world, realists point out, is a much less pleasant place than Americans— raised in freedom and relative wealth—ordinarily comprehend. This makes us reluctant to accept that cruelty, injustice, and suffering are widespread or to acknowledge the limits on what can be done to ease such wrongs. Realists fear that we will devote so much energy trying to construct a perfect world that we will neglect to strengthen the foundation of the best world for which we can hope—that foundation being the preservation of American leadership and power.

In a frequently cited quotation, George Kennan put the case

for a foreign policy that was hardheaded even to the point of seeming coldhearted:

> We have about 50 percent of the world's wealth, but only about 6.3 percent of its population. . . . In this situation, we cannot fail to be the object of envy and resentment. Our real task in the coming period is to devise a pattern of relationships which will permit us to maintain this position of disparity without positive detriment to our national security. To do so, we will have to dispense with all sentimentality and day-dreaming; and our attention will have to be concentrated everywhere on our immediate national objectives.

During the last decades of his century-long life, Kennan complained vehemently about American interventions abroad. He believed it was a mistake for the United States to seek to project its own values into societies that were unprepared to accept them. He would have agreed with Gerald Ford that America should not attempt to go with "hellfire damnation around the globe freeing people."

When, in 2005, Kennan died, realism was back in vogue. President Bush had led our country into a Middle East quagmire and many of his critics suggested that Wilsonian moralism was the reason. Where the senior President Bush was said to have directed a rigorously pragmatic foreign policy, his son argued that America had a "calling from beyond the stars" to rid the world of evil. Where the older Bush refrained from sending U.S. troops to Baghdad at the end of the first Gulf War, the younger didn't hesitate to do so during the second.

Given the results, many have concluded that America will be better off if our next president is guided by realism instead of idealism.

This history is too simple and the facts, as they are commonly understood, not so clear.

It was the senior President Bush, the supposed realist, who envisioned "a new world order" and the dawn of an "era in which nations of the world east and west, north and south, can prosper and live in harmony." It was he who—against Kennan's advice—sent U.S. troops into famine-stricken Somalia because, he said, "Morally, a failure to respond to [such] massive human catastrophes . . . would scar the soul of our nation."

Remember, too, that the younger Bush's decision to invade Iraq—though it would later be dressed up in frilly democratic frocks—was conceived as a tough-minded use of American power for the purpose of protecting U.S. interests. Advocates of the invasion possessed a profoundly cynical notion of how people, and Arabs in particular, respond to the use of force. They told themselves that Arabs respect strength and that a demonstration of "shock and awe" would convince everyone in the region that America was determined to impose its will. They expected that Iraqi extremists, fearful of our might and demoralized by our resolve, would surely either accept defeat or go into hiding, clearing the way for the Pentagon to install pro-American exiles in positions of authority. This was hardly Wilsonian idealism. In fact, Bush overran the signposts commonly associated with idealism—respect for international law, deference to the United Nations, cooperation with allies, and attention to the principles of just war.

It was only after their original rationale began to look foolish that the Bush team settled on democratic transformation as the real reason for invading. Since there were no weapons of mass destruction and no meaningful connections between Saddam Hussein and Al Qaeda, a new theory had to be put forward to justify the war. Not until November 2003, eight months after the invasion, did Bush unveil his "forward strategy for freedom in the Middle East." That pronouncement was followed by a succession of ever more grandiose claims about democracy being the antidote to terror. Although Democratic idealism was summoned to explain why we found ourselves in Iraq, it did not lead us there in the first place. The prevailing dynamic was neither idealism nor realism, but incompetence.

Personally, I have never liked the realist-versus-idealist paradigm because I never know into which category I fit. That is why I advise my students to think of national security as a hot-air balloon. Without the helium of principles, there is no lift; without the ballast of national interest, the balloon would never return to Earth. The best presidents have melded an informed perception of the world as it is with an ambitious conception of the world as it might be—not a Utopia, but a place with a healthier portion of security, freedom, and justice.

My mother used to embarrass me by telling fortunes after studying the coffee grounds left at the bottom of a cup. She also read palms—deciding, with a glance at my hand, that I had no brain line and that I would bear sons (I have three daughters). If I were to try to discern what lies ahead for you, I would begin by looking at the hand of cards you will inherit from Mr. Bush, knowing that these are the cards you will have to pick up and play. As you consider your first moves, it may help you to ask "What would Truman do?" or "What would Reagan do?" in a similar situation. The value of models from the past, however, like coffee grounds, depends on what you read into them. It will be up to you to find the right combination of realism and idealism to guide your policies, and to search within yourself for the raw materials of leadership. It can be a lonely job, for you alone will have to make the final judgments. There is solace, however, in knowing that as you weigh options and search for answers, you will have the assistance of a large and talented team.

CHAPTER 3

Thy Staff Shall Comfort Thee

T he choice of a prince's ministers," counseled Machiavelli, "is a matter of no little importance. . . . The first impression that one gets of a ruler and of his brains is from seeing the men that he has about him."

By prejudice and custom, a sixteenth-century Italian prince was generally limited in advisors to a single sex; you are not. The mandate to choose carefully, however, still applies. The people you select to serve in your administration may not guarantee a trouble-free presidency, but they can surely produce a discordant and disappointing one.

Every major presidential campaign prepares a transition plan in the event it wins. The (lightly thumbed) document prepared for president elect Dukakis, for example, urges that "priority attention be given immediately after the election to the placement of senior campaign staff." This advice, which you will surely receive from your own campaign staff, should be considered with skepticism, especially in the area of national security. Governing skills differ from electoral skills, and loyalty, though essential, is no guarantee of talent. Good friends do not necessarily make good ministers.

The right approach, not surprisingly, was Lincoln's. As president elect, he was warned against putting Salmon Chase in his cabinet because Chase "thinks he is a great deal bigger than you are." Lincoln replied, "Well, do you know any other men who think they are bigger than I am? . . . I want to put them all in my cabinet."

You need not follow Lincoln's lead in assembling a "Team of Rivals," Doris Goodwin's term for a cabinet that featured the president's chief intraparty competitors. A lineup of political all-stars may yield too much grandstanding and not enough honest sweat, but you do need "big" people—individuals who are personally secure, smart, and able to get along with one another. A brilliant thinker who dismisses any idea not his own will be more disruptive than helpful; a charming person who is unoriginal won't help much either. You want team players who are also team leaders—people confident enough to expect they will be right on most issues and humble enough, when they are not, to realize it in good time. Finding the ideal mix of personalities demands intelligent guesswork complemented by luck. The process can be compared to assembling a jigsaw puzzle with many more pieces than you need, no picture on the box to guide you, and half the world peering over your shoulder whispering suggestions.

You know that, once in office, you will need advice that is both shrewd and varied. Your policy-making will be sterile if your appointees have too much in common or if one advisor is so dominant that dissenting voices cannot be heard. The corresponding risk is that you will pursue ideological diversity too avidly, inviting unnecessary interagency disputes. Such differences are by no means the only potential problem. Especially in Washington—and you can trust me on this—two people can agree on every major substantive issue and still fight like scorpions because they are so intent on occupying the same space.

Selecting a cabinet is exhilarating but also aggravating. It is impossible to avoid hurt feelings when choosing one large ego over another. As President Taft complained, "Every time I make an appointment, I create nine enemies and one ingrate." To begin, you must entrust a person in whom you have complete faith with the job of grilling potential nominees about their finances, drinking habits, dysfunctional relatives, medical histories, online chat room activities, collegiate social exploits, and the legal and tax status of their children's nannies. The candidates who survive that ordeal will queue up for interviews at all hours. Depending on how well you already know them, you may or may not need to ask probing questions about how they would respond in specific situations. Your goal will be to look behind the mask the person in front of you is wearing to see how he or she will perform under pressure.

Inevitably, you will make some choices that don't work out, whether for reasons of chemistry or ability. Correct them quickly. Les Aspin, Bill Clinton's first secretary of defense, was a singularly intelligent man but without the organizational skills required to manage the Pentagon bureaucracy; a career in Congress had not prepared him to deal with myriad conflicts involving programs and people. He was asked to step down after a year and was replaced by William Perry, a self-effacing linear thinker who did the job as well as it can be done. According to rumors early in President George W. Bush's first term, Donald Rumsfeld was thought likely to quit or be fired; speculation to that effect evaporated after 9/11. One wonders how different the world might be if Rumsfeld had been replaced early in 2002 instead of late in 2006.

The senior member of the cabinet—the secretary of state—represents America to the world. Her department was intended to be the transmission belt for intergovernmental messages to and from the United States. The concept is a quaint one, given the emergence of so many alternative avenues of communication. Alleged obsolescence, however, is not the only reason the department has become a punching bag. The perception has grown that our diplomats are overly cautious, insufficiently tough, and susceptible to the disease—or, in the view of some, the crime—of trying to think about issues from a foreign point of view.

It was Franklin Roosevelt's feeling, according to one biographer, that "too many of State's upper-level career personnel had been . . . abroad too long; that they had lost the feel of their own country and were neither truly representative of the American people nor the objectives of his own administration." Jimmy Carter called the department a "sprawling Washington and worldwide bureaucracy" from which he "rarely received innovative ideas." Henry Kissinger dismissed it as a backwater whose employees are incapable of conceptual thinking and whose primary function "is basically answering cables." Newt Gingrich referred to it scathingly as a "broken institution" that "appeases dictators and tries to be nice to corrupt regimes."

I have heard such criticisms so often I have come to think of "low morale at the State Department" as if it were one long hyphenated word. The verbal piling on, however, is not justified.

Political leaders thrive on domestic applause and are always looking to generate more. The State Department's job is to serve as a Cordelia to the president's King Lear, speaking truth while others flatter. It must tell the chief executive honestly and accurately how the world will respond to what he proposes to do. In some cases that reaction may be welcoming, but there are less pleasing possibilities, including misinterpretation, surprise, anger, diplomatic retaliation, even violent assaults on our embassies. Providing a frank assessment of foreign attitudes, especially when they are likely to be disappointing, can prevent embarrassment and fend off disaster—provided the president listens.

As early as 1961, Deputy Secretary of State George Ball warned that, in Vietnam, "We're heading hell bent into a mess. . . . Either everybody is crazy or I am." During the Cuban missile crisis, while the Joint Chiefs of Staff wanted to invade, Ball held firm for a diplomatic solution. In 1980, Secretary of State Cyrus Vance, alone among top officials, argued against the ill-fated Iran hostage rescue attempt. On issues ranging from arms control to Central America, George Shultz provided an essential counterweight to ideologues in the Reagan White House. During my own tenure, the State Department led the fight within the bureaucracy to confront Slobodan Milošević and halt ethnic cleansing in the Balkans. More recently, the department drafted a post-invasion plan for Iraq that anticipated virtually every problem that has since arisen—only to be overruled by the White House and Department of Defense.

A secretary of state must do more than understand foreign policy; she must know how domestic and international issues fit together, how to attract allies and disarm adversaries on Capitol Hill, how to communicate with the public, and how to defend her turf within the bureaucracy. She may feel at times that no foreign enemy is a bigger obstacle to doing her job than the White House's own Office of Management and Budget. President Clinton came to expect my annual call, on or about Christmas Eve, pleading for more money to be put in the following year's budget. As I told the president, the State Department was responsible for initiatives that would determine 50 percent of the history that would be written about our era, but we had at our disposal less than 1 percent of the federal budget.

Richard Nixon said, while campaigning in 1968, that "No secretary of state is really important; the president makes foreign policy." The second half of that sentence is true, the first part, nonsense. No president has time to do more than establish the broad outlines of policy except on a handful of issues. If the secretary of state is weak, unskilled, or ignored, American foreign policy will suffer. Even the most confident and internationalist of presidents will want a capable partner at Foggy Bottom.

The National Security Council (NSC) was created after World War II to help the professional bureaucracy rein in strong presidents; ironically, strong presidents have found ways ever since to use the NSC staff to bypass the professional bureaucracy. The NSC's official purpose is to serve as a "policy-forming and advisory body of top government officials to assist the president in making and coordinating overall policies in the political and military fields." In practice, the council has turned into a small empire whose functions overlap and at times supersede those of the agencies it was designed to coordinate.

When Harry Truman was president, most meetings of the NSC were chaired by the secretary of state or vice president.

Eisenhower, arriving at the White House in 1953, sought to mirror the military by creating the equivalent of an international chief of staff, called the national security advisor. Ike's choice was Robert Cutler, a retired brigadier general from Massachusetts. Cutler's successors have ranged in stature and style from the flamboyant Dr. Kissinger to the hawkish and bookish incumbent, Stephen Hadley, who has held political jobs under every Republican president since Nixon. Most national security advisors have been plucked either from academia (Kissinger, Zbigniew Brzezinski, Tony Lake, and Condoleezza Rice) or the military (among others, Colin Powell and Brent Scowcroft). Sandy Berger, one of the best, was a lawyer.

In choosing someone for such a role, you should be sure that your temperaments are compatible, for this is a person you will be seeing, on average, several times a day. He should be someone who can summarize complex issues cogently, serve as an honest broker, and write in a style that works for you. He must be confident enough to listen to other people's ideas without feeling threatened, and willing to knock heads together when necessary. He must be able to excel under pressure twenty hours a day and be available, as needed, the other four.

The structure and functioning of the NSC has changed with each president. Eisenhower used it, as a general might, to analyze problems and prepare options. Kennedy was less formal and preferred smaller meetings. He regularly brought others into the process, most notably during the Cuban missile crisis, when those at the table included his brother Robert, the attorney general, and former government officials from both parties.

Lyndon Johnson, who liked formality even less than Kennedy did, essentially buried the NSC; then Richard Nixon raised it up. Because of Nixon's desire that the White House control every aspect of foreign policy, Kissinger did not merely coordinate the national security agencies, he commanded them. Borrowing from the departments and recruiting bright young scholars, he enlarged the NSC staff by almost 600 percent. A genius at interagency politics, he capitalized on Nixon's distaste for large meetings, penchant for intrigue, and fear of being undermined. Thus it was Kissinger, not Secretary of State Rogers, who negotiated secretly with the North Vietnamese, reached a landmark arms control agreement with the Soviet Union, arranged Nixon's visit to China, and served as the administration's chief foreign policy spokesman. Kissinger's humbling of the State Department reached a climax in Nixon's abbreviated second term, when the charismatic diplomat ruled simultaneously as national security advisor and secretary of state.

By elevating the NSC position, Kissinger also poisoned it. His successors have taken pains to reassure colleagues that they would not try to replicate Kissinger, but some have been unable to resist the attempt. The most embarrassing examples were the Reagan administration's Bud McFarlane and John Poindexter, who sought a clandestine deal with Iran to free Americans being held by kidnappers in the Middle East. By arranging for the shipment of arms to the ayatollahs, the NSC broke laws and undid the president's vow never to negotiate with terrorists. Wrote George Shultz, "Bud always gave me the impression that as National Security Advisor, he wanted to be like Henry Kissinger, to do big and dramatic things secretly. As Henry brought off the opening to China, so Bud had the idea of an opening to Iran."

The arms-for-hostages scandal was ironic given that Reagan had taken office intending to downgrade the NSC. His budget-conscious administration sought to "defang" the Council by eliminating the staff responsible for congressional and press relations. At the time, I was a "fang," managing legislative affairs for Jimmy Carter's NSC, which was run by Brzezinski from a large corner office in the White House West Wing. I had the duty of personally escorting Reagan's first national security advisor, Richard Allen, past a warren of cubbyholes and clutter to the tiny basement office that he had been assigned by the Reagan team. Allen's face fell a foot. Within a few years, however, the impatience and ambition of his successors circumvented Reagan's original intent, and the NSC slipped its leash.

The NSC has retained a somewhat shadowy image in part because detailed accounts of foreign policy deliberations are not always kept. When I was doing research for my memoir, I was struck that although we keep word-for-word transcripts of a president's telephone talks with foreign leaders and precise summaries of most encounters with foreign dignitaries, we do not maintain a similar record of the debates in which the president's top advisors formulate their recommendations. The minutes of an average Rotary Club gathering would tell you as much about who said what as the official records of the NSC. The result is that historians will know significantly more about our international deliberations than our internal ones.

In preparing this memo, I found in my basement a handwritten assessment of the NSC drafted by a fellow member of Brzezinski's staff, Robert Gates, currently our secretary of defense. Although composed thirty years ago, Gates's analysis (unclassified, in case you were wondering what else I have stowed in my basement) remains on target. He argued that the NSC ordinarily reflects rather than shapes foreign policy, and that its role depends on relationships among the president's advisors and, most particularly, on the character of the president himself. Does the president have a clear sense of organization? Does he favor formality or informality? Does he want strong cabinet secretaries? How widely does he search for advice? How much involvement does he personally seek in the process? How does he feel about divided counsel? These questions are still the right ones, and as president elect, you should be thinking about your answers.

The third official at the top of the national security pyramid is the secretary of defense, one of the toughest jobs in Washington. A defense secretary must find time to advise the president while managing a Pentagon bureaucracy so enormous it could swallow the State Department without a burp. Every defense secretary enters office determined to modernize the armed forces, improve war-planning, eliminate redundancy, and curb interservice rivalry. It is as hard to accomplish these tasks, however, as it would be to turn an elephant into a ballerina.

Because management is so much a part of the job, many secretaries of defense have corporate experience, but the indispensable qualification is an ability to persuade senior military officials to trust and support the decisions made by civilian leaders. This can be complicated, because the military has its own perspectives on policy-making. Traditionally, the military's role has been confined to telling the president what it can and cannot do, while leaving to civilians the prerogative of deciding what it should do. There have always been exceptions, from McClellan's refusal to engage with the Confederates in the Civil War to MacArthur's desire to go on the offensive against China in the Korean conflict. Today, much depends on the personal styles of the senior military leaders. Some are inclined to salute and keep doubts to themselves; others insist—even at the risk of harm to their careers—that civilians be made fully aware of military concerns. As president, you should encourage members of the Joint Chiefs of Staff to speak freely, with no penalty for unwelcome views. You don't want to learn after the fact that "Yes, sir" actually meant, "You must be out of your mind."

At first glance, one might anticipate that the secretary of state would clash with the military over whether or not to use force. That does indeed happen, but not always in the expected way. While serving as ambassador to the UN, I was standing outside the White House one day with Gen. John Shalikashvili, chairman of the Joint Chiefs, in full uniform. A colleague approached and commented, "Ah, this must be war and peace." Shalikashvili retorted, "Yes, but which is which?" We had just left a meeting during which I had urged mobilizing NATO to end the civil war in Bosnia, a course resisted by the Pentagon, which was concerned about where such involvement would lead.

The truth is that the State Department has often been quicker than the Defense Department to suggest using force. This was the case during the Reagan years, also under President Clinton, and I suspect it may be true in the future, once our country has put Iraq behind us. When civilian leaders blunder, our armed forces pay the highest price. Understandably, our military is determined to avoid being ordered into quagmires or onto wild goose chases. Our fighting men and women are not game pieces to be sacrificed in pursuit of poorly defined or unachievable goals. On the other hand, a secretary of state is determined to take full advantage of all available assets. When she looks at the Department of Defense, she sees the most capable war-fighting, aggression-deterring, peace-building, troop-training, terrorist-tracking, equipment-moving, disaster-responding institution in history. She will want to make good use of its skills.

You will recall that, during the campaign, you promised to deliver fresh air to Washington, dispel the clouds of partisanship, and bring Americans together. Does this mean you should appoint members of the opposing party to senior positions in your administration?

Sure. Such gestures will advertise your desire to pursue policies that all Americans can support. You may silence critics and even be thought of as bold. There are practical considerations as well. As defense secretary, Republican Bill Cohen helped the Clinton administration communicate with potentially troublesome members of the Senate. FDR and JFK appointed opposition secretaries of the treasury because Wall Street slept better knowing Republicans were watching its cash. Lincoln selected a Tennessee Democrat as vice president in hopes of speeding reconciliation with the South after the Civil War.

Presidents are right to consider appointees from the other party. Members of the opposition, however, will have reasons to keep their distance. A bipartisan appointee is likely to forfeit the trust of old allies without necessarily gaining the confidence of new colleagues. Lacking independent authority, he or she may feel like an ornament used to decorate somebody else's lawn. The most likely candidate for a bipartisan appointment, therefore, is a person with moderate ideas and no future political ambition. Such an appointment will provide more the appearance of bipartisanship than the reality. Too bad, but that is why we have elections.

•   •   •

Few spectacles are more entertaining to Washington insiders than watching ordinarily dignified people audition for senior White House or cabinet posts. As you have discovered, the jostling begins during the early days of the campaign. And it doesn't end even when the foreign policy team is named, because the question remains who, other than the president, will be captain. Aggressive appointees maneuver behind the scenes, offering plans for how the national security decision-making process should work. One prize is who gets to convene the meetings. Under Nixon, there were six senior committees, and Kissinger headed them all. Under Carter, there were two committees, one for policy and one for crises, with the relevant cabinet officer chairing the first and Zbig Brzezinski the second. Since Brzezinski enjoyed being in charge, no one could be sure that a crisis, once declared, would ever end. Al Haig, Reagan's first secretary of state, drafted a twenty-one-page memo designating himself "vicar" of U.S. foreign policy. The memo, which was promptly leaked by the White House, soon disappeared—as did Haig.

You would think that the national security advisor and the secretaries of state and defense, each with a deep stake in the administration's success and chosen by the same president, would find ways to work together smoothly. In fact, relations among the trio have often been strained, at considerable cost to the presidents they served and to our country. Kissinger was a one-man show until Nixon was succeeded by Gerald Ford, after which he butted heads repeatedly with the opinionated young secretary of defense, Donald Rumsfeld. Jimmy Carter had known that Vance and Brzezinski would often disagree, with the former seeking balance in all things and Brzezinski liking to take firm positions. Carter hoped the contrast would prove constructive. Instead, Vance and Brzezinski competed to define Carter, wasting energy and sending mixed messages. In the end, the Carter presidency achieved much yet received credit for little. Under Reagan, George Shultz fought openly with Defense Secretary Caspar Weinberger, except when he and Weinberger teamed up to do battle with the NSC.

While I was often a bemused observer of the Vance-Brzezinski competition, I felt caught in the middle of the rivalry between Brzezinski and Edmund Muskie, who, in the spring of 1980, succeeded Vance as secretary of state. I had worked for Muskie in the Senate before being hired by Brzezinski at the NSC. They were both heroes of mine, but I soon realized that they did not understand each other.

After one contentious meeting, Muskie asked, "Why does your boss feel the need to show off in front of the president? Who cares if he knows the name of every tribe in Nigeria?" "He's not showing off," I replied. "He's a professor, and professors are trained to know facts."

For his part, Brzezinski complained, "Why doesn't your friend Muskie do anything at meetings except ask questions? We need to know what he thinks." I explained, "He's a senator. Senators ask questions. They don't take positions until they have to, and they don't have to until there's a vote." The two even quarreled about who was more Polish—a fight that Brzezinski won because he was born in Poland and knew the language. Muskie had a Polish father but was born in Maine—not the same thing.

The national security decision-making system works best when each of the senior officials is content to do the job assigned and does not try to do all three. The secretary of state should be the president's primary policymaker and the person most responsible for publicly explaining U.S. positions. The national security advisor should manage the daily foreign policy–related activities of the president, coordinate the interagency process, and see that necessary decisions are both made and implemented. The secretary of defense should concentrate on running his own department, make certain that the president has the benefit of military advice, and figure out how to make best use of the agency's resources. There is room for all three to operate without stepping on one another's toes; room, as well, to accommodate our UN ambassador and officials from other departments whose views may be essential on particular issues. The space can become cramped, however, if the bureaucratic equivalent of Bigfoot walks through the door.

According to Woodrow Wilson, "The chief embarrassment in discussing [the vice president's] office is that, in explaining how little there is to be said, one has evidently said all there is to say." Writing in the early twentieth century, the parodist Finley Peter Dunne opined that the vice presidency:

> isn't a crime exactly. You can't be sent to jail for it, but it's a kind of a disgrace. . . . During the campaign . . . the candidate for the vice-presidency . . . goes to all the church fairs and wakes and appears at public meetings between a cornet solo and the glee club. . . . [When in office] it is his business to call at the White House [every morning] and inquire after the president's health. When told the president was never better, he gives three cheers and leaves with a heavy heart.

America grew up on jokes about how powerless the vice president is. Who would have thought that, for the past eight years, we would be hearing jokes about how overbearing the vice president has become?

Recent books are filled with (mostly anonymous) complaints from former Bush administration figures that Dick Cheney has had too many opportunities to sway policy, that he has so many bites at the apple, his colleagues are left with nothing but seeds and stems. The vice president is represented in gatherings of the NSC, sits in every group meeting with the president, and has frequent lunches with Mr. Bush on a one-on-one basis. By tradition, the veep withholds his advice to the boss in front of others, except when directly invited by the president to weigh in. This frees him from the need to justify his views in a group setting. The problem, though, is less institutional than personal. Never before has a vice president exercised as much power as has Dick Cheney. He created his own national security staff of fifteen professionals—a larger staff than John Kennedy's entire NSC—and then sought to keep its activities secret from Congress on the ludicrous grounds that the vice president is not really part of the executive branch.

The Cheney model is unlikely to be repeated in the near future because the impression created—that the vice president is the one really running the show—is demeaning to the chief executive. Al Gore, George H. W. Bush, and Walter Mondale all provide better examples, each discreetly involved in policy-making, assigned serious areas of responsibility, and used as a private sounding board for the president. Gore, especially, was effective as a kind of super-ambassador to key countries such as Russia and Egypt. So much is going on in the world that you will want your vice president pitching in and even demonstrating that he has what it takes one day to be president himself. We will all be more comfortable, however, if before actually assuming the duties of commander in chief, he waits until you have left.

• • •

Each day, the federal government makes thousands of decisions. Issues that cannot be settled at a low level are pushed upward. Only the most significant find a place on the agenda of the NSC's interagency process, which is designed to save the president from being swamped by routine matters. Depending on an issue's gravity, the chief executive will respond to interagency recommendations either by checking a box on a memo or convening a meeting of his national security team. That is a good time to look for blood on the floor, because beneath the polite memos and civil discussions there exists a sometimes vicious struggle to push the president in one direction or another. As questions are considered, informal alliances are forged across agency lines. Like-minded officials in one department may conspire with those elsewhere to defeat the position of their own cabinet secretary. Such alliances can accelerate a decision or block it while influencing how issues are framed, who gets invited to meetings, what information is presented, and whose positions are discredited through stories planted in the media.

Officials who do not like their chances within the system look for opportunities outside it. Shultz sometimes found an ally in Nancy Reagan. Clinton officials turned to the many "friends of Bill." Those seeking to sway the current president have at times sought the help of Christian evangelicals, especially on such challenges as poverty and AIDS.

Even when the system works as designed, there are weaknesses. Isolated at the top, the president may be the last to know why a policy must be changed. His reaction upon receiving a recommendation may well be "Why didn't we do this months ago?" Second, a passive president may rely on the system too much, producing government by bureaucracy, too slow to cope with today's needs. The system also provides no guarantee that a president will know all that is taking place inside his administration. In Clinton's first term, key decisions were made on Somalia and Rwanda that tarnished perceptions of the president's leadership, and yet Clinton was not personally involved in making those decisions. The pivotal choices—thought at the time to be in keeping with settled policy—were made at the subcabinet level. When I received instructions as UN ambassador to vote to withdraw peacekeepers from Rwanda amid the genocide there, my call of protest was routed to a divisional director at the NSC.

Finally, the system is designed to incorporate the views of all relevant agencies. This is both a strength and a weakness. Arguments can be healthy, ensuring that many interests are represented and that the resulting consensus has broad support. The weakness arises when the consensus is achieved by avoiding tough questions or by using so many verbal qualifiers that conclusions are reduced to mush. I expect this was the case with the Bush administration's own response to genocide—this time in Darfur. The president wanted to act; meetings were convened; decisions were announced; still, not much happened.

So, be forewarned. The interagency process provides a means for considering issues systematically and with many views taken into account. It is an aid to leadership—but is not to be confused with leadership itself.

Until 1936, presidents were inaugurated in early March, allowing a period of roughly four months from the November election. This gave the new president ample time to ride his horse up from Virginia or down from Boston. Your transition will last seventy-five days: How best to use your time?

Here's an idea. Prior to his inauguration, Bill Clinton hosted a two-day seminar on the economy, helping to set the tone for his presidency by showing that he was open-minded and determined to make good on promises made to working families during his campaign. You might consider something similar on the relationship between our domestic economy and its global equivalent. As chief executive, you will want to prevent a return to protectionism at a time when resentment toward multinational companies and free trade is high. People in vulnerable jobs are tired of having their concerns dismissed, and yet the prescriptions often put forward to address worker resentment are either unrealistic or likely to invite retaliation. A seminar would not resolve the economic dilemma, but it may help you to deal with the political challenge, which is to gain and maintain the trust of business and labor leaders who have no faith in each other. Let them blunt their swords against one another verbally while you gently push them toward one another substantively.

Remember also that the transition can be a vulnerable time, with the political authority of one president on the wane and the incoming president not yet legally empowered. It would be educational for you—and reassuring to our country—if you and the people you have designated to serve were to take part in a full-scale crisis-response simulation. Our intelligence officials, in association with military and academic experts, would be only too happy to scare the daylights out of you, while you would get a bit of useful on-the-job practice. After Inauguration Day, we will be looking to you for direction in the event of a terrorist attack or public health emergency; it would be unsettling if the first words out of your mouth were "What do we do now?"

One personal suggestion: Stay fit. Leave time for exercise. FDR had his physical therapy, Truman walked, Eisenhower and Nixon golfed, Nixon also liked bowling, and Clinton both golfed and jogged. If all else fails, clear brush. Less advisable is the example of John Quincy Adams, who rose early each morning to swim naked in the Potomac. A female journalist once trapped him there, sat on his clothes, and forced him to choose between revealing himself physically and revealing himself philosophically by answering questions while standing in water up to his neck. He gave the interview.

CHAPTER 4

The Art of Persuasion

I was taught in college that the purpose of foreign policy is to persuade others to do what we want or, better yet, to want what we want. I have learned since that a president has a limited number of tools with which to attempt this. Some are coercive, others offer rewards, still others appeal to shared interests or values. Because relations among countries are so complex, our government ordinarily uses a combination of means. This process has been compared to chess but more closely resembles billiards, where one ball hits another, which may hit two or three more, each of which may carom off a cushion into still others. Every move alters the landscape on which future moves are made. The player with the steadiest hand and the most skill at envisioning future alignments will do best. Adherence to all rules and courtesies is advised, but you always have the option—as in billiards—of bopping your opponent over the head with a stick.

If you grow frustrated in the White House, it will be because no one can win every game and because each victory today is succeeded tomorrow by a new contest at least as stressful. For a president managing world affairs, mere effort is no sure path to reward. Lyndon Johnson tried to make two days out of every one by rising early, napping briefly in the afternoon, and working well into the night. Reagan, on the other hand, joked, "It's true hard work never killed anyone, but I figure why take the chance?"

As president, you will first define your goals, then select the means to achieve them. Foreign Policy 101 dictates that America's top priority should be to protect our territory, citizens, and economic well-being. The protection of territory became more demanding, however, following the introduction of the intercontinental ballistic missile and, more recently, the intercontinental terrorist plot. National security experts used to refer to the globe's "strategic map," showing the location of oil (or, previously, coal), vital navigation routes, and convenient sites for military bases. For decades, this map was colored blue for allies of the West, red for countries within the Soviet orbit, and a pale, suggestive yellow for those unwilling to take sides. We don't draw maps like that anymore. Our strategic interests are no longer bound by geographic limits. The bin Ladens and Zawahiris of tomorrow may even now be reaching the age of maturity in the crowded neighborhoods of Mogadishu, the ancient streets of Peshawar, the markets of Marrakesh, the apartment buildings of London, or the tree-lined suburbs of New Jersey. It sounds like a slogan but still rings true: in the twenty-first century, what happens anywhere can matter everywhere.

During your presidency, the defense of U.S. territory may require disrupting a terrorist cell or restricting nuclear activity in the most remote locations. Similarly, the protection of U.S. citizens will demand constant attention given that American scholars, businesspeople, journalists, missionaries, and humanitarian volunteers are perpetually active in most countries and, on too many occasions, subject to harassment or arbitrary arrest. There are, moreover, literally hundreds of indirect U.S. interests related to our values (promotion of democracy), workers (elevation of labor standards), health (protection of the environment), prosperity (energy prices), and so on.

Priorities are not created equal. Certainly, an Iran equipped with nuclear arms would pose a more worrisome threat than the infringement of intellectual property rights. The rise in Europe or Asia of a hostile superpower would cause more angst than the emergence of a new Caribbean dictator or a dispute with trading partners over the safety of biogenetic foods.

Priorities also change. If you're in a kayak, intent on making good time, your priorities will be altered if you suddenly find yourself heading for a waterfall. During the past forty years, such unlikely places as Vietnam, Cambodia, Afghanistan, El Salvador, Nicaragua, Panama, Somalia, Haiti, Rwanda, Bosnia, East Timor, Chechnya, Sudan, and Burma all dominated our foreign policy agendas for a time. So, in 1999, did a little Cuban boy named Elián González who was found clinging to an inner tube off the coast of Fort Lauderdale. Even the smallest issue or the most distant place can surge to prominence because of the notoriety it receives, the lessons it might teach, or the larger events it sets in motion.

Americans love to identify jobs and check them off before going on to the next one. That is not how the world works. Old issues that seem settled don't stay that way; many problems cannot be solved at all and instead must be managed; meanwhile, new challenges arise and soon start to pile up.

This means that if you do not yet know how to juggle, you soon will. My first year as secretary of state went relatively well; by the middle of the second, I felt like a piñata at a birthday party. The supposedly stable post–cold war era seemed to be falling apart; we were dealing simultaneously with the Asian financial crisis, revolution in Indonesia, the Indian and Pakistani nuclear tests, four separate wars in Africa, an outbreak of violence in Kosovo, reports of a secret nuclear facility in North Korea, deadlocked peace negotiations in the Middle East, and bogus but well-publicized allegations that I was obstructing UN weapons inspections in Iraq. When August arrived, I looked forward to a few days off, traveling to Italy for a friend's wedding. I was awakened to news that our embassies in Kenya and Tanzania had been bombed. As president, you will set a course and pick your fights only to find that some fights have picked you.

Foreign policy begins with diplomacy. The word is derived from the Greek term "diploma," meaning a folded paper used for official purposes, or a license. A diplomat is licensed to negotiate on behalf of a nation. Although originally the province of aristocrats, diplomacy evolved into a profession when royal dominions gave way to modern states. In the hands of such as Tallyrand, Bismarck, and Metternich, diplomacy also acquired the aura of back room dealing as countries conspired one against another and made or broke commitments depending on the needs of the moment.

Diplomacy today is conducted more openly. Unlike Talleyrand and his peers, a modern secretary of state must answer questions in public and before legislators about what she has been up to. She need not say everything, but as we have seen from the recent deluge of tell-all books, even the most confidential discussion may end up in somebody's memoir. The diplomat's job, however, has remained constant: to obtain the maximum advantage at the smallest cost.

The seat of routine diplomacy is the embassy, which represents American interests and serves as a base for personnel from a dozen or more agencies. In times gone by, our embassies were welcoming places, host to Fourth of July celebrations at which the values of liberty were ingested along with frankfurters and beer. This has changed as security fears have forced our diplomats to retreat behind high walls guarded by dogs, metal detectors, and steel doors. A visit to one of our embassies today may feel more like a trip to a prison than to an outpost of liberty. American ambassadors still host parties and do their best to win friends, but they must be protected at all times. No longer do they drive through foreign capitals with miniature U.S. flags affixed to their cars. To a youngster in, let us say Nairobi or Islamabad, the American ambassador is the nice person standing next to the broad-shouldered people with wires in their ears and guns on their belts. Such a loss.

A president's own involvement in diplomacy consists primarily of a steady stream of phone calls and of meetings of various sizes. Over the years, countries have organized themselves into a bewildering array of groups, each with its own acronym. You can look forward to bilats, trilats, quads, quints, G-7s and G-8s, EU, NATO, APEC, and UN summits, plus special events. You may at first begrudge the time required to meet with individual foreign leaders, but you will soon find that you enjoy the company of most. Presidents and prime ministers form an elite club and have much to discuss that goes beyond talking points on cards. Multilateral diplomacy, on the other hand, can be both numbing and odd. Aides choreograph every movement weeks in advance so you may feel less like a giant bestriding the world stage than a puppet being pulled this way, then that. In Asia, you will be asked to pose for photographs while wearing a batik shirt or an outfit resembling pajamas. To understand all that is being said, you will have to adjust your hair to accommodate ear phones, a trickier task for some of us than for others.

You will also learn as you travel that, for a national leader, you live in a comparative hut. Years ago, I showed pictures of Saddam Hussein's palaces to an Arab emir, who exclaimed indignantly, "Why, his palace is bigger than mine!" Arabs are not the only ones who live in palaces. The French have a palace for their president; so do the Poles. The Czechs have a castle, while the Filipinos have a presidential bungalow that was big enough to store all of Mrs. Marcos's shoes. I visited the outgoing leader of Nigeria not long ago; his home is luxurious, and there are giraffes in the backyard.

As comparatively modest as it is, the White House can serve as a valuable diplomatic tool. Most foreign leaders would love to be invited for an official state visit, complete with welcoming ceremony on the White House lawn, a twenty-one-gun salute, a gala dinner, drinks on the Truman Balcony, and perhaps even a night in the Queen's bedroom on the residence's second floor. You can also ask visitors to enjoy the wooded surroundings of Camp David or to spend a weekend at your summer home—if you have one. Whatever the arrangements, an invitation to a summit meeting in America may be used to sweeten or close a deal.

When you travel, you will be crowded by top aides elbowing each other to be allowed into meetings. Ironically, the one person essential to have in the room may not officially be an advisor at all but your interpreter. The interpreter plays a pivotal role, because negotiations demand precision in language and often some degree of personal warmth. An interpreter's job, therefore, goes well beyond the literal translation of words; he must convey the negotiator's desired emphasis, nuance, and tone. This is only possible if he has a sophisticated knowledge of the subjects under discussion. The superstar of American interpreters is Gamal Helal, an Egyptian-born naturalized U.S. citizen, who has coolly translated into and out of Arabic the words of the last three presidents, seven defense secretaries, and six secretaries of state. Often Helal has been the only person in meetings other than the president and his Arab interlocutor. In Geneva in 1991, he translated as James Baker gave his Iraqi counterpart an ultimatum: leave Kuwait or else! During the Clinton administration, we sometimes asked Helal to meet with Arafat one-on-one. An interpreter such as Gamal, who knows not only the language but also the politics, personalities, and culture of a particular situation, can be a unique asset.

In other situations, the interpreter can save a meeting in a different way. When in Saudi Arabia as secretary of state, I was required as a matter of courtesy to meet with old King Fahd, who was chronically ill and sadly incapable of saying much. The role of interpreter was assumed by Prince Bandar, the longtime Saudi ambassador to the United States. A typical meeting went like this: "Good evening, your majesty. I appreciate the opportunity to extend to you the best wishes of the United States." "Harumph," the king would reply (in Arabic). Then, from Bandar, the translation: "His Royal Highness King Fahd says that we are delighted to welcome Madam Secretary to our home and trust that you will let us know if there is any way in which we can make your stay more pleasant."

Aside from formal meetings, a president commonly becomes directly involved in diplomacy either when issues are at their easiest or when they are intractable. If an issue is an easy one, you will be enlisted for the purpose of chalking up a win. If it is intractable, you will be involved because negotiators at a lower level could not get the job done. This will happen frequently, because negotiators are trained to conceal their bottom line until the last minute, and by definition the last minute has not been reached until the decisive questions have reached your desk. The more clearly your negotiators are empowered to speak for you, the less often you will have to step into the breach. You can help by making explicit that your negotiators are authorized to take firm positions and by showing, when tested, that you will drive at least as hard a bargain as they. If you are thought to be more willing to compromise than the professionals by whom you are represented, foreign dignitaries will insist, "We must deal directly with the White House!" To you, the demand may seem flattering, but it is, in fact, no compliment.

Prior to any bargaining, a skilled diplomat will negotiate first with her own government, to secure as many chips and as much leverage as possible. At the same time, she will learn and inwardly digest information about the foreign parties with whom she intends to engage, trying to discern the line between what they will demand and what they can be made to accept. When discussions begin, she will try to assert control by defining the terms, outlining the issues, and tolerating tantrums that may help other negotiators justify compromise. She may adopt the tactful approach practiced by our first diplomat, Benjamin Franklin, who was careful not to contradict anyone but instead quietly asked questions and raised doubts; or she may choose a more dramatic style—storming around, threatening to call in the press, assigning blame for failure. In either case, she will likely seek an outcome that will enable all sides to claim they have held firm on key points.

When at an impasse, it is sometimes useful either to narrow or broaden a negotiation's scope. The United States might, for example, want to talk to a government that is serving on the UN Security Council about its position on an upcoming vote. That government might want to talk to us about its need for economic assistance and help in marketing exports. A negotiation that combines a broad range of issues is more likely to succeed because it can be portrayed by both sides as balanced, with some give-and-take for each.

You may well arrive in the presidency with a short list of diplomatic projects in which you are determined to take a personal hand. You may also find yourself dissatisfied with the way a certain set of discussions is proceeding. In such an instance, you might want to appoint a special presidential envoy to demonstrate your interest and enliven negotiations that have stalled. A fresh pair of eyes can sometimes identify promising new angles to pursue; also, a high-level envoy may have more sway with foreign governments and factions because he or she is known to have the president's ear. Bill Clinton's involvement in Northern Ireland, aided by special envoy George Mitchell, is a good example. Such a tool can be overused, however, adding a layer of bureaucracy for no good purpose. If we have special envoys for every unresolved problem, they will hardly be special. When a challenge is just too much for conventional diplomacy, or if only a small push is needed to get an important job done, such an envoy will make sense. In other instances, it is better to rely on the career professionals, who deserve their own chance to shine.

To some Americans, negotiating is inherently a sign of weakness. The truly strong, it is thought, don't need to talk; they just flex their muscles and *do*. The reality is that not every disagreement is best resolved by flexing. During President Bush's first term, Dick Cheney was asked about the possibility of negotiating with North Korea. He replied that America's mandate was to defeat evil, not negotiate with evil—a tasty sound bite but, as a national security strategy, without substance. While Cheney blustered, North Korea built and tested a nuclear weapon. Lesson learned: much of the president's last two years have been given over to negotiations—and apparently productive ones at that—with North Korea.

Diplomacy is not pursued for its own sake; it is a means of creating change in the existing order, whether by making new friends, mending differences with old ones, or finding peaceful ways to accommodate a rising power. It can be most useful, however, where the road is roughest—clearing the way for adversaries to coexist.

FDR said in the months before World War II that "No man can tame a tiger into a kitten by stroking it." He was referring to Adolf Hitler, and he was right. The 1938 agreement at Munich between Hitler and the Western powers was a betrayal of my native Czechoslovakia and testimony to the folly of appeasement. Ever since, those opposed to negotiating with unsavory governments have pointed to the lesson of that event. This use of history will serve to remind you that evil exists and that some confrontations cannot be avoided.

We must also acknowledge, however, that diplomatic solutions, like human conceptions, are rarely immaculate. As a practitioner of foreign policy, you cannot be more concerned with your own moral standing than with the morality and value of the results you seek to achieve. To solve problems, or ease them, it is sometimes necessary to do business with genuinely villainous people, though you would be well advised, when you do, not to drink toasts or smile in front of cameras. In World War II, Stalin was our ally. In the 1970s, Nixon went to China. Two decades later, I met with Burma's military junta, Slobodan Milošević, and Kim Jong-il. The Bush administration picked up where President Clinton left off in dealing with Libya's Qaddafi. If engagement were identical to appeasement, the art of diplomacy would have no purpose. We have no need to make peace with friends. We have a responsibility to use the full national security toolbox to keep our people safe. That may not be possible without resorting to force, but it begins, as civilization demands, with dialogue.

A second foreign policy tool available to every president is the microphone. Any hour, any day, you will have the option of striding into the Rose Garden or East Room to propose, exhort, or clarify. In so doing, you will have both the obligation to teach and the opportunity to persuade.

The presidents who have excelled as educators have done more than announce three-point plans and appeal to the spirit of 1776. They have used words to paint a picture or tell a story, to explain what they did, why they did it, and what will happen next. Instead of speeches, they have begun conversations or, in the case of Franklin Roosevelt, mastered the art of the fireside chat. As he told Americans near the onset of World War II: "This war is a new kind of war. It is different from all other wars of the past. . . . It is warfare in terms of every continent, every island, every sea, every air lane in the world. That is the reason why I have asked you to take out and spread before you a map of the whole earth, and to follow with me the . . . battle lines of this war."*

By contrast, Lyndon Johnson's efforts to give meaning to U.S. involvement in Vietnam were hampered by his own inner doubts. He feared the war would drain support from his beloved Great Society programs, so instead of being forthright, he promoted the idea of a limited conflict that could be won without mobilizing popular passions. Privately, he conceded that "If you have a mother-in-law with only one eye and she has it in the center of her forehead, you don't keep her in the living room." Richard Nixon, who inherited the war, made a more systematic effort to explain U.S. policy, though he, too, neglected to mention certain details—such as the invasion of Cambodia.

When modern presidents speak to Americans, the rest of the world will eavesdrop, so be careful of your words. Prior to any important speech, I asked my staff, "Is there anything I should not say?" I was told, for example, to refrain from praising Anwar Sadat to Arabs; Americans think highly of the slain Egyptian president for precisely the reasons that many Arabs don't. I was also told not to speak of the Persian Gulf when addressing Arab audiences or of the Arabian Gulf when speaking (from a distance) to the people of Iran. Both terms are possessive, but each refers to the same body of water. It was easier (and safer) simply to refer to "the Gulf." I was told as well not

---

* In 1990, I hosted Czechoslovak leader Václav Havel on his first visit to Washington. Havel returned from a meeting with President George H. W. Bush exclaiming about a set of *National Geographic* maps he had seen in the White House. I called National Geographic and was told that the organization sent a set of maps to the White House each year. The practice began after Franklin Roosevelt complained shortly before the start of World War II that he didn't have any decent maps. Roosevelt liked his maps so much he immediately requested that another set be made for Winston Churchill. After my call, National Geographic sent maps to Havel, who liked them just as much.

to equate America with the United States while traveling in our hemisphere, because that habit is understandably resented by the hundreds of millions of Americans who live south of the Rio Grande. I learned a different type of lesson when, early in my tenure as UN ambassador, I made an offhand comment about a potential threat to oil supplies, only to be startled when gas prices immediately jumped. Not all the advice was helpful. While en route to Beijing, I was counseled not to refer to the coming of Y2K because the traditional Chinese calendar had passed that mark about 2,700 years previously. I dutifully complied, only to have the Chinese foreign minister eagerly describe his country's anticipated role in the third millennium. Jimmy Carter's first presidential foray to Mexico was marred by a reference to Montezuma's revenge; President George W. Bush should not have compared the war on terror to a crusade, an error he readily acknowledged and then repeated; even JFK could cause linguistic controversy—his famous declaration of solidarity with West Berlin ("I am a Berliner") was later characterized as a gaffe by some because "Berliner" is also a German term for "jelly doughnut."

The temptation to try connecting with a foreign audience by speaking its language, if only for a few words or a phrase, can be hard to resist. It is a practice, however, that requires preparation; improvisers proceed at their own risk. Andrei Gromyko, the longtime Soviet foreign minister, prided himself on his grasp of idiomatic English. At a social gathering in Washington, he proposed a toast to his hostess, the wife of Secretary of State Dean Rusk. Smiling at his fellow guests, he raised his glass urbanely, and exclaimed with genial innocence, "Up your bottoms!"

•   •   •

The calendar will offer many chances for you to practice public diplomacy before a global audience. This is a priceless gift, especially now, when America's reputation needs refurbishing. In his second term, President George W. Bush made a diligent effort to explain his policies in terms the rest of the world might accept. He made little headway because, by then, many people distrusted his sincerity. You must find ways (and words) to inspire renewed confidence.

It is no shame to admit that many of the words you will use as president will be written by someone else. Thus it has always been. George Washington's first official message to Congress was drafted by James Madison, who in his capacity as a legislator also drafted the reply. Even Lincoln had help from William Seward, his secretary of state. The ideal partnership between a speechwriter and a modern president was that which existed between John Kennedy and Ted Sorensen. Because they had worked together for years, Sorensen knew how and what his boss thought and the language with which he was comfortable. Sorensen was knowledgeable and experienced enough to serve as a principal advisor to Kennedy, in addition to writing speeches. He didn't create Kennedy's voice, but he did compose arrangements that brought out its full energy and range. The result was a combination of elegance and substance that—jelly doughnuts aside—lifted America in the eyes of the world.

Bill Clinton did not have a similar relationship with any speechwriter because few people can write better than Clinton can talk. Unlike Kennedy, who loved classical references and taut aphorisms, Clinton disdained high-sounding phrases. He spoke like an Arkansas governor who just happened to know more about everything than most people know about anything and who had a story to fit every situation. Clinton may not have matched Kennedy's legacy of memorable quotations, but he, too, lifted America in the eyes of the world.

In the Clinton administration, national security speeches were drafted, and logically so, by writers on the National Security Council's staff. Although the political arm of the White House was consulted, the purpose, language, and emphasis of the president's remarks were set by the foreign policy team. Under President George W. Bush, major foreign policy addresses were drafted primarily by the same trio of writers who worked on domestic and political speeches. The result, especially in Bush's first term, was simultaneously spectacular and catastrophic. Bush's rhetoric captured people's attention across the globe in a manner both riveting and grating. The "axis of evil" reference in the 2002 State of the Union address diverted attention from America's battle with Al Qaeda and complicated life for pro-democracy activists in Iran. The president's insistence that we were fighting terrorists in Iraq so we would not have to fight them in America played well in the United States but not so well in Iraq—where it mattered more. Bush's declaration in his second inaugural that "America, in this young century, proclaims liberty throughout all the world and to all the inhabitants thereof" was so presumptuous that no mainstream national security advisor in either party would have conceived it. Even Peggy Noonan, a conservative who wrote for Reagan, said that the speech was characterized by "deep moral seriousness and no moral modesty."

No one would recommend to any president that he ignore the domestic audience when delivering a speech to the world. I wonder, then, why political advisors sometimes urge presidents to ignore the world when delivering speeches to domestic audiences. Every speech to every audience is both domestic and global—and each should be composed with both audiences in mind. I hope you will use your speeches to convey the qualities we want people everywhere to see in America: toughness blended with compassion, confidence in our own ideals coupled with respect for the ideas and traditions of others.

Foreign aid did not play a major role in your campaign—which explains, in part, why you were elected. Though the American people will generously support particular humanitarian projects, foreign aid, as a whole, is as politically popular as bird flu. It is also, however, a useful national security tool. The purpose of assistance is the same as other tools: to persuade countries to act in ways that we would like. This sounds more calculating than it is, because we genuinely want to help and wish most countries well.

America's first major overseas relief effort was humanitarian: to relieve hunger and assist refugees in the aftermath of World War I. Following the second great war, the Truman administration developed the Marshall Plan to help Europe rebuild. In his 1949 inaugural address, Truman announced a broader initiative, to "make available to peace-loving peoples the benefits of our store of technical knowledge in order to help them realize their aspirations for a better life."

From the start, the altruistic side of Truman's idea was balanced by a desire to influence the political direction of poor countries. The communists were trying to buy support; so would we. At its best, our development aid contributed to a rise in life expectancy, literacy, and basic nutrition. Although foreign aid still conjures up images of waste, the truth is that assistance is now so thoroughly audited and accompanied by so much paperwork that many potential recipients do not think it worth the trouble to accept.

According to Donald Rumsfeld, "The present structure of the U.S. government foreign assistance is an anachronism. A system is needed that recognizes assistance for what it really is, a component of our national security strategy. In simple terms, Defense has resources but not authorities, while State has authorities but not resources. . . . The only choice is to trash the current laws and to undertake a total overhaul of the current system."

If he is implying that the State Department should be given resources equal to its responsibilities, I find myself in rare agreement with Mr. Rumsfeld. While in office, I had at my disposal about one-seventh the level of funds (in real dollars) that were available to the secretary of state half a century earlier. Considering the treasure we invest in fighting wars, the amounts we devote to their prevention are a pittance. As for Rumsfeld's desire to scrap the laws and start over, forget it—we would end up with something even worse. If the executive branch finds it hard to set priorities, the 535 members of Congress are even less capable of that task. It would be like asking the states to design a sensible system for scheduling presidential primaries. This does not mean that improvements are impossible. There are ingenious and dedicated people studying the issue; listen to them, but keep your expectations in check.

You should think of foreign assistance as a lubricant that gives other countries more reasons to help us and improves their ability to do so. At the most practical level, it helps to pay for radiation and bomb-detection equipment at foreign air and seaports through which traffic bound for the United States must transit. Diplomatically, it can sweeten the pot for a government otherwise reluctant to make peace. Politically, it can mitigate the impression that America is selfish. We are second to last among industrialized countries in the amount of our wealth that we share with the poor. We can and should do more because it is right and because others will care more about the extraordinary dangers threatening us if we show we care about the everyday dangers confronting and often killing them.

In any sizable group of foreign policy experts, you will find some who believe international law is civilization's only hope and others who see it as a false god whose worship breeds complacency and may one day lead to our destruction.

The skeptics warn that it is naïve to rely for protection on so-called global norms that are ignored by terrorists, aggressors, dictators, and thugs. The United States must be free, so the argument runs, to do what is necessary to defeat the likes of bin Laden. We cannot allow ourselves to be judged by others. A great power shows its greatness by acting, so why would we allow ourselves to be hemmed in or tied down?

Supporters insist that—aside from the ability to manipulate our thumbs—international law is all that separates men and women from beasts. Force defeated the Nazis, but it was law that convicted them and executed their leaders. Law provides the basis for holding war criminals accountable, for settling disputes without violence, and for conducting the day-to-day business of world affairs. To argue that international law is useless because it is not always enforced is no different than suggesting that laws against murder are without value because murders are still committed. No country gains more from a strong international legal regime than Americans do, precisely because we have so many interests to protect.

When the war began in Afghanistan, Secretary of State Powell argued that enemy combatants should be treated in accord with the Geneva Conventions because the requirements are not burdensome and because we shouldn't give other nations a rationale for mistreating U.S. prisoners. As the world well knows, Powell's reasoning was rejected—at enormous cost to America's standing. The Bush administration's baffling record on prisoners and torture, its allergy to treaties in general, and its appointment of an ambassador to the UN (John Bolton) who expressed open contempt for international law placed the United States in a poor position to argue the importance of law in other contexts. You will, I trust, be far smarter.

America alone cannot solve most problems. International organizations and law enable us to merge our energy and resources with others to achieve shared goals. What is sometimes sacrificed in efficiency is made up for in legitimacy—so it is not just America that supports a particular cause; it is the world. To the extent that global institutions help countries everywhere to pull in the right direction, the burdens on America are reduced.

As critics are quick to point out, many international institutions do not function as well as they might. The global banks have a lesser role to play now than previously, given the greater availability of private capital. The new UN Human Rights Council suffers from the same problem as the old: too many members who do not actually believe in human rights. The UN Security Council is unrepresentative, unaccountable, and in the habit of approving resolutions its members are unwilling to enforce. The UN system as a whole is large and uncoordinated; it is the ultimate committee. I used to joke that the world body is like a corporation with almost two hundred people on its board of directors, each of whom speaks a different language, answers to his own priorities, acts in accordance with his own set of values, and has a brother-in-law who needs a job. As for international law, it has a hard time keeping pace. Politics and technology move more rapidly than global negotiations.

The question for you is whether our response to the short-comings in the international system should be to devise ways to improve that system or to work around it. It would indeed be a mistake to put so much faith in institutions such as the UN that we neglect to take necessary actions on our own behalf. We should have learned in recent years, however, that there can be a high cost attached to going it alone—and that unilateralism in many instances simply doesn't work. This argues for making multilateral tools as effective as we can, whether the purpose is social enrichment, building peace, or doing battle with an un-compromising foe.

CHAPTER 5

Fifty Lady Sharpshooters

In the spring of 1898, as trouble beckoned between America and Spain, a letter addressed to President William McKinley arrived at the White House. "I for one feel confident that your good judgment will carry America safely through without war," wrote the correspondent. "But in case of such an event I am ready to place a company of fifty lady sharpshooters at your disposal. Every one of them will be an American and as they will furnish their own Arms and Ammunition will be little if any expense to the government." This patriotic offer from Phoebe Ann Moses, better known as Annie Oakley, sums up the American attitude toward using force. We expect our leaders to keep us out of war, but we will fight if we must—and so much the better if we can do so at limited cost to the Treasury.

The great seal of the United States features an eagle clutching an olive branch in one set of talons, in the other, spears. Old Abe sits in his grand chair on the National Mall with right hand open and left hand clenched. Herbert Hoover, quoting his Quaker uncle, said, "Turn your other cheek once, but if he smites you again, then punch him."

You get the idea. In our own view of ourselves, we are reluctant warriors. We are like the Great War's mild-mannered marksman Sergeant York, summoned from a small town in Tennessee, doubtful that he should or could ever turn his rifle on a fellow human being. That is, until he saw his countrymen falling beside him; after which he fought with such single-mindedness that enemy soldiers had no choice but to surrender.

We understand well that we are not always as heroic as we would like, but neither do we want to find ourselves too much at odds with the myth. We fight for big causes, we tell ourselves, such as liberty and the defense of home and hearth. We fight because we are forced to, not because we want to or for petty reasons of material gain. We see ourselves as loyal allies and fair but formidable foes.

That is why any U.S. decision to use force should begin with a domestic understanding. As commander in chief, you will be obliged to choose America's fights carefully and to design missions that are worthy and for which our troops are well trained and equipped. You must reestablish America's standing as a nation that desires peace without allowing that desire to be misinterpreted as weakness. You must realize that even if you succeed at every other aspect of the presidency, you will still fail overall if you do not make wise choices about when and how to use force.

Given U.S. capabilities, military coercion can be employed as a blunt instrument, to blast whole cities, or with surgical care, to rescue a lone aviator held captive behind enemy lines. Although war requires force, force does not require war. A traditional conflict against a conventional enemy remains a possibility for which you must plan. More often, force will be needed now in situations where the mythic figure recalled is not the plainspoken infantryman but a more dashing figure—the elite fighter assaulting a terrorist training camp, the intrepid spy using high technology to target enemy leaders, the Navy SEAL intercepting a shipment of arms. As the world changes, still further roles have assumed prominence—that of peacekeeper, nation-builder, and provider of emergency relief.

Force, when most useful, does not need to be used. This is the greatest value of a fearsome defense—to deter potential enemies or at least dictate changes in their tactics. Hence the first commandment of the presidency: be prepared. In the words of JFK, "Only when our arms are sufficient beyond doubt can we be certain beyond doubt that they will never be employed."

During your campaign, you promised to equip our troops with the most effective weapons, the most modern communications, the best antimissile systems, the toughest armor, the most advanced bulletproof vests, the most highly proven bomb-detection equipment, and optimum real-time intelligence. You pledged, as well, to enable our armed forces to meet ongoing commitments and prepare for other emergencies without undermining long-term readiness, relying too heavily on our Reserves, or destroying the morale of the all-volunteer army. You promised to modernize our military's strategy and tactics, take better care of military families, and enhance benefits for veterans. You also vowed to further enlarge the army and, in so doing, cited Gen. Eric Shinseki's (U.S. Army ret.) pithy warning, "Beware the twelve-division strategy for a ten-division Army." How to pay for all this? You didn't quite go into that, but then neither did your opponent—who promised the same things.

•   •   •

While in government, I christened a destroyer, the USS *Mc-Campbell*, and visited with American troops on every continent. I clasped hands and did my utmost to memorize faces. A leader cannot become paralyzed by the prospect that because of his orders people will die, including our own daughters and sons. And yet a leader who is not moved to agonize over this prospect does not belong in the White House.

The decision to use force can be unavoidable when the provocation is obvious—Pearl Harbor and 9/11. It can be harder when aggression is directed at allies or friends. The toughest judgments involve cases where America's interests are significant but less than vital. How do we ask someone to risk death for a cause that is "pretty important"? And yet, if a crisis has to involve the nation's very survival before the military can be brought into play, the advantage of maintaining powerful armed forces is sharply reduced.

When considering force, the first question to evaluate is how foes will react. The answer will hinge on the enemy's military assets, the character of its leadership, and psychology. Force is designed to generate fear, causing an adversary to submit or sue for peace. It can also have the unintended effect of multiplying anger, thereby deepening resistance and prolonging the fighting. In Vietnam, American strategy underestimated both the enemy's will and its ability to absorb punishment. As we slowly increased military pressure, communist leaders had time to adapt—and to mobilize world opinion against us. They also had on their side the two most powerful yearnings in twentieth-century Asia: nationalism and the desire to escape domination by the West. Americans in Vietnam were fighting for freedom as a principle; our enemies were fighting, so they thought, to become free.

The shadow of Vietnam fell forward, creating a period of national self-doubt and altering the U.S. military's own attitude toward the use of force. The defeat, it was felt, was not a military loss but a political one, stemming from civilian misconceptions about the nature of war.

During the conflict, Defense Secretary Robert McNamara claimed that "The greatest contribution Vietnam is making . . . is that it is developing an ability in the United States to fight a limited war, to go to war without the necessity of arousing the public ire."

What McNamara saw as a valuable precedent the military saw as a tragedy never to be repeated. Reflecting later on the lessons of Vietnam, Gen. Fred Weyand (U.S. Army) said:

> As military professionals we must speak out, we must counsel our political leaders and alert the American public that there is no such thing as a "splendid little war." There is no such thing as a war fought on the cheap. War is death and destruction. The American way of war is particularly violent, deadly and dreadful. We believe in using things—artillery, bombs, massive firepower—in order to conserve our soldiers' lives.

The searing experience in Southeast Asia was bracketed by an indecisive conflict in Korea and a poorly conceived intervention in Lebanon that ended in 1984, four months after a terrorist attack on a Marine barracks claimed 241 lives. By that time, the armed forces had grown wary of civilian leaders. They worried about being deployed for goals that could not be achieved, kept changing, or were not fully understood by the American people. They yearned for the days of Sergeant York, when America entered wars with but one purpose: to win.

In the wake of our retreat from Lebanon, Defense Secretary Weinberger proposed a set of preconditions for committing the U.S. military. He argued that a deployment should occur only as a last resort, with a reasonable assurance of public backing, for objectives that were both clearly defined and vital, and with the intent to win and the resources to do so.

Secretary of State Shultz, a former Marine, thought Weinberger's list too restrictive. He felt America might have to use force in situations that were less clear-cut—in fighting terrorism, for example, countering insurgencies, or trying to prevent small wars from growing into large ones. He foresaw the need for what he called "ambiguous warfare," not a term the post-Vietnam military was eager to embrace.

It is unsurprising, therefore, that Weinberger's ideas prevailed over Shultz's when, in 1989, Gen. Colin Powell, a former aide to Weinberger, became chairman of the Joint Chiefs of Staff. The Weinberger-Powell approach guided U.S. preparations for the first Gulf War, in which America deployed massive forces, set limited objectives, assembled a broad international coalition, implemented an exit strategy, and enjoyed overwhelming public support.

It is worth remembering in light of subsequent developments that this coalition was brought together for the purpose of driving Iraqi troops out of Kuwait, not removing Saddam Hussein from power. The George H. W. Bush administration kept to its original goal because it feared that to do otherwise would have destroyed the coalition and left America to bring order to a broken and divided Iraq. For years afterward, this exercise in consistency and restraint was widely viewed as a mistake. Today, it is seen as an exercise in consistency and restraint.

After 9/11, the administration of George W. Bush brought debate over the use of force into a new phase. According to its 2002 National Security Strategy: "Given the goals of rogue states and terrorists, the United States can no longer solely rely on a reactive posture as we have in the past. The inability to deter a potential attacker, the immediacy of today's threats, and the magnitude of potential harm that could be caused by our adversaries' choice of weapons, do not permit that option. We cannot let our enemies strike first."

The brouhaha that greeted this so-called preemption doctrine turned the world's attention at a critical time away from what Al Qaeda had done to what America might do. The mystery is why administration leaders chose to highlight the issue when it was not, in principle, anything new. It was false to suggest that our country had historically been crouched in "a reactive posture." America has used force many times without first being attacked. In the past quarter century alone, we have done so in Lebanon, Grenada, Panama, Somalia, Iraq, Haiti, Bosnia, and Kosovo.

The difference between the current administration's policy and previous ones is that the Bush team established such a low threshold for using force. According to Vice President Cheney, "We have to deal with this new type of threat in a way we haven't yet defined. . . . If there's a one percent chance that Pakistani scientists are helping Al Qaeda build or develop a nuclear weapon, we have to treat it as a certainty in terms of our response."

President Bush himself explained his decision to invade Iraq in these terms: "Saddam Hussein was dangerous with weapons. Saddam Hussein was dangerous with the ability to make weapons. He was a dangerous man in a dangerous part of the world . . . and I believe it is essential . . . that when we see a threat, we deal with those threats before they become imminent. It's too late if they become imminent. It's too late in this new kind of war, and so that's why I made the decision I made."

Bush's message, however inelegantly phrased, was unmistakable: America will attack dangerous people in dangerous places without waiting until they actually threaten us—a straightforward vow that might have been a cure-all if we had the authority to make rules that apply only to ourselves. In reality, a principle that allows country A to attack country B simply because country B may one day attack country A invites anarchy. Every nation with an ornery or well-armed neighbor would have the right to defend itself by striking first. Such a doctrine could cause countries that fear an attack to redouble efforts to acquire a deterrent, especially a nuclear one. A public emphasis on military preemption also downgrades the importance of alliances and disregards diplomatic and other nonviolent means for neutralizing potential threats. Finally, as we have seen, imperfect intelligence is the Achilles' heel of any preemption strategy. The perceived legitimacy of a preemptive strike depends on the accuracy of information a president has about the adversary's capabilities and intentions. It's one thing to say, "Oops, sorry about that," when picking up someone else's suitcase at the airport, quite another to invade a country based on "facts" that aren't facts at all.

President Bush is right that some terrorists cannot be deterred by fear of destruction, and that modern technology creates the possibility of a sudden and devastating attack. To guard against these threats will almost certainly require actions that go beyond the narrow definition of self-defense referred to in the UN Charter. Most reasonable people accept this. One does not have to embrace Vice President Cheney's supposed one percent threshold to support military strikes against known Al Qaeda cells regardless of whether those particular cells are preparing to attack the United States. Most of us would also support operations directed at halting the transfer of weapons to a terrorist group. However, just because some potential enemies are not deterrable does not mean that deterrence will never work. Most people want to live, and most people with power want to keep their power. Preemptive attacks must be limited to cases where the imperative to use force—not just the option of doing so—is clearly indicated by the circumstances. The purpose of a national security policy is to make the world safer, not to legitimize mere anxiety as a pretext for war.

In a speech at West Point in 1993, the senior President Bush advised against trying to establish a set of hard-and-fast rules governing the use of force, suggesting instead nonspecific guidelines: "where the stakes warrant, where and when force can be effective . . . where its application can be limited in scope and time, and where the potential benefits justify the potential costs and sacrifice."

Whole books have been written about this subject, but Bush's summary is as good as any—and not much help. Specific decisions will always boil down to a consideration of costs versus benefits. The difficulty is that judgments about supposedly objective factors—stakes, duration, level of danger, likelihood of success—are all subjective. In weighing them, you should bear in mind several lessons from the past.

First, do not overvalue recent experience. Too often, we are tripped up by what we have just learned. We should not assume that the next crisis will resemble the last or that what succeeded or failed in one case will do so in another. Critics insisted, for example, that airpower alone could not make a decisive difference in Kosovo; they were wrong. This doesn't mean that airpower alone can always be decisive, only that, in the right circumstances, it might be. An overwhelming military deployment was triumphant in the first Gulf War and should have been the strategy in the second. There are, however, occasions when the limited use of force for a carefully defined purpose is necessary and can prove effective. The Pentagon is inherently cautious, which is good, but it cannot be allowed to veto military deployments by always insisting that it will take a battalion of cats to catch a mouse. Similarly, a demonstration of "shock and awe" might work well in one place, but flop elsewhere unless accompanied by a long-term security and reconstruction plan. Study the past but understand that each situation will have its own character.

Second, know your adversary. To risk yet another analogy, foreign policy is not like tennis practice, where you bang the ball against a concrete barrier and the ball bounces back straight and true. It's more like Wimbledon, where your opponent has his own tricks and you are unaccustomed to the court's surface. To score well, you will need to learn as much as you can about the conditions in which you will be operating, the overall strengths and weaknesses of the opposition, and the distinctive fears, vanities, and core beliefs of those leading the other side. This is true whether your opponent is a hostile country, an insurgent militia, or a terrorist group. If you don't see the court of play clearly from their perspective, you will find yourself constantly leaning in the wrong direction.

Third, understand your own objectives. Many military operations fail because it is unclear what they are attempting to do. Vietnam and the second Gulf War are obvious examples, but the rationales shifted for our armed forces in Somalia, Lebanon, and Korea as well. The military is solution oriented; keep changing the mission and the military will become disoriented—a sure path to failure.

Fourth, recognize that the threat to use force loses value quickly unless backed up. A president can say "or else" only so many times. Threats should be an instrument of strategy, not a product of anger or frustration. It was observed of James Cagney, that most American of actors, that his voice grew quieter, not louder, just before he resorted to his fists. Teddy Roosevelt's favorite West African proverb fits here: "Speak softly but . . ."

Fifth, your aims, once established, should be pursued urgently and with the level of force required to achieve them. Gradual escalation rarely works because it allows time for the enemy to recover from setbacks, devise new tactics, and try to turn global opinion in its favor.

Similarly, beware the step-by-step intervention into what is or might become a civil war. Once America begins to favor a particular side, our level of investment is likely to grow, because our credibility becomes involved and we do not want to lose. What begins as moral support alone can quickly extend to financial and nonlethal material aid, then to training and arms, and eventually the deployment of troops. We become the gambler who keeps redoubling his bet, ending up with far more on the table than originally intended. In general, the first rule for intervening in a civil war is don't. The second: when intervening, avoid making commitments. The third: having violated rules one and two, be sure to be on the winning side.

Finally, know that the United States will use force most effectively when we do not have to do so alone. Our alliances in Europe and Asia are among our most valuable national security assets and should be treated as such. Every president gives lip service to NATO; President Clinton actually employed NATO troops in the Balkans. He also took the lead in expanding the alliance and revising its charter to deal with the new global environment.

True, an alliance such as NATO, which now includes twenty-six members, can be hard to manage. You go to a meeting and a representative from each is expected to speak. The old joke—everything has been said but not everybody has said it—applies. The payoff, however, is well worth the investment of time. For the United States, the benefits of a united alliance are less military than political, but the political advantages are huge when compared to unilateral action. Costs are shared, as are risks. More important, when the alliance acts, every member has a stake in success. This is how military clout can be used to create diplomatic pressure leading in combination to a satisfactory result.

The use of force is the bluntest instrument in the foreign policy toolbox. In recent years, America has developed a reputation for being too quick to call on its arsenal. In many countries, we are now thought to be the world's leading threat to peace. So what about nonviolent means of coercion? What is there in our toolbox that may be coercive enough to change the behavior of countries but without dropping a bomb or pointing a gun?

•   •   •

Years ago, I was honored with an invitation to carry the Olympic torch as it made its way from Delphi to Salt Lake City for the 2002 Winter Games. I was assigned to carry the flame for only a few blocks and didn't actually run (though I did walk fast). The torch was heavier than you might think, and we were told to wear gloves, which made it slippery. I was petrified that I would drop it and end up on the front page looking like a klutz. This episode is worth recounting because every prospective torch carrier was given, courtesy of the U.S. Olympic Committee, a special uniform consisting of a nylon sports jacket and matching pants. When my uniform arrived, I glanced at the label, which read "Made in Myanmar," that is, Burma, a country that suffers under one of the most repressive governments on Earth. It was not yet illegal to import clothing from Burma, but public pressure had induced most U.S. retailers to stop doing business there. I had my own grounds for revulsion, having visited the country to pledge support for its courageous democratic leader, the Nobel laureate Aung San Suu Kyi. I was furious about the uniform but knew it was too late to reorder all the clothing, though I did go out and buy my own shirt and pants (Made in America). When I arrived in Salt Lake City, I informed Mitt Romney, head of the U.S. Olympic Committee, about the gaffe; he thanked me kindly for keeping my mouth shut. The following year, Congress approved a ban on all imports from Burma.

Boycotts, embargoes, and other types of economic sanctions are a means short of war designed to persuade a country to do something it would prefer not to. You may find the tool tempting because it allows you to express indignation without resorting to force beyond that required to police the sanctions. Though such restrictions have usually proven effective only when multilateral, U.S. leaders are still prey to the illusion that we can isolate another nation even when we act alone. Sanctions are popular with Congress because they are easy to legislate, giving senators and representatives a rare chance to dictate policy. In consequence, they have been overused.

As president, you will be either authorized or required to impose sanctions when one country invades another, when a democratically elected government is overthrown, when a government confiscates property belonging to a U.S. citizen, when a government is unwilling to protect human rights, or when a government fails to cooperate with the United States in fighting terrorism, nuclear proliferation, the illegal drug trade, or trafficking in persons. You will also be expected to invoke sanctions against countries that are unwilling to safeguard religious liberty, prosecute suspected war criminals, protect endangered species, or ensure that dolphins and sea turtles do not become entangled in fishing nets. In most cases, these requirements are matched by annual reports in which the State Department is compelled to grade every nation in the world—except ourselves—in every category. As a schoolgirl, I once took upon myself the job of policing the hygiene of my fellow students and reported several for having dirty fingernails. The fingernails were cleaned but I lost all my friends.

The United States does not give out demerits to those who violate our standards, but we may, among other penalties, cut off foreign assistance and arms sales, oppose World Bank loans, deny trade benefits, embargo the shipment of certain items, and freeze bank accounts. Especially when we act in company with the UN, the governments singled out are put on the defensive and forced to justify their actions. Still, when it comes to changing a nation's behavior, sanctions often promise more than they produce.

An early test case arose when, in 1935, Italy invaded Ethiopia in violation of the covenant of the League of Nations. Restrictions were immediately voted, but failed because they were neither comprehensive enough nor uniformly observed. Mussolini is reported to have told the German government that he would have ordered his troops out of Ethiopia immediately had the penalties included an embargo on oil deliveries, which they didn't. As to enforcement, when British sales of coal to Italy were cut off, German coal made up the shortfall. Italy's northern neighbor, Austria, also undermined the embargo. The United States, not a member of the League, increased its exports of scrap iron and steel. The Suez Canal remained open, so Italy had no problem resupplying its occupying forces. Eight months after the invasion, Italy formally annexed Ethiopia; the following month, in an admission of failure by the League, sanctions were lifted.

During its first forty-five years, the UN Security Council used sanctions only twice, against Rhodesia (from 1966 on) and South Africa (starting in 1977). In both cases, the crime was racism and, in both, the penalties served their purpose, but only after a decade or more. The end of the cold war led to an increase in Security Council activity, including the application of sanctions (with my support, I must add) in more than a dozen instances in the 1990s. These efforts met with mixed success. Offending governments were often able to adjust, either growing accustomed to doing without, producing goods internally, or finding ways to smuggle in what was needed. In some cases, black markets developed, distorting local economies and creating openings for corruption. In Iraq and Haiti, civilians felt the impact of sanctions more than the governments because the dictators in charge took care to look after their own needs first.

At times, the goal of sanctions—barring weapons shipments, for example—is not realistic. A country such as the Democratic Republic of Congo is a neighbor to nine other nations; its borders are long and dotted with small airstrips. If smugglers are determined to deliver arms there, the Security Council sitting in New York is not likely to prevent them. Another problem with sanctions is that, once imposed, they are hard to remove. This is particularly the case when, as currently with Cuba, the restrictions are mandated by federal statute.

The impulse to penalize someone for a misdeed is reflected in the rules of most organizations, including local communities and even the family. Those who misbehave are punished; those who enforce the guidelines benefit—at least in theory. Real life, though, is not lived in theory. When my daughters were young and less than careful at the dinner table, I warned them not to spill their milk, lest they be deprived of television that night. They spilled their milk, so there was no television. Instead, I spent the evening dealing with tantrums, refereeing fights over toys, rescuing the dog from a session of "dress-up," and reading extra stories because the girls were too charged with adrenaline to sleep. The next time milk slopped out of a glass, I said nothing, but got a towel and cleaned it up.

When I was secretary of state, President Clinton issued an executive order imposing sanctions on Sudan, whose government was violating human rights, bombing schoolchildren, and giving aid and comfort to terrorists. This seemed a simple step, and I supported it; and yet it was not simple—the reason was sap. Gum arabic, which is derived from the acacia tree, is a natural emulsifier used in such products as candy bars, colas, cosmetics, and fireworks. The two leading American processors are located in New Jersey, while 80 percent of the world's supply comes from Sudan. I soon received a phone call from New Jersey congressman Robert Menendez demanding that we exempt gum arabic from the sanctions. I asked him, "How can you ask for an exception to sanctions for Sudan while you oppose so vehemently any exceptions to our embargo of Cuba?" His answer: "jobs." Over my objections, Menendez won his exemption for gum arabic, which remains in law. In 2007, the Bush administration announced plans to seek UN sanctions against Sudan in connection with the genocide in Darfur. Sudan's ambassador to Washington responded by calling a press conference. Standing surrounded by a display of soft drink products, he warned that his country could retaliate against UN sanctions by halting shipments of gum arabic to the United States—thereby threatening to hit us with the same club we had intended to use against Sudan. That's the problem with sanctions: it is often unclear who is penalizing whom.

In recent years, the world community has worked to make sanctions more finely tuned, or as we put it, "smarter." The preferred means is to focus on the bank accounts and visa rights of specific government officials and their families. The theory—logical enough—is that a dictator may be more upset by the loss of shopping opportunities and access to personal wealth than by any hardships experienced by his countrymen.

The use of economic sanctions is no more amenable to a rigid set of rules than the use of military force. Each situation has unique aspects. I suggest, however, that you limit any additional use of this tool to extreme cases and that you analyze in advance the question of enforceability and the potential for the restrictions to backfire. Sanctions should be designed to influence the decisions of leaders not to punish whole populations. They should be part of a comprehensive strategy and should be imposed only with a reasonable understanding of next steps in the event they fail to achieve their purpose. In short, if sanctions are to be effective, thay must be something more than the rain dance we perform when we do not know what else to do.

Diplomacy, speeches, foreign assistance, international organizations, law enforcement, economic sanctions, intelligence, and force are the major tools that will be available to you in pursuing your national security strategy. The measure of your leadership will be found in selecting not which tool to use but in which combination, with what timing, and with what adjustments as the months fly by and each event impacts every other.

CHAPTER 6

Be Sure You're Right; Then Go Ahead

I n my office hangs a framed picture showing a lone soldier. The inscription reads, "Search all the public parks and you'll never find a monument to a committee."

In months to come, you will be surrounded seemingly at every moment by advisors, even people as trusted as your spouse, yet you will stand alone. The oath of office will vest in you, as commander in chief and supreme policymaker, the sole authority to decide and the responsibility to be right. Some presidents thrive as decision makers; others grow accustomed to the role; a few never learn to cope.

During his brief presidency, Warren Harding found himself unable to assess competing arguments. Confronted by debate, he was persuaded by one side and then the other until his head began to spin. In bewilderment, he exclaimed: "Somewhere there must be a book . . . where I could go to straighten it out in my mind. But I don't know where the book is, and maybe I couldn't read it if I found it. And there must be a man in the country who could weigh both sides and know the truth. Probably he is in some college or other. But I don't know where to find him. I don't know who he is, and I don't know how to get him. My God, this is a hell of a place for a man like me to be."

Presidents, like the rest of us, make decisions every day about routine matters, but only presidents make decisions that routinely shape history.

Theodore Roosevelt, a student of the past, separated his predecessors into Buchanans and Lincolns. In his view, a Buchanan was someone who feared to use the powers of the presidency and backed away from every fight. A Lincoln was someone who employed the full powers of the office no matter how stubborn the opposition. No one would (yet) confuse you with Lincoln, but you had better not prove to be a Buchanan or a Harding; you were elected to lead.

This doesn't require instigating change simply to allow you to claim credit for a new direction, nor should you rush to put out new policies in every area. Not everything is broken, and some problems that are broken cannot quickly be fixed. Timing is important from many perspectives: the communication of strategy, the receptivity of Congress, the cooperation of foreign governments, and the ability of executive agencies to follow through. As a candidate for president, you had little choice but to overpromise. As president, the temptation will remain to try to be all things. Resist. There is wisdom in Aesop's story about the donkey who chases the lion—with predictably fatal results. "Alas," says the rooster, "my poor friend did not realize what he could or could not do."

One of the least useful gimmicks in American political life is to announce a bold plan for a presidency's first hundred days, thereby making promises that cannot be kept. FDR originated the idea, but he was focused on the single overriding challenge of lifting America out of the Depression. Taking office in 1977, Jimmy Carter was bursting with ideas, most of them good ones. The enthusiasm prompted his administration to move ahead in too many areas simultaneously. Within the first months, the new president adopted zero-based budgeting, promised every taxpayer a fifty-dollar tax rebate, tried to kill pork barrel water projects, proposed campaign finance reform, announced a comprehensive energy program, offered plans for hospital cost containment, hosted eight heads of government, pardoned Vietnam-era draft evaders, unveiled a new human rights policy, called for a ban on nuclear tests, floated the idea of normalizing relations with Cuba, approved Vietnam's entry into the UN, spoke in favor of a Palestinian homeland, and sent Cyrus Vance to Russia with a drastically revised arms-control scheme. Columnist David Broder observed that Carter was governing less like the captain of a ship of state than a "frantic . . . white-water canoeist."

All this activity produced a monstrous jam-up that obscured priorities, gave Congress more than it could handle, and ignored an elementary rule of public perception: if you propose three ideas and prevail on two, you will be thought a success; if you propose ten and chalk up wins on four, you will be judged a failure, even though you have accomplished twice as much.

Instead of trying to remake the Earth in six or ninety-six days, you should develop a plan for the first two years. What actions are urgent and unavoidable? What decisions can wait? How can you best make use of already scheduled international events? Consider the practice, especially at the outset of your administration, of ordering on some issues a "comprehensive policy review." This will enable you, in a systematic way, to invite and benefit from the comments of all. The exercise will, often enough, yield useful ideas. At a minimum, it will create the impression of action, provide your spokesperson with an excuse to deflect questions, and allow unwise promises to fade from memory.

It is possible, as well, that by the time the review is finished, the urgency of the issue will have eased. Calvin Coolidge was famed for not saying much, but he did advise that "If you see ten troubles coming down the road, you can be sure that nine will run into the ditch before they reach you and you only have to do battle with one."

Good decisions begin with good information, but collecting data is the easy part. We live surrounded by statistics, opinions, and rumor. Each of us has access to the media and can turn to the Internet for answers (sometimes even accurate ones) to every question. Government officials also have access to embassy reports and intelligence briefings in daily, weekly, and long-term versions. The problem for any leader is twofold: how to manage the input so that you know what you need without being overwhelmed, and how to distinguish truths from lies, half-truths, and facts that have passed their sell-by date.

You can help yourself by insisting that you be given information as free from political and other prejudice as possible. Such a directive will guarantee nothing, however, because virtually every source of information is tilted to some degree, and even data gained by technical means must be interpreted. Many is the time I have gazed quizzically at an intelligence photograph until it was explained to me that, for instance, the dark blotch in the corner was in fact a three-story warehouse containing missile parts while the shadows on the side were vans waiting to transport the parts to places we did not want them to go. I hoped we knew enough to tell one blotch from another—after all, we were the United States—but to me they just looked like blotches.

When I was first a professor at Georgetown, I criticized public officials for failing to make perfect decisions. When I became secretary of state, I met with professors who blamed me for not making perfect decisions. In managing world affairs, there is an enormous gap in perspective between the theorist, however sophisticated, and the practitioner. Even those of us who have previously served often forget how complicated the top jobs are. Nothing you can read will adequately prepare you to make good decisions, but certain habits help. Richard Neustadt listed some: "The personal command post, a deliberate reaching down for the details, hard questioning of the alternatives, a drive to protect options from foreclosure . . . and finally a close watch on follow-through."

In this spirit, you might want to keep members of your team on their toes by dropping in on their meetings unannounced, phoning experts in the departments, and visiting the agencies. A little of your energy can multiply the enthusiasm of those working on your behalf. In return, you should insist on truth. There is a tendency within agencies to preserve their prerogatives and protect their backsides by refusing to acknowledge problems. You ask and are told not to worry; the problem is under control. You might reply that it is your job to worry and that the buck doesn't stop with them but with you.

Every decision-making process should begin with a skeptical review of the premises supporting the recommended policy. This is the essence of critical thinking: to test assumptions, probe for bias, and, above all, to understand that asking questions is not a sign of weakness. How strong is the connection between a proposed policy and the results predicted? Are the statistics cited valid? Are the precedents relevant? Will foreign leaders act in the manner anticipated? How will foreign populations respond? The Bay of Pigs invasion went awry in part because the CIA assumed, based on ideological assumptions and the scantiest of anecdotal evidence, that the majority of the Cuban population would rise up against Castro at the first opportunity. Years later, America was stunned by Iran's revolution because we assumed that a radical ayatollah would have little appeal to a modern population. Many of our foreign aid initiatives have fallen short because they have failed to make logical connections—for example, external food aid may feed the hungry but also drive down prices and thereby make it impossible for local farmers to earn a living.

U.S. decision makers have to make a conscious effort to see the world through foreign eyes. We become so steeped in our own political and social culture that we forget that the global majority is poor, a quarter of the world's population is Muslim, more than half is Asian, and much of it is too young to place current events in perspective. We also forget that our power is often resented, even when our help is sought.

In gauging the likely responses of a foreign government, you might ask: What options are open to that government? What is the nature of the country's leadership and political system? How does the country feel about itself? Is it aggrieved and spoiling for a fight or content with the status quo? Is it desperate or confident? What does it expect from us?

As with people, nations are influenced by events to think differently about what is possible and necessary. World War II, fought in the name of freedom, fed Asian and African desires for independence from colonial rule. The Nazi invasion made the Soviets determined to create a buffer of nations to their west. The threat of communist subversion drove Turkey and Greece, otherwise bitter rivals, to take refuge in the same military alliance. The communist revolution in China made Lyndon Johnson unwilling to accept a communist Vietnam. Disaster in Vietnam created a hunger in America for even the smallest victory. In 1975, President Ford sent U.S. Marines to rescue the crew of the U.S. merchant ship *Mayaguez,* seized by Cambodia's Khmer Rouge. Acting on inaccurate intelligence, the Marines landed in the wrong place, encountered stiff resistance, suffered forty-one dead, and nearly had their position overrun. In response, the U.S. bombed Cambodia—but due to a miscommunication, did so after the thirty-nine-member crew of the *Mayaguez* had been released. Despite the confusion and the fact that more lives were lost than saved, battle-weary Americans treated the episode as a triumph.

A nation's collective psychology will make it susceptible to leaders who understand and exploit its needs. A nation's actions, however, will depend on where those leaders choose to go. There is more than one way for a country that feels aggrieved to reestablish its pride. The challenge for the world is to understand in time the character of the people with whom it must deal. Is that charismatic nationalist a single-minded adversary such as Ho Chi Minh or, like Hitler, a threat to all civilization? Is that armed group an irredeemable collection of terrorists or a movement that may be persuaded to adopt peaceful means? There is a world of difference between a Mugabe and a Mandela, a Khomeini and a Sistani. Among all the qualities demanded by your job, none will be more essential than the ability to understand the psychology and capabilities of other leaders and nations.

•   •   •

Let us suppose that you have a decision pending before you as president. Your advisors are sitting around on chairs and sofas, briefing books open, prepared to make their arguments. You swoop in, greet them, then convene the meeting. It is the habit of some leaders to open discussion by expressing their views and asking for a reaction. The problem for you is that you are no longer just some leader. Your counselors may be extraordinarily reluctant to tell you that you are wrong. After all, they are indebted to you for their positions, influence, and chance for a place in history. Once your ideas are on the table, they may clam up, and what good is that? Far better, as Truman and Kennedy did in times of crisis, to withhold your views and encourage your colleagues to share their thinking. If you sense someone is holding back, encourage him or her to speak. Insist that open quarreling is welcome while silent dissent (especially if later shared with the media) is not.

As I can attest, Bill Clinton's first year was marked by undisciplined meetings in which junior political advisors were allowed to participate and the talking went on forever without decisions being made. The bad habits were corrected, however, and by the start of Clinton's second term, we had settled into a businesslike routine. In meetings with the president, CIA director George Tenet often led off, explaining what we knew about the personalities, politics, and probabilities involved in a particular situation. Sandy Berger then explained the specific issue to be decided, thus framing the question and establishing a context for the ensuing debate. As the senior member of the cabinet, I went next, followed by the secretary of defense and chairman of the Joint Chiefs. If I didn't like the way Sandy had described the issue, I said so and restated the question. Al Gore weighed in at appropriate times, but Clinton also liked to listen to Gore's assistant, Leon Fuerth, a shrewd and forward-looking analyst with broad shoulders and the cautionary demeanor of Eeyore. The president's chief of staff, Erskine Bowles or John Podesta, kept us all honest, interposing their own ideas and questions.

When we were done thrashing issues out, Clinton thanked us and we left. He did not tell us what he had decided, or even whether he had decided. This gave him extra time to reflect, confer privately with Gore if he so desired, and pursue answers to aspects of the problem that might still be nagging at him.

Perhaps the hardest part of decision-making is not knowing as much as you feel you should. I can think now of at least five significant questions I asked repeatedly while in office to which I never got a clear answer—because we didn't have good enough sources or because the information we did have was conflicting: Where was Osama bin Laden? Was Pakistan's military our ally in fighting Al Qaeda or part of the problem? Did Saddam Hussein have weapons of mass destruction? Under what arrangements, if any, would Arafat agree to peace with Israel? Did Iran's leadership have any interest in improved relations with the United States? Not having answers didn't mean we could avoid making decisions. It only meant that we were more likely to be surprised by the results.

You should treat the decision-making process not as an inheritance to be preserved but as your own invention. If it doesn't work for you, change or go beyond it. The people in the room when you deliberate should be the people you want to have in the room.

Be aware that your advisors are influenced not only by their perspectives within the bureaucracy but also by their personal histories and beliefs. Each has a self-image to live up to and often certain constituencies to impress. They may have written articles in the past whose conclusions they will seek to justify. They may have future ambitions they would like to burnish. They may want to establish primacy over their colleagues and they may already be thinking about how they would like to be portrayed in Bob Woodward's next book. You have to be alive to all these agendas.

An advisor who is especially adept at framing an argument will often seem more persuasive than one who is less glib but whose ideas may be just as useful. There are brilliant lawyers in Washington, and some are likely to end up sitting around your table. A good advisor will always want to seem objective; the best will appear so regardless of the reality. The point to remember is that an argument can sound compelling and still be wrong because facts not in evidence at the time—or at least not brought to your attention—will make it wrong.

Presidents are not immune from the human desire to hear what they want. If the public is demanding that he act in circumstances where success seems unlikely, he will want to be told how inaction can be explained without loss to his popularity. If he has already committed to a particular course, he will want to be told that he has made the right choice. Clever (and sometimes self-serving) advisors know this and tailor their arguments accordingly. This enhances the appeal of their words but not necessarily their wisdom. An advisor who goes against the grain by telling you what you are loathe to hear should be listened to carefully. When George Ball counseled Lyndon Johnson to shift course on Vietnam, Johnson could not dispute the substance of what he was being told; he simply refused to accept the conclusion. He did not want to be known as the first president to lose a war. As for Ball, he was accused by hawks of advocating a policy of "cut and run."

It will come as no shock to you that most knowledge resides outside of government. You might consider hosting policy dinners with scholars and regional experts where no one is quoted and no-holds-barred discussion is encouraged. You should seek the advice of businesspeople and development specialists who have as much a global perspective as any U.S. official and who may have keen insights into how perceptions of America can be changed. It may also be useful to bring in—or wheel in—respected former cabinet members who can lend a touch of bipartisan gravitas to the policies of your administration.

I have emphasized the importance of critical thinking because its absence can lead even well-intentioned people into disaster. Consider the story of the superpower that decided to launch a preemptive strike.

The time was 2,400 years ago; the superpower was Athens; the intended target, Sicily; the alleged danger, that the people of Sicily might one day unite and take up arms. Athenian leaders were so certain their invasion would succeed that they disregarded the warnings of their military, who said the planned strike force was too small. "What if the Sicilians in terror combine against us and we make no friends?" asked one general. Besides, he continued, "Even if we conquer them, they are so distant and numerous that we could hardly rule them."

In the emotions of the moment, such voices were drowned out. According to Euripides, "although some disapproved, the excessive passion of the majority made them afraid of being thought unpatriotic if they voted on the other side; and they therefore held their peace." The Athenian authorities decided to consult their soothsayers, who, being on the official payroll, reported dutifully that the city-state was favored by the gods and would win simply because it deserved to. So, accompanied by the blaring of trumpets and the clashing of cymbals, the expedition set forth.

When it arrived in Sicily, its leaders proclaimed to the local population that "we come not to enslave you, but to keep you from being enslaved." The Sicilians were unconvinced. Although previously divided, they came together to defeat the Athenians, who complained, "Though we are supposed to be the besiegers, we are to a great extent besieged."

In trying to conquer Sicily, the Athenians overreached; in the process, they transformed a containable risk into a major self-inflicted wound. The invasion exhausted their military, divided their population, disillusioned their allies, and forfeited their global prestige. "When [the Athenians] recognized the truth, they were hard on the orators who had joined in promoting the expedition . . . and furious with the soothsayers and prophets and all who by the influence of religion had at the time inspired them with the belief they could conquer Sicily."

The Athenians' decision to invade also opened the way for a much stronger adversary who would subjugate their empire within a decade. That adversary was Persia—modern-day Iran.

Parallels between classical times and the modern era cannot be exact, nor need the past be prologue. Yet this parallel is worth citing because the Bush administration's decision to invade Iraq violated every principle of wise decision-making. The judgment was made, from all accounts, without the benefit of prior consultations with the chairman of the Joint Chiefs of Staff, the secretary of state, or the director of national intelligence, each of whom was informed that the country was going to war instead of being asked for his recommendation. In the past, the United States has entered a war because it was attacked (as with Pearl Harbor and Fort Sumter) or tiptoed into a war step by step (as with Vietnam), but never in modern times has it decided to invade another country without a thorough balancing of the potential benefits and risks.

The central lesson is that an overdose of certainty can be at least as much a handicap to a president as an excess of timidity. Like the leaders of Athens, Bush decided on his course without bothering to analyze objective factors or to consider the possibility that he might be wrong. Instead of using the decision-making process, he circumvented it. Rather than seek the views of experts, he ignored the warnings that were volunteered.

I bring this up not to belabor an obvious point, but to remind you that the test of leadership is the ability to think clearly in an unclear world and not to leave off thinking once decisions are made. The path ahead of you is littered with traps and landmines. You must be decisive enough to set a course, but also wise enough to adjust that course as more is learned and new dangers are detected.

The Tennessee trader, trapper, backwoods fighter, and Whig legislator Davy Crockett was reputed by his admirers to have been cradled in the shell of a snapping turtle, weaned on whiskey and rattlesnake eggs, and to have grown strong and agile enough to hug a bear to death. When hungry, he preferred his steaks salted with hail, peppered with buckshot, and broiled by lightning. He is best remembered today for wearing dead animals as hats and dying at the Alamo. Separating truth from legend, we also know that he coined the axiom "Be sure you're right; then go ahead." Crockett's advice should be taken to heart, provided you accept that the certainty you crave will always be relative and that being right is not a state of grace but the product of diligent work—asking questions, analyzing information, and seeking out the people who know what you need to know. The possibility of being wrong dictates that, even as you implement the decisions you make, it will be prudent to leave side and back doors open. Having done your best, do not shy from responsibility. The public will forgive you for being wrong; they will not forgive you for standing behind the presidential seal and trying to blame mistakes on somebody else.

CHAPTER 7

The Lion and the Lion-tamers

Y ou have identified an issue, sought advice, tapped every source for information, considered all options, and made your decision. Exhaling, you move on, carefully plucking the next thorny item from the in-box. Six months later, your chief of staff comes to you and says, "Mr. President, we have a problem." It turns out to be the same problem you were sure you had solved. "What happened to my instructions?" you demand. "It's a long story," comes the reply.

To carry out your decisions as president, you will have to rely on the sprawling collection of government agencies known as the bureaucracy. Defying physics, these institutions can absorb jolts of energy without generating an equal and opposite reaction or at times any reaction at all. Career public servants have their own priorities, preconceptions, and ambitions and, unlike you, are not limited to four-year terms. In their own fields, they know a great deal and will want to help by protecting you from mistakes. They also know that blame for delays can be widely dispersed, while actions—even those taken on the president's authority—inevitably involve risk. Thus your decisions will not strike your subordinates as you might wish—like thunderbolts from above; instead, more often, they will descend as doth the gentle rain from heaven, landing with a soft plop.

Jonathan Daniels, an aide to FDR, observed that:

> Half of a president's suggestions can be safely forgotten by a cabinet member. And if the president asks . . . a second time, he can be told that [the matter] is being investigated. If he asks a third time, a wise cabinet officer will give him at least part of what he suggests. But only occasionally, except about the most important matters, do presidents ever get around to asking three times.

Roosevelt himself had this to say:

> The Treasury is so large and far-flung and ingrained in its practices that I find it almost impossible to get the action and results I want. . . . But the Treasury is not to be compared with the State Department. You should go through the experience of trying to get any changes in the thinking, policy, and action of the career diplomats and then you'd know what a real problem was. But the Treasury and the State Department put together are nothing compared with the Na-a-vy. The admirals are really something to cope with and I should know. To change anything in the Na-a-vy is like punching a feather bed. You punch it with your right and you punch it with your left until you are finally

exhausted and then you find the damn bed just as it was before you started punching.

During the Cuban missile crisis, John Kennedy came to appreciate FDR's frustration. At a moment of highest drama, the commander in chief's instructions were either ignored or misunderstood on four critical issues. The president authorized bombing Cuba if an American U-2 plane were shot down; the air force interpreted this as authority to bomb in the event a plane were merely attacked. He ordered a halt to provocative intelligence operations; nonetheless, a U-2 strayed over Soviet territory. He authorized no contact between the U.S. Navy and Soviet submarines; and yet the navy repeatedly forced Russian subs in the Caribbean to surface. Kennedy ordered the air force to prepare for enemy attack, yet our aircraft remained lined up on airstrips, wing tip to wing tip, providing juicy targets at bases across the South.

Although Harry Truman also expressed exasperation while in office, he said in retirement that presidents should not be allowed to use the bureaucracy as an excuse: "[expletive deleted]. If the president knows what he wants, no bureaucrat can stop him."

Truman's claim is most apt to be true in cases where the president's will is unambiguous, his desires widely communicated, and the officials designated to execute his decision both fully empowered and supportive. More often, a presidential decision is wrapped in the swaddling clothes of compromise, susceptible to various interpretations, and open to argument about who should do what and when.

If a decision has been reached only after interdepartmental squabbling, the dispute will end once the president has spoken.

Then it starts up again. In a democracy, people who lose arguments do not disappear or shut up; they look for reinforcements. The tactics used to influence policy remain available even when the president believes he has settled the matter. Bureaucratic alliances may still be created, memos leaked, anonymous sources quoted, and excuses made about why certain actions are, for the present, impractical. To carry out its will, the White House appoints a lead agency, but there is no hierarchy. The secretary of state cannot give orders to the head of the CIA or the secretary of homeland security. The bureaucracy is a band of equals whose members do not always play well together—and it is a large band.

Almost every major U.S. agency has at least some international function. Suppose, for example, that you decide (as you should) to help save the planet by supporting vigorous international action on climate change. This is an issue of massive scope about which you spoke fervently during the campaign. It is also an issue that, almost as much as any other, can help you to rebrand American leadership, marking a sharp departure from the prior administration. Now, as president, you will seek to make good on your promises. Even before Al Gore calls you, you call him. You then announce plans to develop an all-encompassing policy and, to show your seriousness, designate senior officials from the National Security Council and National Economic Council to coordinate. They, in turn, summon representatives from the Environmental Protection Agency and the departments of State, Defense, Energy, Interior, Treasury, Labor, Commerce, and Agriculture. Experts from the National Academies of Science will also likely be involved. Within the State Department alone, officials responsible for global affairs, economic issues, international organizations, Asia, Europe, Africa, Russia, and Latin America will have places at the table. Congressional affairs offices from each agency represented will also have an interest, as will those that provide a liaison to the private sector and civil society. You will sit in the White House having determined that America should be a leader on the issue, but unless you personally and repeatedly demand otherwise, the departments may struggle for months, even years, to agree on the precise manner in which that leadership should be exercised, what it should entail, who should bear the costs, and how Congress and other countries will be persuaded to follow.

No president, however popular or determined, can escape the distorting impact that the federal bureaucracy has on executing decisions. At times, you may end up grateful for this—because the dissenters, delayers, and questioners are occasionally right. At other times, you will feel as if you were steering a vessel the size of an aircraft carrier with a rudder made for a dinghy. Any president confronted by bureaucratic obstruction will be tempted to raise hell and fire people, which will make sense when orders are directly disobeyed. Creating an atmosphere of hostility between the White House and the departments, however, will not ordinarily be in your best interest.

Limitations on the president's power extend well beyond the bureaucracy. Constitutional checks and balances create an invitation to struggle, giving Congress control of the purse, a consenting role on treaties and nominations, and the opportunity to help or hinder trade negotiations. The judicial branch has historically accorded the president broad authority in conducting world affairs, but it can still compel policy changes in, for example, the treatment of detainees apprehended in the course of fighting terror. Revelations in the media can also disrupt your plans, creating an atmosphere in which the decisions you have so carefully reached must be scrapped and new policies devised. Every president tries to master events, but even the commander in chief must sometimes ride the whirlwind.

From a president's viewpoint, much of what happens on Capitol Hill is either annoying or destructive. You will ask for money and get it, but not in the amounts requested or for the purposes you desire. You will ask to have your nominations approved, but some will inevitably be held up because a senator is feeling disrespected or thinks she can trade her vote for a favor. You will ask for an unfettered chance to carry out your foreign policy, but Congress will be determined to micromanage, adding conditions and restrictions to much of what you attempt. You try to make every moment count, but you will have 535 friends on Capitol Hill who want their phone calls returned.

Congress is at its best when it is holding the executive branch accountable for policies that have been misrepresented to the American people. Investigatory and oversight hearings can be excruciating for those required to testify, but public give-and-take between the people's representatives and those wielding administrative power is the essence of democracy. A senator or representative who asks probing questions usually speaks not only for himself but for millions of Americans. During George W. Bush's first term, Congress was partisan and feckless. Since the 2006 midterm elections, our national legislature—though still partisan—has been appropriately nosy on the public's behalf.

It is common to mourn the old days when Congress was supposedly populated by statesmen rather than the politicized creatures with whom we are allegedly saddled today. I find it hard to compare across the decades. I do know that Daniel Webster, in the early nineteenth century, was every bit as parochial about the interests of the New England fishing industry as Maine senator Edmund Muskie was when I worked for him in the 1970s. A glance at past Senate debates shows a mix of the high-minded and long-winded that does not vary much from the occasionally brilliant but more often mediocre debates we see today on C-SPAN. Commentators have poked fun at our national legislature since its earliest days. There is little that David Letterman, Jon Stewart, or Stephen Colbert can say that wasn't said in a prior era by the likes of H. L. Mencken, Mark Twain, or Will Rogers ("The country has come to feel the same when Congress is in session," Rogers observed, "as when the baby gets hold of a hammer.").

Do not, therefore, neglect the more uplifting qualities of members of Congress. It is true that some members could not be uplifted with a steam shovel, but most are diligent and searching to do what is best for the country. Moreover, in each generation, there are a handful of congressional leaders with the seriousness and stature to be what they should be—the strongest partners and toughest critics of a president. These are not people who ignore political labels but who at least know when partisan considerations should be suppressed for the nation's good. They are smart, experienced, influential, patriotic, and not all scheming to replace you. Seek them out. Invite them to share meals at the White House. It will be refreshing personally and helpful to your administration.

I also hope you will educate the public about the value of congressional travel. It is a myth, and a damaging one, that when legislators travel abroad, they spend most of their time sightseeing, shopping, golfing, and sipping exotic drinks. When in government, I urged members of Congress to travel so they would know what I was talking about when I asked them for help. We cannot in any case lead a world we do not understand. A senator or representative who has been confronted for the first time by abject poverty will not want to believe it but will never forget it; he or she will change instantly, and almost always for the better. A congressperson who hears firsthand the stories of families that have lost homes and of women who have been raped in the course of civil strife will bring a different frame of mind to future debates about America's role. A senator who sits down with leaders of civil society in Pakistan, Colombia, or Burundi will learn quickly that informed decisions made in Washington can turn life right side up for millions and that our mistakes can get thousands of good people killed.

It can be useful, in thinking about Congress, to separate what always happens from what can be made to happen. You know that Congress will approve a budget and pass judgment on your nominations. Those routine processes can hurt or help and will demand attention. The larger challenge is to enlist key legislators as advocates on controversial questions. This requires consultation, the right timing, and a willingness to give leading legislators a stake in your success. Senator Vandenberg promised Truman that he would approach issues in a bipartisan manner provided he were "involved in the takeoffs as well as the landings." Under Clinton, we let Jesse Helms take credit for stopping us from doing several things we never intended to do, such as give Russia a decision-making role in NATO. This enabled Helms to support our priority (NATO enlargement) while preserving his well-honed image as a right-wing curmudgeon.

•   •   •

For more than two hundred years, Congress and the executive have argued over the checks and balances involved in decisions to deploy American troops. Ordinarily, the executive is jealous of its authority, but in one case it decided cleverly to defer.

The year was 1954; Dwight Eisenhower was being pressured by conservatives to rescue French colonial forces encircled by North Vietnamese communists at Dien Bien Phu. This was in the McCarthy era, when a refusal to act on Eisenhower's part would have invited allegations of softness, even betrayal. The French cause was essentially hopeless, however, as was the larger and even more dubious struggle to preserve European dominance in Asia. Eisenhower, therefore, thought it unwise to commit U.S. troops to help the French but politically imprudent to say so. Instead of doing either, he promised to consider American military involvement but only as the result of constitutional processes requiring congressional support. This put the responsibility for action squarely on Congress, which, as Eisenhower expected, preferred talking to acting. In this way, the president was able to assume a principled position until the issue became moot, as it rapidly did, with the French surrender.

Eisenhower did not want to deploy the U.S. military when many in Congress did; more often the situation is reversed. The original conception, that Congress declares war and the president wages it, is obsolete, and not only in the United States. Formal declarations of war occur rarely, military interventions frequently. Modern vocabulary accommodates a range of actions that are neither peaceful nor exactly war: counterinsurgency, covert strikes, punitive bombing, police actions, humanitarian interventions.

In 1973, Congress approved the War Powers Resolution, designed to limit the deployment of U.S. forces into combat situations without legislative consent. Although the executive branch has been unwilling to concede the resolution's constitutionality, administrations have found ways to comply with it in spirit. One method is to encourage a supportive vote prior to a deployment. This was the case with the two Gulf Wars and the U.S.-led NATO intervention in Kosovo. The question debated more recently is whether Congress can place restrictions on the authority of the president to manage a conflict already under way and, if so, whether it is wise to do so. As president, you can minimize such controversies by consulting with Congress regularly and by being honest; you can avoid them altogether only by making decisions about the use of force that turn out well.

Every president feels the media is unfair; some consider it reckless to the point of treason. George Washington wished that "our Printers were more discreet in many of their publications." Jefferson, champion of the free press, observed that "The man who reads nothing at all is better educated than the man who reads nothing but newspapers." John Quincy Adams characterized reporters collectively as "a sort of assassin who sit with loaded blunderbusses at the corners of streets and fire them off for hire or for sport at any passenger they select." Martin van Buren was more plaintive: "Why is it that they have such an itching for abusing me? I try to be harmless."

Even Lincoln referred to "villainous journalists" and took countermeasures to improve his image. In Pennsylvania, he procured kind coverage from the *Philadelphia Press* by appointing the publisher's son, brother-in-law, cousin, and the publisher himself to government jobs, while awarding lucrative printing contracts to the newspaper.

Woodrow Wilson was the first to schedule regular meetings with "the gentlemen of the press." He abandoned the practice during his tumultuous second term, and his three reticent successors, Republicans all, did not revive it. The modern tradition began with the ebullient Franklin Roosevelt, who held a news conference four days after his inauguration. The task of preserving an official record was left to FDR's personal secretary, who quickly became so interested in the discussion she neglected to take notes. Roosevelt continued to meet with the press regularly, refusing to answer only what he called "iffy" questions—that is, hypotheticals. The president's answers were for background purposes only; he could not be quoted without permission. The convenience of anonymity gave way to the march of technology, however, when Eisenhower began televised news conferences in the 1950s. When asked to list Vice President Nixon's contributions to his administration, Eisenhower told reporters, "If you give me a week, I might think of one."

The courting of the media is a hopeless undertaking, in the sense that no president is long satisfied with the results. No matter how thick your skin, you will rebel at much of what is written about you. In the White House, you will desire to play the role of Prospero, the artist-magician directing events. You will want your strategies to unfold smoothly and according to schedule. Journalists, at least the good ones, are not paid to sit patiently by; they will do all they can to pull back the curtains prematurely, while the actors are out of costume, putting on their greasepaint, and still learning their lines.

Since you know your motives are for the best, you will blame the press not only for ruining your show but also for hurting the country. From a president's perspective, any breach of confidentiality undermines American interests, and may even jeopardize people's lives. From a reporter's standpoint, disclosing information, whether secret or not, is both a fast track to career advancement and a professional duty. Writing about the job of the Washington correspondent, Walter Lippmann had this to say:

> We make it our business to find out what is going on under the surface and beyond the horizon, to infer, to deduce, to imagine, and to guess what is going on inside, what this meant yesterday, and what it could mean tomorrow. In this we do what every sovereign citizen is supposed to do but has not the time or the interest to do for himself. This is our job. It is no mean calling. We have a right to be proud of it and to be glad that it is our work.

Of course, in doing their job, reporters thrive on unauthorized disclosures and quotes from anonymous sources. You will hate such breaches (except those you have orchestrated yourself) because most will come from members of your own team. Kennedy said that the ship of state is the only ship that leaks from the top. Nixon ordered wiretaps placed on the phones of members of his own staff. Reagan's national security advisor talked him into demanding that top aides—including Vice President Bush and Secretary of State Shultz—take a lie detector test. As soon as this directive became public, it was rescinded—if the president couldn't rely on his most senior advisors, why should anyone else? As for the current administration, it has denounced leaks, threatened to fire those responsible for them, and then been caught purposely exposing the identity of a covert CIA agent. If there is any principle other than self-interest at work, it is hard to identify.

I expect that you will find enforcing rules against leaks to be arduous because so many people violate those rules and for such varied reasons. You should lay down the law every so often to keep the spillage from swamping your administration, but if you allow each such episode to upset you, you will not have many good days.

Your press secretary will be among the most prominent and visible members of your team. The choice you must make is whether to keep her fully apprised of administration plans or whether, on sensitive matters, to leave her in the dark. In the former case, she will be accused by the media of withholding information, in the latter, of not being in the loop. The wiser course, by far, is to select a spokesperson who can be trusted with the truth and who will tell reporters when she is not at liberty to speak. Such an approach may not satisfy the press, but it is better to have a representative who is criticized for not saying what she knows than ridiculed for not knowing anything worth saying.

The inherent tension between the White House and the press should not worry a president who is disciplined about observing certain elementary tactics of survival: take responsibility, admit mistakes, put out bad news quickly, and acknowledge inconsistencies before others point them out. The press alone can only rarely frustrate a president's wishes. It is when the press, Congress, and elements of the bureaucracy combine to oppose a policy that the strength of the executive is truly tested. Once the momentum builds, something must be done to let the air out. During Vietnam, Johnson and Nixon took numerous steps to quiet opposition, such as bombing halts, troop withdrawals, and declarations that the turning point had been reached. When Nixon eventually gave in, he claimed to have achieved "peace with honor." When Reagan pulled U.S. troops out of Lebanon, his advisors insisted that "Nothing has changed. We are not leaving Lebanon. The Marines are being deployed two or three miles to the west." It was left to the press to observe that two or three miles to the west meant the marines were now on ships.

When I was UN ambassador, I referred to CNN as the sixteenth member of the Security Council because the cable network had more influence on Council decisions than most governments. The sight and sound of Christiane Amanpour at the scene of a massacre in Sarajevo or inside a refugee camp in Africa generated questions to which the public would want answers. For better or worse—and I think for worse—time has dulled the edge of such reports, as we have seen so many.

The bureaucracy, Congress, and the press all restrict the power of the president—as they should, for they are all democratic institutions. There are other checks, as well, most particularly the public itself, which can deny reelection to an unpopular president or create such a clamor as to preclude certain courses of action.

As is well known, President Bush and especially Vice President Cheney entered office determined to push back the boundaries of presidential power. They claimed legal authorities they did not possess to tap phones, detain terror suspects, and interrogate prisoners. They repeatedly invoked executive privilege to block congressional access to documents, and hijacked legislative and judicial prerogatives by appending their own questionable interpretations to newly signed laws. Their approach, bold to supporters and arrogant to the rest of us, is more likely to weaken your authority as president than to strengthen it. From your first day in office, you will be under pressure to distance yourself from the abuses of your predecessor. This you should do, but no more. Hire legal advisors who will labor to preserve every iota of your rightful powers, but who will also tell you bluntly what the limits are. This is the right approach both in principle and in practice. History has been unkind to timid presidents; it has been downright cruel to those who thought themselves above the Constitution.

Political scientist Clinton Rossiter referred to the president as a "magnificent lion who can roam widely and do great deeds so long as he does not try to break loose from his broad reservation. . . . He will feel few checks upon his power if he uses that power as he should. This may well be the final definition of the strong and successful president: the one who knows just how far he can go in the direction he wants."

These are words worth remembering when your instructions are being disregarded by your own cabinet, Congress is issuing subpoenas, the media is competing to win Pulitzer prizes at your expense, and you can't give a commencement speech without scores of students (and half a dozen faculty members) standing up to protest. Keep thinking, "I am a magnificent lion." Given the work that lies ahead, let us hope it's true.

PART TWO

CHAPTER 8

New Foundations

A president inevitably shapes perceptions about our country through what he says and does but also through personal qualities. No individual can fairly represent a whole population, yet notable leaders often seem to embody national traits—Churchill's perseverance, De Gaulle's pride, Nehru's independence, the dignity of King Hussein, the single-mindedness of Deng Xiaoping.

What traits are emblematic of the United States? For the answer, writers often turn reflexively to a Frenchman (Alexis de Tocqueville). I will cite a German and a Swede.

Paul Tillich, the eminent Protestant theologian, was among the many German intellectuals who emigrated to America after Hitler seized power. At the midpoint of the last century, he wrote appreciatively of his new home:

> There is something astonishing in American courage for an observer who comes from Europe: although mostly

symbolized in the early pioneers it is present today in the large majority of people. A person may have experienced a tragedy, a destructive fate, the breakdown of convictions, even guilt and momentary despair: he feels neither destroyed nor meaningless nor condemned nor without hope. . . . The typical American, after he has lost the foundations of his existence, works for new foundations. This is true of the individual and it is true of the nation.

A second assessment, also midcentury, is that of a journalist, Victor Vinde, who traveled extensively in the United States:

> The greatest asset of the Americans, so often ridiculed by Europeans, is his belief in progress and his profession of democracy. . . . The Depression has left traces in most people in the USA, perhaps not so much because of the troubles which accompanied it as because of the despair and hopelessness for the morrow which characterized it. It was the first time in history that the American doubted himself or the future of his country. Belief in progress, however, is stronger in America today than it has ever been.

America at its best is mirrored in these testimonies: optimism, resilience, faith in freedom, and, one might add, confidence that our national experiment matters to all the world. And yet who today describes Americans in such flattering terms?

Powerful myths emerge from revolution and resistance; present-day America is identified with privilege and the status quo. Tillich credited Americans with courage, but it is hard to appear brave when we are so advantaged; we consume a quarter of the world's resources with 4 percent of the population and can afford to spend as much on defense as the rest of the world combined. Though we are still admired for our scientific and material accomplishments, even friends have become reluctant to follow our lead. In the language of the playground, many feel that we have become too big for our britches; they want us brought down a peg.

Strong leaders often generate resentment, but stirring resentment is no proof of strong leadership. Success is sustained through respect, trust, and a measure of affection. Those assets are invaluable now, when major problems can be solved only through the work of many hands. The renewal of American leadership will depend on whether you deploy the tools of the presidency in ways that inspire cooperation. So from the first day, stress your desire to listen to others, knowing that you will invite more complaints than solutions. Listening is essential, nonetheless, for though few countries expect America to do what they tell us, all want us to care what they say.

When you first sit down with your advisors, you will find them concerned, sensibly enough, with the most pressing issues in their particular area of responsibility. It will be your task to make the right choices in each arena while keeping in mind what the overall picture should look like. Anxious as you are to make your mark, do not rush. Your first months should be used to hone your priorities and gauge the lay of the land internationally. By late spring, you will have met and exchanged views with most other world leaders. You will have a better feeling for the strengths and weaknesses of your national security team and will have established new relationships on Capitol Hill. Tested by early battles, you will develop an even more sophisticated grasp of foreign policy tools and of what it means to be head diplomat and commander in chief. When you have found your stride, the time will be right to outline in public a comprehensive national security strategy.

One precedent to consider is that of John Kennedy, who, four months into his presidency, delivered to a joint session of Congress a special message on "Urgent National Needs." Kennedy used the occasion to unveil forward-looking initiatives on diplomacy, development, military reorganization, and arms control. He also announced, with fanfare, a commitment by decade's end to land a man on the moon.

You must be conscious, as you prepare to introduce your own strategy, of the need to do more than describe; you must persuade. On paper, you will have a list of ideas and priorities. On the podium, you will require a story. The particular problems we face are well enough known. These are issues, in the case of nuclear weapons, that have preoccupied the world for decades and—with respect to the dilemma in the Middle East—for centuries. To be heard, you must speak of old problems in new and surprising ways.

As you do, be aware that you are not the only storyteller on the street. Hundreds of millions of people have been conditioned to believe that the American president is a hypocrite and liar. Words, if they are in fact to persuade, must be linked to action; yet words matter if they speak to universal aspirations, reassure the wary, and cause the hostile to think twice. In the film *Cabaret,* a young Nazi, blue-eyed and blond, rises from his seat to sing "Tomorrow Belongs to Me." America, with its hair and skin of many colors, must stand up for a different principle—that tomorrow belongs not to any one nation or faction, but to us all.

• • •

Survival and the desire for economic improvement were preoccupations of America's first European settlers and then of the pioneers who pressed relentlessly (and sometimes ruthlessly) westward. In our era, these same instincts have driven hundreds of millions of people in the developing world from rural areas to urban. These modern pioneers have turned already large cities into massive concentrations of humanity. In Africa and Asia, the combination of mobility and fecundity is expected to cause the urban population to double during this century's first three decades. By the end of your presidency, more than fifty cities in developing countries will have in excess of five million people, with the majority living outside any effective system of legal protections and rights. If these populations are left jobless and without hope, they will threaten political upheaval with rising fury. It is unsettling that America today is not seen as part of the solution to this problem but as one reason the rich and poor are so far apart.

The president of the United States is, ex officio, a symbol of globalization. We have more influence in the international financial institutions than any other country. An American has always held the top position at the World Bank. Ever since the Great Depression, our leaders have preached the merits of free trade. Our wealth and power mean that we are held responsible for the world as it is—and to people who have nothing or very little, this does us no credit.

With communism essentially dead and the victory of capitalism presumed, we might think that Marxism could safely be forgotten. Yet Marx predicted that capitalism would fail pre-

cisely because it concentrated wealth in the hands of a few. Increasingly, this is happening both within and among nations.
Globalization, though celebrated for increasing productivity,
has been accompanied by growing inequality. Critics allege that
this split is caused by corporate interests who have used their
power to impose unfair rules governing trade and tax policies.
Because the rules are unfair, the Western prescription for economic health, embodied in the so-called Washington consensus
(disciplined budgets, privatization, liberal rules for investment
and commerce) can seem the wrong medicine. Governments
are forced to curtail social spending and give higher priority to
pleasing foreign investors, so it is said, than to meeting the needs
of their citizens. When this happens, policies intended to aid development are perceived as marginalizing the poor.

This might not occur so often if governments were run by
enlightened technocrats who could institute needed economic
reforms over a long period without fear of being turned out
of office. The leaders of fragile democracies, however, cannot
afford such patience. If an economic program doesn't yield dividends right away, it's likely to be supplanted by another that
promises more, even if—as is often the case—the new policy
ends up delivering even less.

Bill Clinton responded to these issues by embracing what he
called "globalization with a human face." He favored a bargain
through which relatively honest and democratic governments
would benefit most from debt relief, trade concessions, and aid.
Similarly, George W. Bush sent more aid to fewer countries,
rewarding those that met a list of benchmarks for good governance. After some foot-dragging, he endorsed the UN's Millennium Development Goals, which call for a 50 percent reduction
in extreme poverty by 2015 along with parallel gains in such

areas as maternal health, child survival, and universal access to primary education.

Reducing poverty should be a central theme of your administration. This is smart politically, right morally, and makes sense economically. With this goal in mind, you should reevaluate our policies on trade, aid, farm subsidies, the environment, and women's rights. To dramatize your commitment, you might visit some of the poorest countries early in your term and, while there, draw attention to the linkages that exist among disease, hunger, corruption, and conflict. Visit Mali to shine the spotlight on a place with few natural assets but blessed by an honest and democratic government dedicated to helping farmers become self-supporting. Take advantage of the global antipoverty movement, which includes rock stars, billionaires, evangelists, students, and the producers of *American Idol*; don't underestimate the power of their enthusiasm—some jobs can best be done only by people too inexperienced to know exactly how hard the jobs are.

You might also consider the insights of a friend and colleague of mine, a man who can only be described as a walking, talking oxymoron: a charismatic economist. Twenty years ago, Hernando de Soto developed an economic strategy for Peru based on the extension of legal rights to participants in his country's informal economy—that is, farmers without deeds, businesspeople without certificates of incorporation, and families without title to the houses in which they lived. Backed by the government, de Soto's program gave new legal standing to people in areas preyed upon by a violent guerrilla group, Sendero Luminoso, the Shining Path. De Soto's approach, dubbed El Otro Sendero, the Other Path, proved so threatening to the guerrillas that they bombed his offices and tried to assassinate him. Today, Sendero

Luminoso has few followers, and de Soto has taken on a new enemy: poverty across the globe. He and I serve as co-chairs of an international panel of experts that is considering how best to apply more broadly the principles of legal empowerment for the poor.

As de Soto's research reflects, families living in poverty already have assets many times greater than amounts received through foreign aid. They possess trillions of dollars in wealth in the form of livestock, houses, small businesses, and the products of their own labor. The catch is that many of these assets exist outside the formal legal economy, and thus cannot be leveraged into capital, investments, or loans. More than one-third of the developing world's GDP is generated in the underground economy. Disturbingly, this proportion has risen steadily over the last decade, with the largest increases in the poorest nations.

The key to capitalism is capital; the key to obtaining and using capital is the law. Yet the law, even in countries where free enterprise is supposedly practiced, can be the enemy of capitalism. Mr. de Soto's team found that months, even years, can be required in some countries to establish legal title to a house or to register a new business. This leaves millions of small entrepreneurs—such as cabdrivers, jitney runners, street-side vendors, laundresses, small farmers—without enforceable rights at home or on the job. Many don't even have a birth certificate or proof of identity. Lacking power, they are vulnerable to those with power, including criminals, predatory government officials, and single-minded developers, who may, for one reason or another, want to move poor people out of the way. In Africa recently, I saw an entire neighborhood where each house was marked with an X, indicating that it was to be destroyed. The local families had built those houses with their own hands yet had no papers to demonstrate ownership and no legal means to seek compensation or redress.

Not long after that trip to Africa, I had cause to look at the deed to my own farm—a retreat a couple of hours outside Washington that my family has long used to relax and commune with cows. Instead of the legalese I expected, the language setting out the farm's boundaries read as it might have hundreds of years earlier: "Beginning at a pile of stones . . . proceeding over the mountain in a northwesterly direction to another pile of stones . . . continuing beyond the hanging rocks to a birch tree by an old stump; south past a Black Oak Chestnut to an iron pin set in the easterly edge of a private road." The lesson in this is that the law need not be complex; at its most basic, it simply reflects what our senses tell us.

Most past efforts to extend legal protections to the disadvantaged have nevertheless failed because they have required unrealistic levels of documentation. De Soto tells of walking through a rice field in Bali. There were no official papers or physical markers to tell which portion of the vast field was cultivated by which family, but he noticed that as he moved from one area to the next, a different dog began to bark. The dogs knew what the law did not. The goal (and it would be a good one for you to espouse) is to find ways to give the poor the same rights as the rich and then see what happens. It may be that free enterprise has not delivered because inequity at the starting line has made fair competition the exception, not the rule.

There are many who blame globalization for inequality and a host of other ills; while some see it as just the opposite: a remedy for economic backwardness and intercultural misunderstanding. Neither view bears scrutiny. Globalization, according to *Webster's,* is defined neutrally as "the act, process or policy of making something worldwide in scope or application." Whether globalization is positive or negative, therefore, depends entirely on what is being made "worldwide in scope or application": Disease or access to medicine? The exploitation of workers or the establishment of fair labor norms? Peace or war?

The spread of new information technologies may improve efficiency, but that is an economic virtue not a political one. I fear that Thomas Friedman, best-selling author of *The World Is Flat,* is wrong when he predicts that "No two countries that are both part of a major global supply chain, like Dell's, will ever fight a war against each other. . . . Because people embedded in major global supply chains don't want to fight old time wars anymore. They want to make just-in-time deliveries of goods and services—and enjoy the rising standards of living that come with that."

Such thinking places the logic of material self-interest on too high a pedestal. Governments do not make decisions solely on the basis of what is best for standards of living. According to one study, "Contrary to popular belief, the most impressive episode of international economic integration which the world has seen to date was not the second half of the twentieth century, but the years between 1870 and the Great War." In that era, political stability and technological change caused trade to expand and capital markets to become integrated to an unprecedented degree. This was particularly the case in Western Europe, where Great Britain and Germany were major trading partners and Lloyd's of London insured the German merchant marine. These cozy arrangements nevertheless failed to check nationalist passions, leading to a level of destruction that was also without precedent. World War I was a disaster for business interests in all of Europe—except for the manufacturers of armaments and tombstones.

Globalization is supposed to make us more alike, but it can also cause people to cling ever more tightly to the identities and beliefs that separate "us" from "them." Uplifting ideas may now be transmitted instantaneously from one mind to millions of others, but so can lies, boasts, stereotypes, and threats. Perhaps Friedman and other global enthusiasts are right, but I suspect each modern generation has believed something similar—that, on their watch, the world had become more advanced and more tightly linked than ever before. We may all hope that humanity has advanced to the point that nothing is beyond our reach, but consider this prediction: "It is impossible that old prejudices and hostilities should longer exist, while such an instrument has been created for the exchange of thought among all the nations of the Earth." Tragically, international conflict did not cease on that day, in 1858, when the first transatlantic cable was connected.

Time does bring change, astonishing things do happen, technology steadily pushes back the boundaries of what can be imagined—and yet unimaginable tragedies still occur: the Somme and Belleau Wood; the Ottomans and the Armenians; Guernica, Nanking, and Pearl Harbor; Auschwitz and Buchenwald; the North Korean invasion and No Gun Ri; Tet, My Lai, Srebrenica, Idi Amin, Rwanda, 9/11, Darfur. Everything has changed but has anything changed? The world may be flat or it may be round, but it sometimes seems as if we haven't learned a thing.

Even though our country was the first to build nuclear weapons and the only nation to use them, American presidents have laid claim to the moral high ground from the earliest hours of the nuclear age. With the Soviet Union, we developed the means to end life on the planet, and yet we also led a global effort to keep the force we had unleashed under control. What kind of force? Lest we forget, here are two statements; the first is eyewitness testimony from an American aviator aboard *The Great Artiste* (which bombed Nagasaki), and the second, a narrative (necessarily speculative) from a visitor to Hiroshima soon after it was bombed:

> Observers in the tail of our ship saw a giant ball of fire rise though from the bowels of the earth . . . next they saw a giant pillar of purple fire. . . . Awe-struck, we watched it shoot upward like a meteor coming from the earth instead of from outer space, becoming ever more alive as it climbed skyward . . . [then] there came shooting out of the top a giant mushroom . . . even more alive than the pillar, seething and boiling in a white fury of creamy foam . . . like a creature in the act of breaking the bonds that held it down.

> Within a few seconds the thousands of people in the streets and the gardens in the centre of the town were scorched by a wave of searing heat. Many were killed instantly, others lay writhing on the ground screaming in agony. . . . Every living thing was petrified in an attitude of indescribable suffering. . . . About half an hour after the explosion . . . a fine rain began to fall . . . caused by the sudden rise of over-heated air to a great height, where it condensed and fell back as rain. Then a violent wind arose and the fires extended with terrible rapidity, because most Japanese houses are built only of timber and straw. By the evening

the fire began to die down and then it went out. There was nothing left to burn. Hiroshima had ceased to exist.

These fearful explosions were preceded by prayers and motivated by anger and the urgent desire to end a war. During the past sixty years, a big part of the job of the American president has been to see that it does not happen again.

Dwight Eisenhower, in his 1953 "Atoms for Peace" address to the UN, pledged America's "determination to help solve the fearful atomic dilemma—to devote its entire heart and mind to find the way by which the miraculous inventiveness of man shall not be dedicated to his death, but consecrated to his life." In the same spirit, John Kennedy proposed to prohibit atmospheric nuclear tests; Richard Nixon authored a ban on antiballistic missile defense; and Ronald Reagan stunned advisors by telling Mikhail Gorbachev that his suggestion to eliminate nuclear weapons "suits me fine." When the Berlin Wall fell, the Clinton administration helped remove nuclear weapons from Ukraine, Kazakhstan, and Belarus and began a program to prevent loose nukes by safeguarding nuclear materials and expertise.

Most important was the Nuclear Nonproliferation Treaty (NPT), negotiated by Lyndon Johnson, ratified under Richard Nixon, and signed by every country except Israel, India, and Pakistan. That agreement was based on a grand bargain: the nuclear haves (the United States, the USSR, the United Kingdom, France, and China) promised to eliminate such weapons over time, while everyone else pledged not to build or acquire them. For more than a quarter century, the pact held. Dozens of countries that could have developed nuclear arms refrained from doing so. The number of proclaimed nuclear weapons states froze at five—with Israel, outside the system, a probable sixth.

As UN ambassador in the mid-1990s, I participated in negotiations to extend the NPT indefinitely. The talks succeeded, but the allegations of hypocrisy were hard to counter. Egypt's representative took the lead in demanding that we support a nuclear-free zone in the Middle East—a seductive proposal aimed at embarrassing Israel. Indian negotiators were angry about the unwillingness of the nuclear states to destroy their weapons. Having conducted a nuclear test in the 1970s, India had paused, but eventually ran out of patience. In 1998, first India and then Pakistan announced that they had crashed their way into the nuclear club—though without accepting the club's rules.

The fear of a nuclear-armed Iran has since set off a chain reaction among Arab states, half a dozen of whom have announced plans to begin developing nuclear power—including the oil-rich Emirates and Saudi Arabia. The Arab programs are advertised as civilian and commercial, but then so is Iran's.

The NPT made it easier for governments to do without nuclear arms. Subsequent developments are causing some countries to reconsider. The director of the International Atomic Energy Agency (IAEA) complains that until the world commits to eradicating nuclear weapons, we will "have this cynical environment that all the guys in the minor leagues will try to join the major leagues. They will say, 'If the big boys continue to rely on nuclear weapons, why shouldn't I?'"

Although any degree of proliferation concerns us, we are most alarmed when governments hostile to us prepare to go nuclear. The irony is that this threat is magnified by our strength. Hostile countries may see the nuclear option as the only way to deter us from doing to them what we did to Iraq. In their view, Saddam Hussein was toppled not because he had weapons of mass destruction, but because he did not.

There is also a risk that, as more countries produce the components needed for nuclear arms, a portion of these materials will be bought or stolen by terrorist groups. This would be doubly dangerous, because some terrorists claim to welcome death and are therefore impossible to deter and because many lack an address against which retaliatory or preemptive action might be taken.

For all these reasons, you should restore America's vocation as an architect of peace. That means recognizing that nuclear weapons threaten the survival of all and so the concerns of all must be addressed. The core of the dilemma is that we are preaching what we do not practice. Since the knowledge of how to make atomic bombs cannot be unlearned, we will be reluctant to give up our arsenal. These weapons help protect us, we believe, and therefore the world, because we see ourselves as defenders of stability and right. If we disarm, and others cheat, we would be vulnerable to nuclear blackmail.

Under George W. Bush, our policies have focused appropriately enough on problem countries but have paid little attention to the overall effectiveness of the nuclear nonproliferation regime. Instead of trying to strengthen the IAEA, we have picked fights with its leadership. Worse, our credibility has been undermined by the president's proposal to build a new and unneeded generation of bunker-busting nuclear bombs. Your administration can remedy this by forgoing the bunker-busters and instead supporting the goal of a nuclear weapons–free world (even if we are not sure how to arrive at that destination). Diplomatically, you can seek further cuts in existing arsenals and the elimination of loopholes in the NPT that allow countries to jump quickly from legal civilian nuclear programs to illegal military ones. Financially, you should devote additional resources to safeguarding materials that could be used to build bombs. Militarily, you should step up efforts to prevent the smuggling of sensitive equipment and technologies. On Capitol Hill, you should seek the Senate's consent to the Comprehensive Nuclear Test Ban Treaty. Politically, you might find it helpful to cite the wisdom of the Great Communicator himself: "I can't believe," said Ronald Reagan, "that this world can go on beyond our generation and on down to succeeding generations with this kind of weapon . . . without someday some fool, or some maniac, or some accident triggering the kind of war that is the end of the line for all."

Not long ago, I was invited to the White House along with other former secretaries of state and defense. President Bush asked for our support, emphasizing the importance of promoting freedom. We were sitting in the Roosevelt room and as we rose to leave, the president invited us to visit the Oval Office to see how Laura had redecorated it. I took the opportunity to thank Mr. Bush and politely, I hope, to chide him. "Mr. President," I said, "I applaud you when you ask us to support democracy, but I do have one small bone to pick. Sometimes you act as if you invented democracy. The truth is that I did." Bush laughed. As chair of the National Democratic Institute (NDI), I felt able to joke that I had first claim to the patent. The reason the issue was on my mind, however, is that democracy-building under President Bush has not achieved its purpose. On several occasions recently, I have talked up democracy in Arab countries only to be rebuked by leaders who exclaim in horror, "We do not want our country to look like Iraq."

As Mr. Bush's successor, you are uncomfortably placed. It

would be a dereliction for any president to refrain from touting democracy. You cannot, however, ignore what has gone on these past eight years.

For a time, what President Bush called his "forward strategy for freedom" had momentum. Elections in Iraq, Afghanistan, Georgia, Ukraine, and Lebanon combined to generate a rising tide, but one that crested prematurely. In fact, democracy is having its worst decade since the 1930s, when elections in Germany yielded infamous results. While visiting Egypt in 2005, Condoleezza Rice bravely endorsed democratic reforms. Two years later, when she returned, she was silent on those same issues. The lesson learned in the interim is that many Arabs, when given the freedom to choose, do not choose as we would like. Instead of West-leaning modernists, they tend to favor candidates whose views we consider extreme. Thus the same administration that claimed it was a historic error to rely for stability on unelected Arab leaders has turned to unelected Arab leaders—now referred to as "moderates"—for precisely that purpose.

One reason the administration has found itself at odds with its own rhetoric is that freedom has more than one meaning. Americans tend to equate freedom with democracy; Arab populations relate it to their own sense of personal and cultural identity. So when President Bush talked about a democratic transformation in the Middle East while simultaneously occupying Iraq, many Arabs interpreted the combination less as a plan to spread political liberty than as a threat to their independence. Western interventions in Arab lands have an inglorious history, thus Western intentions are widely mistrusted. This does not mean that we should abandon support for democracy, but it does mean that we should express our support in ways that do not question the right of Arab societies to decide their own future. We can offer ideas, but not issue demands, and we must accept that transforming the Arab world is not our job.

A second source of confusion is that democracy means far more than choosing a leader at the ballot box. The distinction is striking in many countries where democracy is accepted in theory but limited in practice to the holding of dodgy elections and the enumeration of rights that then go unprotected. Democracy's reputation is dragged through the mud when self-described democratic leaders fail to deliver on promises to clean up government, improve standards of living, or respect human rights.

In Nigeria, for example, satisfaction with democracy has plunged from 84 percent to 25 percent over the past seven years. This despite the leadership of Olusegun Obasanjo, easily Nigeria's best president to that time but still in many ways a disappointing one. In April 2007, I witnessed the selection of Obasanjo's successor in the first electoral transition from one president to another in that country's history. It was not a happy event. Polling stations in many areas opened late, closed early, or never opened. Turnout was low because of threatened violence. The anger was fed by the public's perception that the authorities are neither honest nor fair. Exhibit A is that the benefits from Nigeria's oil reserves are not widely shared. The hotel my delegation stayed in was freezing because the air-conditioning was set too high, yet the country has so little energy that the popular nickname for the state Power Holding Company is "Please Hold Candle." Manufacturers cannot create jobs because without power they can't compete against foreign imports, and as I discovered, vote-counting becomes complicated as well. When it grew dark in the village where I was, local officials had to ask if anyone had a generator they could borrow. One man volunteered, and I watched as he fetched the device and strung up a single lightbulb to allow the clerks to tally votes. Little wonder that protestors during the balloting had chanted, "No job! No food! No light! No freedom! No election!"

Yet even in Nigeria there is hope. The electoral process may have been disheartening, but the courts, parliament, and press are independent and relevant. Civil society is growing. In Africa as a whole from 1960 until 1990, only three presidents or prime ministers left office voluntarily or after losing an election. In the years since, that number has climbed to forty. Democracy may not be on the march but it is still upright, fending off the rocks thrown from left and right.

As president you can rally democratic forces without seeming to re-create the crusader mentality associated with your predecessor. The way to do that is by strengthening regional institutions and by urging democratic friends within the developing countries to take the lead. You should be honest in stating that political liberty is no guarantee of prosperity and that free elections are just the beginning of the democratic process. Democracy promotion fits well with efforts to alleviate poverty and also to improve the climate for global peace. This is the right agenda for you to set and will help you in addressing a broader challenge: how to inspire the world to join with you and our country in a common cause.

In January 1941, America confronted a defining choice. The Nazis were in control of much of Europe. Great Britain was under siege. Across the ocean, Churchill warned, "If we fail, then the whole world, including the United States, including all that we have known and cared for, will sink into the abyss of a new Dark Age made more sinister, and perhaps more protracted, by the lights of perverted science." Europe, however, was thousands of miles away. When Franklin Roosevelt went before Congress for his annual address, he could have focused on the domestic economy, still recovering from the Depression. He might have adhered to his campaign promise to keep America as separate as possible from Europe's desperate plight. He could perhaps have tried to bargain with Hitler by implying that Germany, if it ceased to advance, could keep the territory it had gained without fear of U.S. intervention. In living rooms, on street corners, and in bomb shelters across the globe, people listened anxiously: What would FDR say? What kind of role for America would he envision? Roosevelt, of course, rose from his wheelchair and, in so doing, lifted the world. His message went far beyond the provincial norms of such an address to outline universal principles, goals for which America—before the year was out—would take up arms.

FDR spoke of a world founded upon four essential freedoms—the freedoms of speech and religious liberty, and freedom from want and fear. He told Congress and a global audience that this was "no vision of a distant millennium. It is a definite basis for a kind of world attainable in our own time and generation. That kind of world is the very antithesis of the so-called 'new order' of tyranny which the dictators seek to create with the crash of a bomb."

True threats to civilization come from ideas that are, like fascism, both powerfully seductive and profoundly wrong. Such ideas compress all of life into a simplistic pattern that identifies a supposed source of evil against which to unite, and creates a flattering self-image for those otherwise unsatisfied with their lot. These ideas answer the same questions that great religions try to answer—which is why religions, when interpreted narrowly, can be so inflammatory.

To respond effectively to such threats, you will have to do more than draw up plans to fight poverty, supplement the NPT, or devise new ways to zone real estate in Jerusalem. You will have to explain, as FDR did (and Lincoln before him and Jefferson before him), the very basis upon which society should be built. You must help do for the world what Paul Tillich said Americans have historically done for themselves: work for new foundations of existence once old foundations have been shaken or even for a time destroyed.

No one expects you or any president to lead us to some promised land; we do count on you to point us in the right direction. Ideally, you will show the qualities of integrity and courage that reflect our country at its best. You must also search out the best in others, beginning with those we have long counted on and whose trust we must regain: our allies and neighbors.

CHAPTER 9

Hoops of Iron

Through four decades of cold war, the Soviets tried without success to drive a wedge between Europe and America. The danger now is that we will divide ourselves.

When the cold war ended, we felt sure that America and Europe together could accomplish anything. By facing down the communist empire, we had ended the superpower confrontation, extracted the barbed wire from Europe's heart, and made possible the dream of a continent whole and free. When people from both sides of the Atlantic sat down together, we did not have to explain whom we meant when using the word "we."

Tony Blair, visiting Washington, reaffirmed his belief that so long as Europe and America remained a team, "the other great nations of the world, and the small, will gather around in one place, not many." The assumption that the West still provides the organizing principle for the globe is comforting (to us) and is backed by enough wealth, military clout, and technological prowess to remain arguable. Less tangible but even more in-dispensable are the shared ideals of respect for human rights, liberty, law, and faith in the power of reason; these are the hoops of iron that have seen the West through periods of extreme trial and that remain our tightest bond.

The Euro-Atlantic partnership evolved from a common heritage and is centered on a joint perception, arrived at over centuries, of the ideal relationship between government and the individual. Our friendship goes deeper even than military alliances ordinarily do, for it was conceived not simply to oppose a mutual enemy or as a matter of temporary convenience. John Kennedy characterized transatlantic unity as the basic objective of postwar American foreign policy, and succeeding presidents, down through Bill Clinton, both expressed such sentiments and meant them.

As I can testify, maintaining close relations with Europe was a centerpiece of U.S. foreign policy in the 1990s. Even when there were disagreements, we were able to work through NATO or with the European Union (EU) to resolve them. As always, our relations with France were prickly; the French are prone to criticize America's hegemonic tendencies to the same degree they mourn the loss of their own imperial capacities. Nevertheless, the alliance stood together through grueling tests in Bosnia and Kosovo, embraced the new democracies of postcommunist Europe, and broadened its purpose to deal with threats arising outside the region. Though fear of the Soviet Union had dissipated, Euro-Atlantic ideals endured and a lively sense of common purpose was retained.

Enter George W. Bush. Europeans expecting a younger version of his father were startled by the new administration's blunt rejection of their concerns on such matters as climate change, arms control, the role of the United Nations, the international criminal court, Guantánamo, and, of course, Iraq. Never before had Europeans been asked to embrace a U.S. president who seemed so uninterested in advice and so unilateral in asserting American prerogatives. The response was applause from a few, bewilderment on the part of many, and much criticism—some thoughtful, some excessive.

When, in 2005, British dramatist Harold Pinter accepted the Nobel Prize for Literature, he railed, "The crimes of the United States have been systematic, constant, vicious, remorseless, but very few people have actually talked about them. You have to hand it to America. It has exercised a quite clinical manipulation of power worldwide while masquerading as a force for universal good."

Pinter's claim that "few people have actually talked" about the shortcomings of the United States is hard to fathom; my impression while traveling in Europe was that people were talking about little else. Though most Europeans are less hyperbolic than Pinter, even my normally pro-American friends fear that the United States has become simultaneously besotted by power and unnerved by terror; or, as one plaintively asked, "Have you lost your minds?"

It is not that Europeans fail to appreciate the trauma of 9/11; it's just that they were baffled by the choice of Iraq as the cornerstone of our response. Saddam Hussein was a villain, they concede, but no imminent threat to us—and blameless for 9/11. European governments that cooperated with Washington on secret arrests and detentions found themselves on the defensive because America's standing as a champion of due process and human rights has been soiled. In consequence, America and Europe have begun to speak with separate voices. Our sense of collective identity, as the West united, has been weakened.

Though years have passed, many Americans have still not forgiven European critics of the Iraq invasion either for opposing it or—what is worse—for being right. Many Europeans have not forgiven Americans for reelecting Mr. Bush. These are, however, far from the only issues.

Since the era of Jefferson and Franklin, the United States has been Eurocentric. In recent decades, the country has evolved, its population becoming more Latin, Asian, and African. When I travel to American college campuses now, I find students more preoccupied with the latest developments in China, South Asia, the Middle East, and the hot spots of Africa than with what is transpiring directly across the Atlantic. Most Americans don't have a clear idea of how the European Union operates or what it was designed to accomplish. The whole idea of opening national borders, adopting a multinational currency, and ceding lawmaking power to a supranational entity is alien to our ethos—something that might have made sense for American colonies two and a quarter centuries ago but would be anathema today. How many times during the campaign were you even asked by our national press about such issues as Turkey's controversial EU candidacy, Poland's turbulent domestic politics, or the future orientation of Ukraine? The falling value of the dollar, meanwhile, has made it more attractive for Europeans to visit America and more expensive for us to visit the continent, creating yet another reason to avoid learning about our European cousins.

When Americans do indulge in cross-Atlantic thinking, it is usually to complain that Europeans are not stalwart enough in confronting terror, opposing Iran, or bolstering NATO. To many Americans, and certainly to the Bush administration, Europe is seen as a junior partner and, as such, obliged to follow our lead.

As for the European perspective, it is unfair to generalize.

There is no single European point of view, just as no one person, not even a president, can speak for every American. The Scandinavians top the charts as world citizens, generous in aiding others and enamored of multilateral approaches. The Baltics and Central Europe, having survived decades behind the Iron Curtain, still bear scars and so are more nervous about Moscow and less critical of America than their Western counterparts. Similarly, the stouthearted Dutch, champions of law, signed up to fight in both Afghanistan and Iraq. They do not doubt that the United States is on their side. This attitude, refreshing to Americans, can lead to arguments within Europe. During the tempestuous run-up to the Iraq war, the leaders of ten Central and East European countries signed a letter favorable to the United States. This bit of cheek caused Jacques Chirac, the sometimes overbearing French president, to sniff that the countries involved had "missed an opportunity to shut up."

Even as they argue about America, Europeans are engaged in a seemingly endless process of sorting out their own identity. The European experiment is at an awkward point—too committed to unity to back away, too attached to national distinctions to embrace union without misgivings. The EU (or originally, the Common Market) was conceived both to spur economic integration and to respond to communism and the fear that fascism might one day revive. That first Common Market had half a dozen members; today's EU has twenty-seven, making it, depending on your view, either impressively inclusive or hopelessly unwieldy. To complicate matters further, the EU presidency has traditionally shifted to a new country every six months; though an effort to change this is in the works. Let's hope it succeeds. Imagine how confused Americans would be if the White House changed hands twice a year.

None of this would matter much to you as president, except

for two possibilities: Europe may become so consumed by internal squabbling that it is unable to help America; or it may find unity by defining itself as a balance to our power. To Americans, the idea that Europe might come together for the purpose of opposing us seems absurd; to some Europeans, it appears both logical and necessary.

From Caesar's Rome to Hitler's Germany, Europeans have suffered the excesses of ambition before. Many feel that it is unhealthy to have a single superpower. Iraq reinforced this view, but even before the U.S. invasion, many Europeans did not look upon America as quite civilized. After all, the United States has one of the world's largest prison populations, a horrifying murder rate, a fascination with guns, and the curious notion (in some quarters at least) that candidates for high office should prove their toughness by executing people. Where American mythology centers on the role of the heroic individual, the modern European sensibility concerns itself with societies acting humanely. American morality demands that everyone be given a chance; European morality, that everyone be given a share of what society has to offer. Europe believes it has learned the lessons of the twentieth century; America believes—its critics allege—that it taught the lessons of the twentieth century.

As a child of Europe who grew up in America, I like to think that with longer legs I might have a foot on both sides of the Atlantic. I felt I could understand either place. I began to question this, however, when, in 1997, I delivered a speech in Prague upon returning to my native city for the first time as secretary of state. It was one of the more emotional moments of my life. The audience was full of friends, the setting grand, the reception all I could ask, and my speech a celebration of the cold war's end, coupled with a description of Europe's bright future. Václav

Klaus, then prime minister, brought me back to Earth when he told me that no Czech leader would ever have given such a speech—it was so optimistic.

At the time, I was surprised; who could fail to be full of hope at such a moment? In the years following, I came to accept that American attitudes were generally sunnier than European. Perhaps we had a more favorable view of human experience because our country had not—in modern times—been occupied by foreign troops and because we had accumulated so much influence and power. Perhaps that is why 9/11 and the many setbacks since have been such a shock. Today, we are not so sure about our prospects. In fact, a smaller percentage of Americans now think the next generation will be better off than do Czechs and, for that matter, Bulgarians, Poles, and most populations in the developing world. This is a stunning and disturbing change.

In recent times, the British have taken on the assignment—harder than it should be—of explaining the United States to Europe and Europe to the United States. Americans still love the British; the Europeans have been disappointed in Britain's inability, at times, to bring America along. Tony Blair gambled that by joining forces with Bush he could make the president appreciate the European point of view. He lost.

Under Blair, the British led or joined four major military interventions—in Kosovo, Sierra Leone, Afghanistan, and Iraq—in each case contributing to a tyrant's demise. Gordon Brown, in his first days, was tested by terrorist bomb plots in London and Glasgow. His low-key response reflected what is likely to be a shift in the personality of British foreign policy. Out of self-interest and personal conviction, Brown will be inclined to emphasize diplomacy and law over combative declarations and military action. Made wary by the British experience in the Gulf, Brown will steer clear of adventurism; so will the bulk of Europe. For most of its history, the United States sought to remain apart from the conflicts that engulfed the continent. Now much of Europe would prefer to remain aloof from wars involving the United States.

Hubert Védrine, my engagingly cynical counterpart in the French foreign ministry, loved to irritate me by calling America a "hyper power." I was upset the first time I saw the term in print, although when I heard Hubert say it in French, it didn't sound so bad. I didn't even mind when the French press referred to me as "Hyper Madeleine." In alliance politics, France is a squeaky wheel. My own experience, however, was that French leaders would be reasonable in public if given an opportunity to complain in private. Denied that chance, they would accentuate differences just to create a stir. During the Clinton years, we never stopped arguing with the French—and they never failed to act with us when it truly mattered.

The French yearn for earlier times—when Charlemagne or Napoleon ruled and their language was spoken at royal courts from London to St. Petersburg. In May 2007, when Nicolas Sarkozy was sworn in as successor to Chirac, he rode in a motorcade up the Champs-Élysées, rekindled the flame at the Tomb of the Unknown Soldier beneath the Arc de Triomphe, and laid a wreath at the statue of de Gaulle. Sarkozy's policies, however, are refreshingly forward-looking. He did not campaign on a plan to recapture past glory but on the Kennedyesque platform "Get France moving again." With his plebian education and an ancestry that includes a Jewish grandfather, a Greek grandmother, and a Hungarian father, Sarkozy is unlike any previous

French president. He has set about shaking up the government, exhorting his country to work harder, and showing a populist touch. He has even earned—I am gratified to say—the nickname "hyper president."

Unlike Chirac, Sarkozy doesn't see the need to try to inflate his support at home by distancing himself from the United States. Should this attitude hold, it will create an opening for you to bring relations to a level not enjoyed since the days of Washington and Lafayette. For reasons of history (and language), the French can provide particular help in dealing with Lebanon, Syria, parts of Africa, and sometimes Russia. To move Europe itself, however, will also require the cooperation of Germany, Europe's largest country.

In 2000, almost eight out of every ten Germans had a favorable view of the United States. In 2007, the number had dropped to three out of ten. The reason, of course, was Iraq. With President Bush declaring that countries were either with the United States or with the terrorists, Chancellor Gerhard Schröder lined up with his colleagues in Paris and Moscow to oppose the invasion, leading to Condoleezza Rice's supercilious comment that America should "punish France, ignore Germany, and forgive Russia."

These events, the most damaging rupture in U.S.-German relations since World War II, are best forgotten. Schröder's successor, the sensible centrist Angela Merkel, has been comfortable working with President Bush. When I first met Merkel, she was still a parliamentarian and seemed quiet, almost meek. As Germany's first woman chancellor, and the youngest of either gender since before World War II, she has rapidly found her footing on the world stage. Provided she can hold her balky governing coalition together, she has the wherewithal to establish Germany as the economic and political leader of Europe while serving as a critical intermediary between the United States and Russia. You should look to her (along with the British and French) as keys to your European strategy, but militarily there will be limits. Germany is still in the process of emerging from the pacifism thought appropriate after World War II. Over the last decade, it has begun deploying peacekeepers to international trouble spots, including places such as Afghanistan, where real fighting is going on. No country deserves more praise than Germany for learning from and atoning for the past. You should warmly endorse its candidacy for a permanent seat on the UN Security Council. We have not yet reached the point, however, where a strong Deutsche military is desired—either by most Germans or their neighbors.

In April 2009, NATO will observe its sixtieth anniversary. The event looms at a moment of severe testing both on the battlefield and in the minds of leaders and publics on both sides of the Atlantic. Here again, the world is paying a high price for the unilateral instincts of the Bush administration, especially in its first years.

After 9/11, the members of NATO responded the way allies should, invoking the collective defense provisions of the alliance charter and treating the attack on the United States as a strike on all. President Bush rejected this help, deciding instead to rely on a U.S. force supplemented by Afghan mercenaries, who promised but failed to corral bin Laden and the Taliban's top leadership. The administration, ideologically averse to the concept of nation-building, thought it could remake Afghanistan on the cheap; relatively few troops and funds were committed. When the strategy was questioned, the Defense Department told Afghan leaders that more soldiers were not available. The reason for this soon became apparent: the Pentagon was already planning for Iraq. Only after that invasion turned sour did the administration seek to engage NATO fully in Afghanistan. The delay was inexcusable. There is no more elementary a principle in warfare or politics than to press your advantage so that an enemy, once forced to retreat, is not given a chance to recover. In Afghanistan, during the first years of fighting, the Bush administration could have laid the groundwork for lasting success if it had taken advantage of NATO's offer and concentrated its resources there instead of diverting the lion's share to the Persian Gulf.

Now, belatedly, NATO is fighting a resurgent Taliban in a struggle with no definable end point and no early likelihood of victory. With NATO undergoing a test of its relevance, and the fate of a pivotal country on the line, one would expect a fierce sense of urgency throughout the alliance. Instead, because of Iraq, Afghanistan has been treated as if it were a sideshow. Although some countries, such as Canada, deserve particular credit for courage and sacrifice, other allies have limited their troops to passive assignments. The situation demands a NATO leader who can effectively synthesize a variety of views, but listening, let alone synthesizing, is not one of President Bush's strong points. He has also done a poor job of convincing the populations of NATO countries that they have good reasons to care about alliance success. Because of these shortcomings, the Taliban—despite its unappealing social doctrines—has made inroads throughout southern Afghanistan. NATO has the advantage in firepower, but the Taliban has all the benefits of an insurgent force: time, familiarity with terrain, knowledge of language and culture, ideological fervor, and the ability to regenerate itself. It also has strategic depth, due to support from fellow Pashtun tribesmen in neighboring Pakistan.

This mess is part of your inheritance and may well comprise a portion of your legacy. NATO could be in Afghanistan for a decade or more, which will strain both the patience of allied troops and the tolerance of Afghans, who dislike armed foreigners running around their country, too often killing the wrong people. It will be up to you to keep the alliance together—and to develop a strategy either for defeating the Taliban or helping the Afghan government to contain it.

You might use the sixtieth-anniversary celebration to set your course. Unfortunately, the alliance remains lopsided. Europe has as much wealth and a comparable number of people under arms as the United States but spends only about half as much on defense. Reducing the disparity between U.S. and allied capabilities has long been a goal, but much work remains—and our setbacks in Iraq and Afghanistan have done nothing to generate enthusiasm. The effort is diluted in any case by Europe's insistence on developing a separate defense arm under the authority of the EU. When I was secretary of state, Europe's announced objective was to create a rapid response force sixty thousand strong. That scheme was soon abandoned, and the current plan is for a baker's dozen of smaller formations, called battle groups, of fifteen hundred each. If this initiative improves Europe's military capability, well done; but the results thus far have not been impressive, either for the EU or NATO.

·   ·   ·

For the past eight years, we have wondered whether Euro-Atlantic antagonism was due primarily to President Bush or to a permanent clash of cultures and interests. My European friends assure me that the problem is Bush, and that everyone across the Atlantic is dying to see a fresh face in the White House. They may well be telling me what they think I want to hear, or perhaps what they wish themselves to believe. Now, we will find out.

From the first day, your goal should be to stress your belief that the United States, Canada, and Europe are engaged in a common enterprise. The stakes are such that we must not allow ourselves to be distracted by cultural disagreements. Differences are certain to persist over lesser issues but these will matter little if we can agree again on larger questions of terrorism, peace, law, and human rights.

Certainly, you should distance yourself from President Bush's least defensible acts of unilateralism. One field where a coordinated Euro-Atlantic strategy is needed stretches across energy security and the environment. Few controversies have done more to damage America's reputation than the perception, invited by Bush's policies, that we are too selfish to care about the atmosphere and too wedded to wasteful habits to concern ourselves with sustainable energy practices. These matters are plainly linked, since curbing climate change depends on reducing the emission of greenhouse gases, which hinges, in turn, on conservation, the development of clean energy resources, and according to reputable studies—a decline in our consumption of beef from flatulence-prone cattle. These imperatives are intimately connected to the future health of the global economy and to Euro-Atlantic prosperity, which is increasingly dependent on oil suppliers of dubious politics and questionable stability. The global dimension is obvious, as well, given the vulnerability of oil production facilities to terrorist strikes and the potential impacts of climate change on food production, water supplies, natural disasters, and disease.

To lead in these areas, you must first acknowledge that America has fallen behind. As president, you should work with Congress to restore our credibility as a responsible steward of the global environment, while simultaneously establishing a joint planning team with the European Union. The goal should be to coordinate policies on an array of issues, from cutting carbon emissions to the development of energy-efficient technologies to negotiating agreements that accommodate without giving a free pass to the rising economies of China, India, and Brazil. Angela Merkel, a former physicist, would be an ideal partner.

The moment has come to remind ourselves who "we" are and what Europeans and Americans can accomplish together. The quartet of Euro-Atlantic leaders—Merkel, Brown, Sarkozy, and you—can create a new foundation for global progress through the restoration of mutual trust and the implementation of cooperative projects. For inspiration, I encourage you to cite the Berlin airlift—because I fear the tale has been forgotten and because it, too, will have its sixtieth anniversary during your first year.

After World War II, West Berlin was isolated within the communist half of the country, connected to the rest of free Germany only by rail and a single highway. In June 1948, the Soviets blocked ground transportation routes to the Allied sectors of the city, leaving the population with no source of fuel or food. If the Allies did nothing, West Berlin would become a permanent part of the Soviet sphere. The alternative was to try supplying two and a half million people solely by air, using the relatively small, slow-flying planes of the era. Nothing similar had ever been attempted, but Truman was determined to try. They called the airlift Operation Vittles; it began with ponderous C-47s, called Gooney Birds, and later C-54s stacked to the ceiling with coal and food, flying despite worn instruments, failing lights, leaking windshields, and jammed communications. Two towering Russian radio transmitters created hazards for pilots at the airfield in the French sector. The airfield commander, after repeated warnings, ordered the destruction of the towers. Shortly thereafter, a Soviet officer rushed into the French headquarters screaming, "How could you do that?" "With dynamite" came the reply.

Exhausted pilots—American, British, Australian, Canadian, New Zealanders, South African—flew around the clock from summer through winter (complete with Bob Hope's Christmas caravan) and into spring, reaching a climax with the Easter Parade, when 1,398 flights took place in twenty-four hours, with planes moving across the sky like a line of winged ants—proving beyond a doubt that the blockade would never succeed. The airlift even had its own anthem, composed by Irving Berlin:

Operation Vittles, we'll soon be on our way,
With coal and wheat and hay, and everything's okay.
Operation Vittles, as in the sky we go,
we won't forget to blow a kiss to Uncle Joe.

Finally, in May 1949, after some 320 days and more than 250,000 flights, the Soviets yielded and the blockade was lifted. The Americans, British, French, Germans, and other allies had refused to be bullied and, because they stayed together, defied the odds and saved West Berlin. A common enterprise indeed.

•   •   •

Perhaps in the future, as John Lennon imagined, the world will be as one. Until then, divisions will remain and the United States will want and need most of Latin America to engage with us in a common enterprise of our own. This is as it should be. We share a colonial upbringing and a commitment to constitutional democracy that stretches back to Washington and Bolivar. We have been members of a regional organization since the founding, in 1890, of the International Union of American Republics (later superseded by the Pan American Union and then the OAS, or Organization of American States). We have, with few exceptions, stood together in fighting totalitarianism.

We have also survived periods of intense strain. At times, the United States has been accused of indifference toward its neighbors to the south; at others, of intervening and trying to boss everybody around. On occasion, both accusations have been justified. At the moment, relations are not good.

One reason is the regional variation of a global theme. The gap between rich and poor in Latin America is wider than anywhere else. Further, economic growth has been uneven—rising by 82 percent between 1960 and 1980, by only 9 percent between 1980 and 2000, and by just 4 percent in the first five years of the new century. One in two Latin Americans live in poverty; one in four on less than two dollars a day. Especially in rural areas, conditions remain almost primitive. Children are brought into the world using methods and technologies a century old. Health care consists of tiny clinics stocked with a few bottles of past-date medicines. Farmers grow food with their bare hands and the help, if lucky, of a burro. These were not the results promised a couple of decades ago when Latin America's democratic revolution, replacing military governments with elected leaders, was launched.

The resulting disenchantment has caused a weakening of support for liberal rules of investment and trade. Many people do not feel democracy is delivering, because they are unable to see the benefits in their lives. Beginning with the election, in 1998, of Venezuelan president Hugo Chávez, political leaders who promise radical change have done well at the polls. Leftist politicians have taken office in Argentina, Bolivia, Ecuador, and Nicaragua, while failing by narrow margins in Mexico and Peru.

President Bush cannot be blamed, after 9/11, for giving top priority to terrorism. Iraq, however, was avoidable. It has warped many aspects of U.S. foreign policy while devouring resources that could have been invested more wisely elsewhere. Mr. Bush, who had once accused Bill Clinton of neglecting Latin America, virtually ignored the region on his watch, until an effort to catch up midway through his second term.

In March 2007, Bush took a six-day swing, stopping in Brazil, Uruguay, Colombia, Guatemala, and Mexico. His theme, peculiar for his administration, was social equity. The president posed in front of Mayan ruins, touted the benefits of ethanol, hoisted lettuce crates in front of cameras, and sought to take credit for U.S. aid to the region—which equals in a year about what we spend per day in the Persian Gulf.

The tour—though welcome—stirred memories of the cold war, when America used a combination of aid, diplomacy, and support for anticommunist dictators to dampen Latin American ardor for Cuba-style revolution. President Bush's itinerary was designed to counter the anti-U.S. policies not of the ailing Castro, but of Chávez, the exuberantly hostile Venezuelan.

While in office, I had made the acquaintance of Chávez's predecessors and found them to be old, tired, and out of touch. President Clinton and I met Chávez himself in New York during a session of the UN General Assembly. Our initial reaction was favorable; Chávez was friendly and eager to describe his plan to use oil money to help the poor. His energy impressed me, while Clinton recognized a fellow political natural. We were therefore disappointed by his decision, evident soon after, to adopt an antagonistic approach toward the United States and anyone else who failed to share his views on two topics: the need for radical reform and the infallibility of Hugo Chávez.

In 2002, an abortive coup was launched against Chávez by foes within the Venezuelan military. The putsch failed, but not before President Bush implicitly endorsed it, this despite a standing pledge by OAS members to uphold constitutional procedures. The episode enabled Chávez to pin an imperialist tag on Bush in a region where anti-imperial chants are learned in kindergarten. Add to this the usual sources of resentment in U.S.-Latin relations, and the Venezuelan leader had abundant ammunition to fire at Washington.

Chávez loves to speak about broad themes of poverty versus privilege. He urges Latin Americans to unite in fighting Washington, which he demonizes, literally, as "the devil that represents capitalism." Chávez has a televangelist's knack for working a crowd and a taunting style that elicits laughter and whoops, especially when the targets are *yanquis* or Bush. He talks about the poor as if they were not a problem but, rather, emblematic of national ethics and values. He doesn't promise handouts; he promises justice. That is why people cheer.

Chávez has another asset, and that of course is oil. One wonders how many problems Fidel Castro might have created if

Cuba had sat on 6 percent of the world's petroleum reserves. Venezuela's international customers, led by the United States, pour tens of billions of dollars annually into the country's bank account. This allows Chávez to play the role of Santa both at home and abroad. Domestically, he has won support from the poor through price controls, expanded subsidies, the expropriation of large farms, the creation of favored cooperatives, and health care provided by twenty thousand Cuban doctors, dentists, and sports trainers. Free marketers may scoff, but these policies have reduced poverty significantly. At the same time, Chávez has consolidated power by rewriting the Venezuelan constitution, weakening the judiciary, intimidating the political opposition, steering public contracts to cronies, and using his oil money to build up security forces and buy arms. He is clearly wedded to the presidency and has shown every intention of retaining it "till death do us part."

Regionally, Chávez has given bundles of aid to Bolivia, Argentina, and Cuba, while providing cut-rate oil to the poor in, among other places, the United States. To capture attention during Bush's spring trip, Chávez pledged to invest more in a single Nicaraguan refinery than the sum total of annual U.S. assistance to all of Latin America.

Chávez claims to be guided by the voice of the people, which he publicly equates with God. His listeners are receptive to a populist message, especially when it comes from a smiling figure bearing money, anti-gringo slogans, and still more money. There are signs, however, that Chávez lacks a sense of when to stop. His decision to shut down independent television programming sparked angry protests. His campaign, in 2006, to win a seat on the UN Security Council fell flat when his sarcasm-laced speech to the General Assembly struck many delegates as undignified. He supported Bolivia's plan to nationalize its oil industry—a direct affront to Brazil, whose state-owned Petrobras is heavily invested in that country. Chávez's globe-trotting style has earned him photo opportunities with foreign dictators, but has done nothing to address the domestic problems of inflation, corruption, and crime. Further, his pretensions to Latin leadership do not always go down well with his fellow presidents, particularly Brazil's Luiz Lula, Colombia's Álvaro Uribe, and especially Felipe Calderón of Mexico, the world's largest Spanish-speaking nation.

Calderón won election in 2006 by a contested whisker over a leftist very much in the Chávez mold. An economic reformer who is tough on crime and drugs, Calderón is a man with whom any U.S. president should be able to work. The partnership will be tested, however, both by his domestic political situation and by yours. Calderón's party, a minority in the Mexican parliament, faces two strong opposition parties that would be pleased to see him fail. If Calderón feels the need to rouse popular support, he will be tempted to criticize the United States, particularly on the issues of trade and immigration. Like others in the region, many Mexicans feel that free trade policies, including NAFTA, harm small farmers. While Mexicans would like to renegotiate NAFTA to make the treaty more favorable, many in the United States feel the agreement is already tilted in a southern direction. North American labor organizers would like to scrap the pact altogether.

Under President Bush, U.S. immigration policy has been hard for Mexicans to interpret. The president favors a legal guest worker program and has spoken—with considerable courage—in favor of comprehensive immigration reform. On the other hand, he endorsed a congressional decision, unpopular in Mexico, to build a seven-hundred-mile wall along the U.S.-Mexican border.

Meanwhile, immigration remains a white-hot political issue in the United States. Jay Leno captured the mood of some when he joked that "According to a recent poll, anti-American sentiment is running high in Mexico. Half of Mexico's population say they have a negative view of the United States. The other half are already here."

During your campaign, you took a principled position on immigration and have pledged when president to continue in that vein. More power to you. As an immigrant myself and a lifelong believer in the American Dream, I am not neutral on the subject. The pundits and politicians who try to blame the bulk of America's problems on illegal immigrants are misinformed; these critics do no favors to American taxpayers or workers, and do not speak for the majority of our people.

Most Americans understand that our nation was built by individuals and families who arrived here from elsewhere, some—to our permanent shame—in shackles. Today, most of us believe that we should take reasonable measures to prevent illegal immigration so we are not flooded. People who do arrive illegally and are caught should be treated humanely and returned. Those who have already established themselves should be given a path toward citizenship. Those who would like to come in the future should have a fair chance to do so legally—just as most of our ancestors did. We should remember that the reason immigrants come to the United States, however they arrive—is to work. They, too, believe in the American Dream.

For Mexico and countries in Central America, the treatment of their people is a human rights issue. There is a significant moral difference between a person who commits a violent crime and a person who tries to cross the border illegally in order to put food on the family table. Such migrants may violate our laws against illicit entry, but if that's all they do they are trespassers, not criminals. They deserve to have their dignity respected. To say there are hypocrites among us is to understate the case. In 2006, one Orange County congressional candidate was asked to withdraw after sending a letter to residents with Hispanic surnames saying that immigrants who tried to vote would be deported. The offending candidate's name? Tan Nguyen.

In approaching Latin America, Washington should refrain from presenting an all-or-nothing choice between the untrammeled free market and the state-centered populism of Hugo Chávez. Instead, we should support governments that place a high priority on alleviating poverty but which do so without discouraging foreign investment or running up massive debts. Rather than insist that free trade is the solution to all problems, we should work to ensure that the benefits of expanded commerce and outside investment are broadly shared. We should encourage inventive social programs, such as those in Mexico and Brazil, that reward families who keep their children in school. We should strive to dissuade governments from falling too far under Chávez's spell, not by comparing him to Hitler, as Donald Rumsfeld did, but by being generous in our own assistance and by relying on cooler heads around the region to prevent lasting harm. Given the politics of the moment, the ideal way to slow Chávez (publicly, at least) is to ignore him.

As president, you will need a positive agenda in Latin America, but the reality is that its problems are hard to get around. When the number of new babies regularly outstrips the number of new jobs, the math tells the story. Although liberal economic policies have not always been effective, radical policies have never worked. It is likely that there will continue to be dissatisfaction directed at the powers that be, including us.

The best response is not to deny this but to acknowledge and deal with it. The Summit of the Americas process, launched by Bill Clinton in 1994, is the right vehicle through which to engage the region in a common enterprise. The process is focused on issues that both right and left can agree are important: education, development, good governance, crime, and democracy. Early on, you should announce your intention to attend the fifth summit, to be held in Trinidad and Tobago during your first year in office. To prepare, I recommend four steps.

First, you should appoint a special envoy for Latin America and the Caribbean; this should be someone close to you who combines pizzazz and smarts. The envoy should ensure that your interest in the region, and knowledge about it, is communicated every day.

Second, you should recognize that our so-called war on drugs is not working. After years of effort and tens of billions of dollars spent, the price and purity of cocaine available on U.S. streets is essentially unchanged. The fault is to be found less among Andean coca growers than with us. Our yen for illegal narcotics is the most pernicious form of Yankee intervention in the internal affairs of Latin America. We should admit that—and act on it—by devoting the majority of our narcotics-related dollars to education and treatment within our own borders. Drug syndicates can't hurt us if we don't buy what they sell, but as long as thirty-five million people in the United States are abusing illegal drugs, the criminals will find a way to supply our needs.

Third, we need a policy toward Cuba that is free from the political wrangling of the previous half century. The embargo may have served a purpose originally, but it has outlived its usefulness. It currently has no international support and little function except to provide a convenient justification for Havana's repressive policies. The United States has no license to dictate Cuba's future, and heavy-handed attempts to do so will only sabotage those inside Cuba who are working for democracy and human rights. Our approach should be one of friendship toward the island's people, and support for increased contacts between our two countries at every level. Cubans do not need us to point out that Castroism is an insufficient answer to the demands of the global economy. In the post-Fidel era, they will inevitably have to adjust. Let us encourage them to do so through increased political openness, but let us also deprive Castro's successors of the excuse of *yanqui* bullying.

Finally, when planning for the summit, schedule time in Trinidad to meet with people away from your hotel and outside the protective bubble created by your advisors and the press. If you push hard enough, the Secret Service will allow it. When President Bush was in Guatemala, part of the welcoming tradition was to throw at him, and his limousine, small kernels of corn. After his entourage had passed by and the people lining the streets had dispersed, other figures appeared. Bent low, peering at the ground, they gathered up the kernels for something to eat. That is your constituency, Mr. President. Speak to them in ways that truly inspire hope, and Latin America will be on your side.

CHAPTER 10

America's Place in the Asian Century

Europe has NATO, and the Western Hemisphere has the Organization of American States; the leading countries of East Asia have not come together in the same way. Past conflicts still haunt these nations, leaving them without a common vision of the future, thereby complicating our relations with the region. You will have to step carefully, for sensitivities are always on edge where tradition and modernity compete. America's interest is to secure its place as a Pacific power in what may well become known as the Asian century. The path to success is not through an attempt to command—which would surely fail—but by acting as a kind of friendly referee. One advantage of such a policy is that it positions us to keep a close eye on all the players.

When you first visit East Asia, you are likely to have China uppermost in mind. Your initial destination, however, should be Tokyo. A loyal ally deserves precedence. For the past sixty years, Japan has been a leader among industrialized countries, a supporter of international law, and generous to the poor. Japan has also been a reliable friend to the United States with which it values close relations in part because it does not always get on so well with its neighbors. Though the country is respected, it is also resented. Logically, Japan should long ago have become a permanent member of the UN Security Council; it has been blocked by China, a victim of Japanese atrocities before and during World War II.

In the dozen years prior to 2001, Japan meandered along under ten different prime ministers; then Junichiro Koizumi came to power. Where one of his predecessors had been nick-named "cold pizza," Koizumi was full of energy, with unorthodox ideas (and fabulous hair). He revived a lethargic economy by upending the policies of his own party and by being honest about both the need for reforms and the pain of adjusting to them. Outspoken and stylish, Koizumi was unlike conventional Japanese politicians who, though polished, tend to be so dull that one U.S. diplomat complained he could stay awake during dinners only by sitting on his fork.

Koizumi's idiosyncrasies were popular in Japan but less so with other Asians. By the time the prime minister's five-year term expired, neither the Chinese nor the South Koreans were on cordial terms with him. Koizumi insisted on making regular public visits to the Yasukuni Jinja, a Shinto shrine in Tokyo, where the souls of soldiers who died in service to the emperor—including fourteen war criminals—are honored. Exhibits at the site characterize the wartime Japanese as heroic defenders of Asia and lovers of peace. Japan's neighbors, who have a different take on the past, protested the visits. They raised a ruckus, as well, about changes in school texts that downplayed Japanese responsibility for World War II.

Koizumi reacted to such criticism with disdain. Instead of trying to mend fences locally, he drew even closer to the United States. An obliging President Bush invited Koizumi to cap his time in office with a visit to Graceland. There, the sixty-four-year-old bachelor donned Elvis's sunglasses, hugged Lisa Marie Presley, swiveled his hips, and sang "Love Me Tender."

Koizumi's successor, Shinzo Abe, tried initially to repair relations by exchanging visits with leaders in Beijing and Seoul. Somewhat perversely, he then incited anger by denying evidence that Asian women were coerced into providing sexual favors for Japanese soldiers during the war. Abe also raised regional doubts about his intentions when he signed a security pact with Australia, upgraded his country's defense agency, and talked favorably about rewriting Japan's postwar "peace constitution" to loosen restrictions on the military. Under Koizumi, Japan had already inched its way toward a more robust military posture by participating in theater missile defense, deploying high-tech destroyers in the Indian Ocean, sending noncombat personnel to Iraq, and agreeing to establish a joint command with the United States at Yokota Air Base.

One question for you is whether to encourage Japan to become an even more capable and visible military partner. Our defense planners have pointed out the obvious: Japan has the money and skill to be a formidable ally in maintaining stability in East Asia. America, meanwhile, has global responsibilities and could use help. The Japanese, or at least some of them, are pressing to break free from postwar limitations. Shinzo Abe's grandfather, also a prime minister, was forced to resign way back in 1960 for presuming to suggest that Japan become a full security partner of the United States.

Why shouldn't we push the idea of a new constitution and

welcome the development of a modern Japanese military force?

There are several reasons. America's military presence in the Asia Pacific has rarely been contested, even by the Chinese. This is because our forces—although in Asia to protect Japan—are also credited with restraining Japan. The lifting of restrictions on that country's military would likely spur China into an even more rapid buildup of its own, while pushing both Koreas into a closer relationship with Beijing. We cannot assume, moreover, that an independent Japanese military would always be responsive to U.S. interests. Abe's main selling point for a new constitution was less pro-alliance than nationalist; the new document, he emphasized, would be truly Japanese, replacing the one forced upon the country by the American occupation.

The depth of Abe's desire for Japan to become more assertive internationally was matched by the shallowness of his domestic political skills. By September 2007, he was gone, forced to resign because of an incompetent cabinet and a midterm electoral disaster for his party. So when you arrive in Tokyo, you will be greeted by Yasuo Fukuda, an old-style Japanese leader with a strong political pedigree and a more respectful approach toward China. The expectation is widespread that Japan in the post-Koizumi era will fall back into the habits of the pre-Koizumi era, which means a succession of leaders who cater to influential factions instead of tackling structural economic problems. You can nevertheless expect a warm reception in Japan, and wide-ranging discussions conducted with a high degree of intelligence on the part of Prime Minister Fukuda and other senior officials. Be sure to arrive with a smile on your face, a gift in your hand, and a fork in your pocket.

• • •

The cold war has yet to end on the Korean peninsula. Battle stations and barbed wire still separate North and South along the thirty-eighth parallel. We would like to see North Korea, officially the Democratic People's Republic of Korea (DPRK), become a constructive member of the Asia Pacific community, but we lack the power—absent the risk of massive bloodshed—to compel that outcome. Thus, policymakers in Washington and Seoul must grapple with the classic foreign policy challenge of bringing aims into balance with capabilities. The best we can realistically hope for, in the near future, is a North Korea that does not threaten its neighbors or us. That should be your primary goal.

From the beginning, the alliance between the United States and South Korea has been more a marriage of convenience than passion. The traditional American attitude is that South Koreans should be grateful to us for saving them from the North. Some are. Ban Ki-moon, secretary general of the United Nations, remembers as a child being given biscuits, chocolates, and chewing gum by U.S. soldiers, adding that "all our clothes were given to us by America." More than thirty-six thousand American servicemen and women died during the Korean War; tens of thousands have been deployed there since, striving to prevent another conflict.

South Koreans, however, remember other aspects of the past that we generally don't. For example, nineteenth-century U.S. efforts to open Korea to trade were resisted, causing a clash that Koreans referred to as "the barbarian incursion of 1871." In 1906, Theodore Roosevelt received the Nobel Peace Prize for helping to settle a war between Russia and Japan; in so doing he gave America's blessing to Japan's occupation of Korea. When, in 1919, Woodrow Wilson championed the cause of national self-determination, Koreans thought he would insist that their country be set free; he didn't, and the occupation continued. Some Koreans also blame Washington for their country's division after World War II. It was U.S. and Soviet negotiators who split the peninsula, the Koreans having no say.

Today's South Koreans are proud of having built the world's eleventh largest economy and do not plan to stop there. They are intent on asserting a national identity that is separate from the United States and other Asian countries. They still value their alliance with Washington but do not wish to be patronized. Especially during President Bush's first years, disagreements over tactics in dealing with the North generated anti-American feelings, with many in the South concluding that the United States is a graver threat to peace than Pyongyang. Thus President Roh Moo-hyun deemed it advantageous during his 2002 campaign to say that he had never visited the United States. "I don't have any anti-American sentiment," he said, "but I won't kowtow to the Americans either."

To us, North Korea is a rogue state. To South Koreans, it is a rogue state whose citizens share their history and blood. In earlier decades, South Koreans were unreservedly anticommunist and more inclined even than Washington to adopt a belligerent stance toward the DPRK. In recent years, attitudes have softened. Despite having nuclear arms, the North seems less menacing because it is so isolated. South Koreans have no desire to impose sanctions or otherwise make life even more difficult for the North's deprived population. There is also little enthusiasm for the prospect, hoped for by some in the United States, that the dictatorial government of Kim Jong-il will implode. Having observed the reunification of Germany, South Koreans don't think they could afford a sudden reunion with their own wayward half. Seoul hopes instead to encourage a gradual evolution in North Korea that would make any ultimate reunification both nonviolent and less expensive.

The official view in the South is that the North is more likely to remain dangerous if it feels threatened, and more likely to become a law-abiding country if it is treated like one. Thus, over the past decade, the South has pursued what it calls a "sunshine policy" toward the North, characterized by cooperative industrial projects, tourism, family reunions, Olympic partnerships, and two cordial summit meetings.

The Clinton administration welcomed the sunshine policy because we, too, believed that Pyongyang would have to be dealt with; Kim Jong-il was not about to retire or disappear. During Clinton's tenure, we persuaded the DPRK to freeze its known nuclear weapons program and suspend its tests of longer-range missiles. In the hopes of achieving additional progress, I had the experience, in 2000, of visiting North Korea's capital. Because of the possibility that you may—at some point in your presidency— have good reason to go there yourself, let me take a minute to tell you what I found.

Pyongyang is a city of monuments honoring the worst government on Earth. Stadiums, statues, and towers serve to celebrate Kim Jong-il, the so-called Dear Leader, and his late father, Kim Il-sung, who founded the DPRK. The city boasts little commercial life and few cars or scooters—even the rare bicycle seems rickety and in poor condition. There are no cats or dogs wandering the streets nor, from what my ears could detect, any songbirds in the trees. In the lake outside the guesthouse where I was assigned, there swam a single forlorn duck. In the absence of streetlights, my motorcade was guided to the correct road by a pair of fluorescent sticks waved about by a policeman whose body was invisible in the darkness. It is an eerie, joyless place where crowds applaud like automatons in response to staged entertainments, and even five-year-olds dance in perfect unison.

From the moment they are old enough to hold a thought, the North Korean people are conditioned to give over their hearts and minds to a fantasy. Among other falsehoods, they are taught that, in World War II, their land was liberated from Japan by North Korean freedom fighters led by the intrepid Kim Il-sung; purportedly, American troops had no role in Japan's defeat. As for the Korean War, it was the product of a brutal and unprovoked attack—by the South against the North.

The Dear Leader and his father are accorded the status of all-knowing, all-caring gods. Stories, biblical in tone, are recited about the leaders' many acts of kindness. Similarly, every innovation, from the words of the national anthem to the design of school desks, is attributed to the great men. Like most religions, North Korea's myth matches good against evil, with evil in this case embodied by Japan and its ally, America. For North Koreans, this is reality. Those who believe differently are guilty of impure thinking and suitable only for gulag-style reeducation camps—or death.

Kim Il-sung ruled for forty-eight years. Through most of that time, his doctrine of national self-reliance was sustained, ironically, through dependence on aid from the Soviet bloc and the Chinese. The end of the cold war left the North truly on its own, and it has proven unable to cope. Today, the country lacks fuel, fertilizer, and modern equipment. This impoverishment has led to a degree of desperation that has made the country even more dangerous. One reason it builds weapons is to sell them. Missiles and advanced weapons technology are its cash crops. It would benefit us as well as North Korea if the country could find a way to get along without peddling the means of destruction to whoever will pay.

In our meetings in Pyongyang, I found Kim Jong-il to be rational, intelligent, and well informed. He is a short, somewhat spherical man who, in an effort to appear taller, wears platform shoes and puffs up the hair on his head. Like Shakespeare's Prince Hal, he was a playboy when young, known for conspicuous consumption and, as a movie producer, his casting couch. Unlike his father, Kim lacks the credentials of a military hero. He inherited power despite communist dogma condemning personality cults and hereditary leadership. To survive, he has had to manipulate the armed forces and party system so that potential rivals end up fighting one another while remaining loyal to him—or else too scared to mount a challenge. As the son of a figure who was made to appear larger than life, his own life has been distorted by privilege, leaving him oblivious to the suffering of the North Korean people while still craving their affection. In person, he can be chivalrous, as I learned during an official dinner when he ordered the circulating wine-pourers to desist, thereby shielding me from the North Korean practice of competitive drinking.

In our meetings, Kim and I mixed tough talk about human rights and military intentions with more reflective discussions about the reasons for our lack of mutual trust. He allowed that it was perhaps not helpful for North Korean children to be taught to refer to Americans as "American bastards." It became evident to me the longer we talked that Kim was prepared to trade military concessions for a combination of economic help and security guarantees. He felt that establishing full diplomatic relations with the United States would put his government on level terms with the South and validate both his father's legacy and his own leadership. The toughest unresolved issue was verification of military promises. Kim had been unreceptive to any questioning of North Korea's trustworthiness, while I made it plain that we would only believe what we could see.

Leaving office, I expected the Bush administration to pick up where we had left off, as the incoming secretary of state, Colin Powell, indicated would be the case. It didn't happen. President Bush refused to do what Clinton had done, for no better reason than that Clinton had done it. This was the ABC (Anything But Clinton) attitude. Instead of negotiating with North Korea, factions within the Bush team fought with each other. At first, they completely refused to talk to the North; then they sent diplomats, who were forbidden to say anything more than "Disarm or else." North Korea responded by kicking out the IAEA inspectors, removing the plutonium from eight thousand spent fuel rods, building nuclear warheads, and, on October 7, 2006, conducting a nuclear test.

This last event finally shocked the administration into taking a serious diplomatic approach to North Korea. The result was an agreement under which North Korea froze its nuclear programs and allowed inspectors to return in exchange for help meeting its energy needs. This essentially restored the situation to where the Clinton administration had left it, except that the North has had time to generate plutonium for eight or nine additional warheads. Subsequent negotiations, to secure the North's nuclear weapons and dismantle its capacity to produce more, are ongoing. The challenge of dealing with Kim Jong-il now falls to you.

As president, you will be asked by human rights activists and Christian evangelists to view North Korea as much more than a security issue. North Koreans have been beaten down by years of occupation, war, and totalitarian rule; they deserve help. It would be immoral, you will be told, to do anything that would in any way legitimize Kim Jong-il's government or strengthen his hold on power. At a minimum, you should secure a commitment to allow freedom of worship and a chance for religious charities to operate.

Christian activists argue, and I think Kim Jong-il may fear it is true, that the end of his dictatorship will come when the mythology of the Dear Leader is challenged by another powerful way of explaining the world. The gospels provide just such an alternative. After all, South Korea is home to many of the world's largest Christian churches, and Pyongyang was once known as Korea's Jerusalem. Even Kim Il-sung was raised in the faith, a fact he later thought it necessary to deny, though he ended the preface to his memoir with the words "praying for the souls of the departed revolutionaries." As the journalist Bradley K. Martin, author of a voluminous study of North Korea, has observed, the correlation cannot be accidental between the Christian Holy Trinity and "Kim the father, Kim the son and the holy spirit" of self-reliance. To fend off critics, North Korea has allowed Christian evangelists, notably the Rev. Billy Graham, to make brief visits. There is no evidence, however, that anything resembling religious freedom in the country is allowed.

Clearly, the United States cannot have a conventional relationship with the DPRK as long as its government remains totalitarian. Your administration should push for progress on human rights. The hard question is whether a security arrangement that lowers the risk of a nuclear confrontation but also benefits Kim

Jong-il would be defensible. In considering that, bear in mind that reducing the risk of a devastating war certainly has moral value, and that failing to achieve that purpose provides no guarantee that Kim Jong-il will relax his policies. In other words, if we refuse on moral grounds to negotiate with the North Koreans on security matters, we may end up with no improvements on either security or human rights—hardly the outcome you will desire.

Seventy-five years ago, No Yong-Park, the closest Chinese equivalent to de Tocqueville, wrote that Americans "study history only to find the faults of their ancestors, so that they may not repeat the same mistakes. . . . The old-fashioned Chinese revered their ancestors so much as to worship them, and feared to do anything that their ancestors did not do. . . . The Chinese notion of progress has been to struggle to catch up with their fathers, whereas the American idea has been to do something which has not yet been done."

Does this contrast still hold up? I think not. Americans remain forward-looking, but nostalgia, as well, exerts a strong grip. We often refer to our ancestors in glowing terms—witness, for example, our fascination with the founding generation and our reverence for the heroes of World War II. As for China, No Yong-Park would be astonished. His people are no longer struggling to catch up with their fathers; instead, they are rapidly gaining on us. The adjective "rising" is used so routinely in association with China that it seems part of the name. In 2007, a survey reported that the Chinese were more optimistic about the future than any of the other forty-six populations sampled; the Japanese, sadly, were the least hopeful.

Although Nixon went to Beijing, it was left to the Carter administration to establish formal diplomatic relations. The Sino-Soviet rivalry was at its height, so the preoccupation at the time was with cold war politics. The subtext, however, was globalization. When, in 1979, Deng Xiaoping became the first communist Chinese leader to visit Washington, he informed Carter of his plans to open his country's economy. He blamed China's backwardness on his ancestors' decision to shut themselves off from the West. Deng, by no means old-fashioned, systematically dismantled the "House That Mao Built," ditching communist orthodoxy and introducing what was called "market socialism."

I had visited the People's Republic of China (PRC) myself the previous year, accompanying a U.S. Senate delegation led by Edmund Muskie, my old employer. At the time, Beijing was a city of fast-pedaling bicyclists and brisk-walking pedestrians. Now, as proof of progress, its streets are choked with almost stationary cars. Since competitive markets took hold, the Chinese economy has grown at a sustained rate unequaled by any country in history. Extreme poverty has declined sharply, the middle class has broadened, and Chinese industrial centers have become irresistible to foreign investors. Nor is China's success due merely to its plentiful supply of low-wage labor. China is producing an increasing number of scientists and engineers; in 2003, it became the third country to launch a man into space; its research budget is growing; and it is experimenting with new designs in such fields as environmental technology, civilian nuclear power, and bioengineering.

This economic transformation has altered China's political outlook. Growth requires fuel, and the Chinese are prowling the international market for petroleum, timber, and minerals. They have established new supply relationships on every continent. Among their partners are the governments of Iran,

Sudan, Burma, and Venezuela—not a savory quartet. China is also making its diplomatic presence felt. President Hu Jintao has traveled widely, and has often been received with more enthusiasm than President Bush. To underscore its independence, the PRC has begun pulling together regional meetings from which the United States is excluded: an African summit, an East Asian conference, and the Shanghai Cooperation Organisation—a body that coordinates energy policy, conducts military exercises, includes Russia, and has demanded the withdrawal of U.S. forces from Central Asia. China's leaders are cleverly asserting a dual identity. When issues such as trade or climate change are on the table, the Chinese insist that they be given special treatment because theirs is still a developing country. When the issues are political, they demand that China participate—as befits a leading power—in writing global rules. This is not, in fact, an unreasonable claim, for China is indeed both a developing country and, by any measure, a major one.

As president, you will welcome China's economic integration while worrying about the eventual impact of its ascendancy on peace, democracy, and our own leadership.

The worries begin with the fact that the gap in international stature that has existed between the United States and China has narrowed appreciably. In the decades after World War II, most Asian nations felt closer to America than to an impoverished and turbulent PRC. Few people envied the bloody madness of the Cultural Revolution or Mao's Great Leaps Forward, which flopped. Today, China is associated with success, even attracting a growing number of immigrants (legal and otherwise) who see it as the land of opportunity. The government is credited with advancing the economic prospects of its people, which are considered more important by many who are poor than the right to hear campaign speeches and vote. Throughout history, Americans have felt that we offered an example to the world of how to govern. Now, more people in more countries have a favorable view of China than have a favorable view of the United States.

The twentieth anniversary of the massacre in Tiananmen Square will be marked in June of your first year in office, but with what significance? Chinese leaders, determined to prevent a renewed democratic uprising, have turned aside repeated pleas, both domestic and international, to permit a more relaxed and competitive political system. For them, the lessons of Tiananmen are clear: Stability is the ultimate good. Dissident movements should be crushed. Foreign criticism cannot be allowed to jeopardize internal order.

True, the country's economic openness has led to more expansive social and political commentary in Internet chat rooms and the press. The leadership has felt the need to co-opt the language of democracy by equating it with the current Chinese system. There is considerable competition within the Communist Party, including term limits and elections, but dissidents are still arrested, religious liberty circumscribed, political organization prohibited, and the Internet censored.

While in Beijing recently, I was watching cable news in my hotel when the broadcaster announced the start of a congressional hearing on China and the Internet; immediately, the screen went blank. A friend accidentally opened an unmarked door in a different Chinese hotel only to behold a row of startled young men seated in front of monitors, spying (via concealed cameras) on guests in their rooms. Big Brother requires a large labor force, and, in China, he has one.

Disturbingly, the decline in America's reputation has reduced pressure on the PRC to improve its record. As secretary of state, I once flew through the night to deliver a speech on China before the UN Human Rights Commission in Geneva. The Chinese delegates were so angry at my remarks that most of them stomped out of the hall; indignation was the only argument they had. Today, the Chinese merely have to observe that Americans are in no position to lecture others—and heads nod in agreement.

The Chinese system of governing is especially admired by leaders who want their countries to find a niche in the world economy but who do not want to risk losing their own power. This model is supported by Chinese financing, which helps governments in Africa, for example, to undertake capital projects without the kind of accountability that is required by the World Bank. The Europeans have a name for this—rogue aid.

Leadership in China is a many-hatted thing. Hu Jintao became general secretary of the Communist Party in 2002, president of the PRC the following year, and chair of the Chinese Military Commission in 2004. Though he has yet to demonstrate the vision of a Deng Xiaoping, he has shown himself to be adept at climbing and staying atop the ladder of political power. His advance has had less to do with what he has done than with what he has not: advocate new ideas or offend powerful factions such as the military. Even now, after years in office, he seems more a technician than an ideologue; his speeches draw on the slogans of all his predecessors. His own signature summons to the country is to build a harmonious society, a theme with echoes of Confucius, Karl Marx, and Dr. Phil. His caution may stem from his predicament: China is so big and moving so fast that the job of steering takes all the time and attention anyone can give.

There is no rule that economic growth, especially when rapid and uneven, will produce social contentment. Though a problem everywhere, the widening gap between rich and poor in China clashes acutely with socialist values, which emphasize egalitarianism. There is a huge divide between urban areas, which have boomed, and rural regions, which have not. Inequality breeds resentment, especially when people suspect the rich obtained their wealth, not through diligence and ingenuity, but through official corruption. People are also angry about pollution, bitter about industrial projects that drive them off their land, and worried about uncontrolled outbreaks of disease.

What is more, China is headed into a demographic no-fly zone. For years, its people have been having fewer babies while living longer lives, causing a steady increase in the average age. A decade or two from now, the typical worker—who is an only child—may find that he or she has to support children, parents, and grandparents simultaneously. Those who fear that China's new-found wealth will be diverted to the military may be assured that some of it, at least, will be allocated to medicines, bedroom slippers, Mah Jong games, and oxygen tanks. China will get old before it gets rich.

As the country grows, it will take more than respect for ancestors to keep it together. The communist leadership must stay one step ahead, striving to prevent small expressions of dissent from coalescing into large protests. To succeed, it must answer an obvious question: How does a Communist Party that includes capitalists and presides over a robust stock market explain what it is doing? So far, Chinese leaders have responded deftly, articulating at great length a philosophy that rewards free enterprise (up to a point), nationalism (without overdoing it), and stability.

For any U.S. president, the dilemma in dealing with China is that domestic politics will push in one direction and the desire for fruitful diplomacy in another. During the campaign, you found that China-bashing drew applause from most Americans; the exceptions being businesspeople, foreign policy specialists, and our military. In the White House, however, you will try to avoid unpleasantness because China has become so important— it owns three hundred billion dollars in U.S. Treasury bonds, is a permanent member of the Security Council, has diplomatic leverage in places we do not, and, if you believe critics of China's economic policies, has the power of life and death over millions of American jobs.

Prior to your first meeting with Hu, you will receive conflicting advice about what issues should top the agenda. Political counselors will urge you to voice objections to China's monetary and trade policies. Diplomats will stress the need for Beijing's help in curbing nuclear proliferation. The Pentagon will seek a green light for more extensive contacts with the Chinese military. Business leaders will be concerned about the rules for foreign investment and the protection of intellectual property. Activist groups will insist that you address the issues about which they care the most: human rights, democracy, worker standards, religious liberty, the environment, Tibet, the Falun Gong.

When, finally, you do sit down with Hu, you will find him most insistent about hearing your assurances on Taiwan. If you fail to oblige, all other business will become secondary. Though Taiwan has the wealth and organization to thrive as an independent nation, it is not recognized as a state—and has been pressured not to declare itself one—because Beijing insists that Taiwan is part of China. Since Nixon's 1972 opening, the United States has acknowledged China's claim without rejecting or endorsing it. Taiwan was part of China from the mid-seventeenth century until the end of the nineteenth. The fact that the island was lost to the Japanese only deepens China's determination to recover it, even though the Japanese are long gone. Those serving in the Chinese Communist Army, which was created during World War II to liberate the country from Japan, are taught that returning Taiwan to the mother country is the last unfulfilled aspect of their mission.

The Taiwan issue has been around so long we may be lulled into assuming that it will never explode. More than one million Taiwanese businesspeople and their families now live on the mainland, guiding the factories and firms in which they have invested. Those who believe that economic self-interest determines how political and military leaders behave assure us that a conflict over Taiwan is impossible because it would be unprofitable.

Yet, in 1996, the United States and China nearly came to blows after we granted a visa to the Taiwanese president, who then went to Cornell University (his alma mater) and delivered what was considered by Beijing to be an inflammatory speech. China responded by firing missiles and carrying out military exercises near the island. This prompted the Clinton administration to send two aircraft carrier battle groups toward the Taiwan Strait. After a few tense weeks, the situation settled down. Reportedly, Chinese leaders backed away because they didn't think they could prevail in a confrontation with the United States, but promised their armed forces the resources needed to win should a similar crisis arise in the future. A decade later, Beijing has nine hundred missiles lined up on the Fujian coast opposite Taiwan. China's armed forces are equipped with fighter jets, guided missile destroyers, and attack submarines and are in the process of learning how to wage information warfare. Although its military remains far inferior to that of the United States, China is modernizing with a single contingency uppermost in mind, while our armed forces are stretched thin.

Through history, the rise of a new power has often led to war, whether caused by the desire of that power to spread its wings or the attempt by rivals to smother it in the nest. China's rise need not lead to war, but this doesn't mean war or other violent clashes won't happen.

The United States is not formally committed to rescuing Taiwan in the event of attack because we don't want the Taiwanese to be so sure of our protection that they provoke Beijing. Similarly, we don't want the Chinese to think they can attack Taiwan and get away with it. The situation resembles the three-sided showdown at the end of *The Good, the Bad and the Ugly,* but before the shooting starts. So long as we just stare at each other, nobody gets hurt.

It is clearly part of China's military strategy to make us—and Taiwan—think twice about any sudden moves. We must follow a similar strategy. In the words of China scholar Susan L. Shirk:

> Keeping U.S. forces deployed in the Asia-Pacific region
> to deter potential aggression is all the more necessary once
> we are aware of the domestic pressures that could drive
> China's leaders to behave rashly. We want China's decision
> makers, when faced with a crisis, to look out to the Pacific
> and see a U.S. military with the will and capacity to defend
> Taiwan, our allies in Japan and South Korea, and our other
> Asian friends.

The good news is that China's leadership appears patient. There is little reason to expect that you will be awakened one morning with news that the Red Army is swarming over factory outlets and four-star hotels in Taiwan. Though every successor to Mao would like to be remembered as having united the country, President Hu has shown no inclination to march into a bloodbath. The status quo should be acceptable to Beijing for the moment; you will need to persuade Taipei to live with it, too.

The U.S.-China relationship is based on a wary balancing of interests. Though personal friendships may be plentiful, there is not much in the way of affection or trust between our nations. We see, overall, the opportunity for a relationship that will benefit both countries, especially in such areas as commerce and nuclear proliferation. Still, we are nervous about China because we don't know what the upper limits of its influence will be. The country was the leading power in its region, and the largest economy in the world, for most of the past thousand years. If the twentieth century proves to be merely an exception to that, where would that leave us? We don't fear a strong China, but neither do we want Beijing to dominate East Asia—blackmailing Taiwan into surrender, intimidating its many neighbors, or threatening the security of Japan. The Chinese interpret our unease (not without reason) as a desire to contain them. Some believe our plan is eventually either to Westernize their country or divide it. Thus, our criticisms of Beijing's internal policies are thought cynical, part of a strategy to browbeat China into making the same mistakes that led to the breakup of the Soviet Union. I know from experience that if you ask questions about Tibet, you will see that China's diplomats—though no longer really communist—can still turn red.

Chinese foreign policy is based on the principles of sovereignty and nonintervention in the internal affairs of others. Its leaders are not interested in our ideas on morality or in upholding universal norms. It is impossible to conceive, for example, of Beijing issuing annual reports each year assessing the practices of other governments in such areas as human rights, narcotics enforcement, terrorism, trafficking, or religious liberty. This is an important difference between China and the United States and, diplomatically, a significant advantage for China.

I do not anticipate an eruption of hostility between our two countries during the next several years. Tensions will simmer, not boil. The same is likely throughout the region.

East Asia will be stable provided one country does not try to intimidate another. Neither China nor Japan seem possessed of imperial ambition, yet neither will be content to be seen as the lesser state. South Korea wants to be taken seriously on its own terms; North Korea is looking for a way to perpetuate its tattered myth of self-reliance. Taiwan continues to face a choice between self-restraint and the danger of provoking Beijing—an arrangement that is unfair but no obstacle to its democracy or prosperity.

American policy should benefit from the fact that Asian nations will be concerned primarily with one another. China wants Japan kept in check, so do the Koreans and nearly everyone else. Vietnam and Mongolia have been ruled by the Chinese in the past and would fight before being subjugated again. Smaller countries will try to avoid having to choose between the United States and China and will therefore try to maintain good relations with both. If the United States is seen as trying to preserve a stable balance in the region, we will be viewed positively; if we are seen as trying to establish the rules by which everyone else must live, we will create problems that, given headaches elsewhere, we would be well advised to avoid. With a light hand, we should encourage the development of a regional security framework, in which we participate. Although the conditions are not right for an alliance such as NATO, there would be value in a more formal means for building confidence, sharing information, organizing humanitarian missions, and resolving disputes early, before harsh words lead to hot wars.

Pride and Prejudice in Russia and South Asia

Since the cold war ended, America has often been referred to as the world's sole remaining superpower. Most Americans are comfortable with this designation and think that others should be as well. After all, if we were not atop the global pyramid, who would be? Yet we sometimes forget that pride is a sin and, like most sins, widely distributed. Our own pride grates against that of others, prompting many foreign leaders to insist on portraying the world in multipolar, not unipolar terms. The French and Chinese are perhaps the most pointed, but there are other countries that wish—for reasons of past glory, present ambition, and future hopes—to claim for themselves a higher status. Among those you will encounter are a resurgent Russia, a booming India, and a Pakistan that is both aggrieved and accused.

•   •   •

The authors of a 2006 Council on Foreign Relations study theorized that "a more democratic, open, transparent Russia would be behaving differently on many issues." Specifically, such a Russia would be more helpful in halting the spread of nuclear weapons, more in agreement with America on the Middle East, more hospitable to democratic forces in Central Asia and the Caucasus, and more inclined to tailor its energy policies to suit Western needs.

If only it were true. We have cause to regret Russia's retreat from democracy, but little reason to believe that its voters are aching to pursue policies more pleasing to the West. Indeed, we could expect extreme nationalists and perhaps even communists to fare better at the polls than liberal reformers—or, for that matter, compassionate conservatives. The idea that we could, with sufficient help and hugs, turn Russia into an oversize but otherwise typical European country has never been realistic. Consider its history: Russia has sometimes forged connections to the West but has never truly been part of it.

Modern Russia evolved through three transitions: the first from medieval Muscovy into a sprawling empire; the second from a decaying empire into a communist superpower; the third from a declining superpower into a new entity whose nature is still being defined.

The engineer of the first transition was Peter the Great, an eighteenth-century czar who combined despotism with admiration for things European. Upon returning from his first continental tour, he personally cut off the beards of his attending nobles and ordered them to replace their conical hats and flowing cloaks with Western dress. To symbolize the new Russia, he (and several hundred thousand serfs) built a shimmering new capital, St. Petersburg. The czar is credited with changing the watchword of his rustic land from "Guard well the treasure of yesterday" to "Fear not change; strive that tomorrow be better than today."

There was much about the West that entranced Peter, but he was particularly fascinated by its weapons. He built the first Russian navy and dispatched freshly equipped armies outward in all directions, where they clashed with the Asiatic tribes of Siberia, the Catholics of Poland, the Lutherans of Sweden, and the Muslims of Persia and Turkey. To hold his domain together, he asserted firm control over Russia's nobility, created a far-reaching internal security network, established a close alliance with the Orthodox Church, and banned political dissent. Before Peter, not even educated Russians knew much about modern science, the Renaissance, or the Age of Exploration. After Peter, Russia became a full participant in the intrigues of global diplomacy and blossomed into one of the world's great powers.

It is no accident that when Russia for the first time hosted a meeting of the G-8, Vladimir Putin chose to do so in St. Petersburg, his home city. If a new Russian empire were to arise, it would be supported by the same pillars that propped up the old one. It, too, would feature a strong central government, a modern military, support from the clergy, and tight internal controls. It, too, would take the best from the West while maintaining a Russian identity, and it, too, would press outward—if not by the sword then through other means.

As president, you will find that the new Russia is neither a sure friend nor a certain foe; it is instead a unique and willful force that deserves respect but whom we cannot fully trust because one of its stronger instincts is not to trust us. This is because leaders in Moscow are of a naturally suspicious bent, and also because of what Russia has experienced these past twenty years.

In the time just before the breakup of the Soviet Union, I participated in a survey of Russian attitudes toward democracy and free enterprise. What we found was a population fed up with communism but with little understanding of what democracy actually entailed. Reliance on the state was deeply ingrained. People had no knowledge of competitive markets, while the concept of rewarding more productive work with higher pay was alien. Freedom of the press was equally unfamiliar, and the population was deeply divided by ethnicity, level of education, generation, and gender.

My conclusion was that the legacy of seven decades of communism could not be shed like a worn-out trench coat. Democratic institutions would be slow to develop. It did not help that the early years of the new Russia were a disaster, as the country rode the locomotive of change in one direction—straight down. Few societies have crashed harder and faster without war.

By the end of the 1990s, Russia's central government was barely collecting taxes, foreign investment had dried up, and much of the economy was operating on a barter basis. Russians were working less, getting sick more, and dying sooner. Meanwhile, privileged insiders were enriching themselves by buying government companies at a bargain price, draining the assets, and lodging the profits in offshore accounts. As a knockout punch, the Asian financial crisis depressed the price of oil, the country's primary source of hard currency. Before Mr. Putin became president, some in the Russian press had begun referring to their homeland as "Upper Volta with rockets."

I met Putin in Moscow a few weeks after he took power. He

struck me as exceptionally bright and refreshingly eager to get Moscow's finances under control. He spoke in language I welcomed about the need to enforce contracts, curb corruption, and increase accountability. On other issues, however, he showed little desire to please. In his view, American policies had been aimed at keeping Russia down. We had preferred Gorbachev to Brezhnev, and Gorbachev dismantled the USSR. We had preferred Yeltsin to Gorbachev, and Yeltsin left office with an approval rating of 8 percent. We had supported a ban on anti-missile defense systems when the Soviet Union was strong; now that it was weak, we wanted to explore ways to build such a system. Putin was particularly annoyed by our expressions of concern about human rights in Chechnya and Central Asia. He said the entire region was under siege by terrorists and that only uncompromising action could bring it under control. "Do not try to squeeze Russia out of these countries," he warned me, "or you will end up with another Iran or Afghanistan."

I did not have the time while secretary of state to keep a regular journal, but I did try during long trips to type up some observations; these were my first impressions of Putin:

One of the major subjects among foreign ministers and presidents is who is Putin? More than any other new leader, he is being analyzed and dissected. We all agree he is a change from Yeltsin, who was bombastic and larger than life and one was never sure what would come out. Putin is small and pale, so cold as to be almost reptilian. He is clearly a complex individual, someone who wanted to be a KGB agent from the time he was sixteen or seventeen. His father's service in WWII made a great impression on him. He was in East Germany when the Berlin Wall fell and has said that he understands why it had to happen—a position built on walls and dividers couldn't last; but he expected something to rise in its place, and nothing was proposed. The Soviets simply dropped everything and went away. He said that a lot of problems could have been avoided if they had not made such a hasty exit. Putin seems to me a proud Russian, who is so embarrassed by what has happened to his country that he is determined to restore its greatness.

Putin has since been rightly criticized for establishing a "managed democracy"—which is to say, no real democracy at all. Political parties exist, campaigns are conducted, elections held, legislation considered, and judges hand down opinions—but the government always wins. Throughout his eight years in office, Putin sliced away at the power of the provincial governors, the parliament, the courts, and the private sector, systematically adding the slices to his own oversize plate. More troubling is that a number of his outspoken critics have been jailed on dubious charges or murdered in circumstances that remain unexplained. He may be a single-minded manipulator of power; he may also have been—and may still be—something far worse.

Whatever his tactics, Putin has by many measurements done well. Poverty and unemployment have been substantially reduced, the middle class has grown wealthier, foreign reserves have increased by a factor of fifty, and Putin has enjoyed more domestic popularity than most of his major Western counterparts. True, he benefited from high oil prices, but he also captured Russia's mood and did much to revive the country's confidence.

The problem for U.S. policy is that a confident Russia is also an assertive Russia and, to a degree, still a bitter Russia. While

America has talked about the dream of a democratic and united Europe, Moscow persists in seeing Europe as a zero-sum competition, a place where big countries strive to bring smaller countries within their sphere of influence. Thus Russians saw NATO enlargement as an attempt by the United States to expand its sway at their expense. NATO overrode Yeltsin's objections in the 1990s when it confronted Milošević and ignored Putin's warnings in the current decade when invading Iraq. Since 9/11, the U.S. military and its allies have been deployed in nearby Afghanistan. To combat terror, the United States established military bases in neighboring Uzbekistan (temporarily) and Kyrgyzstan. To support democracy, we have participated in efforts to ensure the integrity of elections in Ukraine, Georgia, and Azerbaijan while endeavoring to strengthen civil society within Russia itself. To guard against Iran, the Bush administration announced plans to install antimissile facilities in Poland and the Czech Republic. In short, when Russians have looked out their living room window in recent years, they have seen Uncle Sam, uninvited (at least by them), bustling about their front yard.

In February 2007, Putin decided to make plain his objections to our efforts. Speaking at a security conference in Munich, he accused America of overstepping its boundaries, provoking a new nuclear arms race, undermining international institutions, mishandling the crisis in the Persian Gulf, and trying to advance its own interests through the guise of support for democracy. He said Washington was responsible for "an almost uncontained hyper use of force in international relations" and of trying to create a world with "One center of authority. One center of force. One center of decision making . . . one master, one sovereign." He later added an exclamation point where none was needed by comparing U.S. policies to those of the Nazis.

The Bush administration responded calmly and began trying, through quiet diplomacy, to patch the relationship. The president had already concluded that public criticism of Putin's domestic policies was imprudent, not to mention galling, since early in his tenure the president had formed a positive impression of Putin's soul. Even a visit to the Bush family homestead in Kennebunkport, however, failed to sweeten Putin's season of discontent. He persisted in finding fault with American policies on missile defense and Kosovo, then decided to send Russia's nuclear bombers back into the air on regular patrols.

Required by the constitution to vacate the presidency, Putin will nevertheless find ways to continue exercising power. President, prime minister, or manipulator behind the scenes? You may not be able to tell the difference. This means that any U.S. moves in Russia's neighborhood—for example, inviting Ukraine or Georgia to join NATO—will be opposed. You could try to duck the problem by deferring to Moscow, but that would betray promises made to Russia's neighbors and likely lead to even more difficulties later. In Putin's view, "the collapse of the Soviet Union was a major geopolitical disaster." This is not an opinion widely shared in capitals such as Tallinn, Vilnius, Tbilisi, and Warsaw. So if the Kremlin persists in its recent course, there will be a constant testing of nerves. I fear that a new demarcation separating West from East will be etched into the land, a line reminiscent of the Iron Curtain, if not so stark. Such a division could easily deepen over time, amplifying distrust, and aggravating tensions with every military exercise or contested election.

In any diplomatic showdown, Russia will have two advantages. First, its permanent membership on the Security Council gives it the ability to frustrate our attempts to work through that body. Second, like Venezuela, Russia has oil and gas. America and Europe have urged Moscow to allow more foreign investment in its energy industries and to give the world unfettered access. The Kremlin has moved in the opposite direction, concentrating control in large state-run companies. Putin has turned Russia's natural gas spigot off and on to remind Europeans that he could curtail supplies at any time. Russian companies have also become the leading builders of civilian nuclear reactors, an industry starting to bloom due to angst about global climate change. If Russia returns to superpower status, one reason will be that the world needs energy and Moscow has it to burn.

It is neither in our interests, nor Russia's, to revisit the cold war. As president, you will have no choice but to accommodate Russian pride and deal correctly, if not warmly, with Putin and his surrogates. Officially, our two countries ought to be able to develop a common agenda on global security—fighting terrorism and cutting our nuclear arsenals while discouraging other countries from developing their own. To minimize rancor, you should encourage intergovernmental, academic, and cultural engagement with Russia both in Moscow and other regions. You must be firm, however, in insisting that Russia refrain from challenging the independence of its neighbors. You will need to be alert to the revival of Russian diplomacy in the Middle East, which will be motivated by the opportunity for business deals and arms sales. You should worry, as well, that Moscow and Beijing will put aside past differences in an effort to counterbalance U.S. power.

As for Russia's domestic situation, we are right to be appalled by the halting of democratic gains, the concentration of power in a small number of hands, and the thuggish approach Putin's regime has adopted toward critics. You should not hesitate to condemn these trends and to look for appropriate ways to support advocates of democracy and human rights inside Russia's borders. At the same time, you may have to acknowledge that there will be limits to what we can effectively do. Years ago, when the cold war was just beginning, George Kennan was already looking forward to the end of the communist era and the birth of a new Russia. He predicted then that well-wishers in the West would try and fail to help Russians develop democratic institutions. His advice: "Give them time; let them be Russians; let them work out their internal problems in their own manner. The ways by which peoples advance toward dignity and enlightenment in government are things that constitute the deepest and most intimate processes of national life. There is nothing less understandable to foreigners, nothing in which foreign interference can do less good."

Speaking as a well-wisher to the people of Russia and to democracy, I hate to accept this advice; but as president, you should understand that even Kennan—with his modest view of America's ability to transform others—was sometimes right.

India has all the elements of national greatness and yet it has not been an acknowledged leader in world affairs since the height of the Mughal empire three to four hundred years ago. It has our attention now.

In the cold war, India refused to join with either side, instead sculpting out an independent role in keeping with the vision of its founding prime minister, Jawaharlal Nehru, who conceived and headed the nonaligned movement. A few years after the Berlin Wall fell, India reasserted its independence by becoming a nuclear power.

During that same decade of the 1990s, the country's leaders realized what Deng Xiaoping had earlier concluded in China; it would be impossible to prosper in the twenty-first century with a state-controlled economy. The competitive edge enjoyed by India's newly unleashed private sector includes a surplus of educated English-speakers, many with an aptitude for engineering. Today, more than half of America's Fortune 500 companies acquire some of their information technology from India and 30 percent of software engineers in Silicon Valley are of Indian heritage. Not only is the country's economy racing ahead at a China-like pace (8 percent for the past fifteen years), it is doing so with balance and diversity. Compared to China, India imposes fewer restrictions on information and provides more opportunity to air and resolve problems through debate. Indians are also, on average, several years younger than the Chinese and therefore less burdened by the demands of caring for an aging population.

India, then, is feeling good about itself. What does that mean for us?

Presidents Clinton and Bush each visited India in their second terms; you should visit in your first (and, unlike Bush, find time to visit the Taj Mahal). Both your predecessors claimed to have opened "a new chapter" in relations with India. You should act in the same spirit but with a different cliché—perhaps emphasizing India's newly designated role as our "strategic partner."

In 2006, the Bush administration negotiated a deal that recognized India's status as a nuclear power with full rights to develop a civilian nuclear industry while maintaining a separate and uninspected military program. From the perspective of the NPT system, the arrangement was a step backward. India refused to sign the NPT, developed and tested a nuclear weapon, and was now being accepted by us, without penalty, into the nuclear club. Given that China might reach the same kind of agreement with Pakistan, and that stopping North Korea and Iran from obtaining nuclear weapons is one of America's top priorities, the deal would seem a disaster—and yet it quickly won preliminary approval from Congress, endorsed by members of both parties.

One reason is that Indian Americans are increasingly influential in U.S. politics—the Congressional Indian Caucus has more than 175 members. Second, the U.S. nuclear industry sees India as a lucrative market, and in Washington, money shouts. Third, the United States is in need of friends. We did not wish to drive India further in the direction of Russia or China. Instead, the administration argued for the agreement on the grounds that, in return, India would become our strategic partner.

Calling a country a strategic partner does not, of course, make it one. During the Clinton administration, NSC officials referred to China in this context in order to please the Chinese—and perhaps seduce them into becoming something they are not. The same approach is being used now with India, but with more grounds for optimism.

India and the United States are—as boosters of the relationship never fail to point out—the world's two leading exemplars of multiethnic democracy. Our businesspeople, scientists, researchers, and scholars have created an intricate web of connections. We both depend on imported oil and so want to keep supplies available and prices reasonable. We share a desire for stability in Afghanistan, opposition to terrorism, and a hope that China will not rise so high that it becomes a threat to the advancement of others. Indians and Americans also generally like each other. When Americans think of India, we envision Gandhi, colorful clothing, and great food, except when our minds are distracted by outsourcing, which we blame on multinational corporations, not the earnest young voices on the other end of the phone. A recent survey of Indians showed that 59 percent had a favorable opinion of the United States.

All this is to the good, but it may not mean as much as you might wish. India has made no specific commitments about what a strategic partnership might entail. Precisely because it is a democracy, its government cannot be expected to disregard public opinion, which means it will require good reasons to act differently in the future than it has in the past. Already India has rejected U.S. complaints about its proposed multibillion-dollar gas pipeline project with the government of Iran, whose friendship New Delhi still loudly proclaims. Further, the Communist Party within India's governing coalition has denounced the proposed nuclear deal as an assault on their country's sovereignty.

Some American strategists would like to cast India as a kind of Asian Great Britain, whose actions and policies we could almost always count on to support ours. It is hard to imagine a role less congenial to Indians, who see their country as a champion of the developing world and a leading power in its own right—certainly, nobody's surrogate state.

We should remember that, while increasing numbers of Americans worry about losing jobs, hundreds of millions of Indians still worry about obtaining enough to eat. The nation may seem like a big winner in the globalization sweepstakes, but the reality is not so satisfying—India today remains a far poorer country even than China. In the West, the wealthy are often able to seal themselves off from the sights of misery. As I have been reminded on my visits to India, the contrast between wealth and poverty there is inescapable. The country has the world's largest middle class, but also more poor and illiterate people than any other nation. For travelers stuck in traffic, it is painful to see children crowd around the outside of cars, pointing to their mouths. Visitors are warned not to roll down the windows, for fear of starting a riot or never getting out. Nudging aside the children, the cars crawl on.

For all its freedom, India is also patriarchal and class-conscious. Officially, the country has more Muslims than any nation except Indonesia; in reality, it may have twice as many Muslims as it admits. The government holds to the fiction that the proportion of Muslims has not changed since independence—this is unlikely, given Muslim birth rates. Whatever their number, Indian Muslims tend to reside near the low end of the social and economic spectrum. Of special concern to the United States, many in the Hindu majority show particular disdain toward their Muslim neighbors in Pakistan.

Here we arrive at a dilemma. If India is our strategic partner, what is Pakistan? Surely the rival of our partner is our rival? No, Pakistan, too, is an ally and in some ways more vital to us— albeit even more complicated—than India. For Pakistan and its capital of Islamabad is where the migraines of the twenty-first century all come together: nuclear weapons, terrorism, a lack of functioning democracy, corruption, and poverty.

For this collection of ills, neither Pakistani nor U.S. policymakers have yet to find an effective prescription. Franklin Roosevelt spoke of his exasperation while pounding away without results at the "Na-a-vy," comparing it to punching a feather bed. Especially since 9/11, the United States has given billions of dollars and dozens of lectures to Pakistan, but the core problem you will confront as president—a safe haven for terrorists in the country's rugged northwest—is not shrinking but growing.

Editorial writers in the United States regularly assigned the blame for this danger to Pervez Musharraf, the Pakistani general who assumed the country's presidency in 1999 the old-fashioned way, through a military coup. Musharraf is a complex figure, unburdened by personal humility, who saw no distinction between Pakistan's well-being and his own ambition. In his memoir, Musharraf confesses to being kind to small children, incorruptible, patriotic, unflappable under pressure, and beloved by his soldiers. He says that he decided to seize power only with great reluctance because the times were desperate and because the Pakistani people had habitually looked to the army in an emergency.

Musharraf is a hero only in his own memoir and mind. It is doubtful, however, whether any other Pakistani leader would have been in a position to fight Al Qaeda harder or with more immediate success. Musharraf was the target of four separate assassination attempts. In 2004, he sent eighty thousand troops—of whom six hundred were killed—into the rugged regions near Pakistan's border with Afghanistan in an effort to eradicate Al Qaeda. The operation was professionally executed but indecisive. It was also wildly unpopular with the local citizenry and with the Pakistani army, which felt it was being asked to sacrifice its soldiers at the behest of the United States.

The villagers and herders who inhabit Pakistan's federally administered tribal areas have their own customs, languages, and codes of honor and are markedly more loyal to family and faith than to the government in Islamabad. When, in 1947, Pakistan was founded, these mountainous areas were included but subject to only nominal control. Partly for this reason, social services are poor: health care is primitive; the literacy rate is 17 percent. The border between Pakistan and Afghanistan is an unnatural dividing line, conforming to no distinct topographic or demographic feature. It was drawn by the British for the purpose of splitting and thereby weakening the Pashtun tribes that have long inhabited the region. Accordingly, the border has never officially been recognized by Afghanistan. For those familiar with the terrain, slipping from one side of the border to the other is as easy as breathing.

This matters because, too often, those transiting the boundary are terrorists. Al Qaeda and Taliban training camps have been assimilated into population centers on the Pakistani side. Insurgent operations have been launched from Pakistan into Afghanistan, where NATO is fighting alongside government troops. In an effort to stop diplomatically what he had been unable to halt militarily, Musharraf, in 2006, pledged to withdraw the army from some areas in return for a promise by local leaders to halt the infiltration of militants back into Afghanistan. The agreements, though well intentioned, proved neither permanent nor enforceable. Al Qaeda's presence continued to spread, leading to new rounds of fighting, with less than satisfactory results.

In analyzing events in this region, you should be conscious of the distinction people often fail to make between the different and the dangerous. Pakistan's rural clans practice a traditional brand of conservative Islam laced with cultural values that do not fully accord with our conception of human rights. This does not make them international terrorists. On the contrary, they have lived according to their traditions for centuries without bothering those who do not bother them.

The problem for us, for them, and for you, is that the current politicization has pitted ideological warriors against tribal chiefs. The ideologues include members of Al Qaeda—who may be Pakistani, Uzbeki, Chechen, or Arab—and remnants of the Taliban, which is primarily Afghan. For the past several years, the militants have been competing with traditionalists for control of villages and the minds of the young. This has embroiled the chiefs in a struggle that extends far beyond the boundaries of their own concerns. Most have no interest in fighting in Afghanistan, nor in attacking Americans, but they also oppose any outside military presence. During a visit to Washington, the chief minister of the North-West Frontier Province told me that many of his people believe that America had invaded Iraq because it was Muslim and was thought to possess nuclear weapons, two criteria that describe Pakistan, as well. He said that the United States, a supreme country, should not be so quick to use force. His own concerns, he emphasized, were internal—how to provide education, health care, and law and order for his people. Unfortunately, wars can be hard on groups that want to be left alone; hundreds of local leaders have been murdered for failing to appease the violent extremists within their midst.

The silver lining in this cloud is that Pakistan as a whole is sick of violence and unsupportive of Al Qaeda or the Taliban's rigid doctrines. At least until recently, Pakistani voters have rejected militant political parties whenever mainstream candidates have been allowed to compete. Pakistanis do, however, have grievances against the West; they do not feel they have been treated fairly.

In 1948, my father served as a member of the United Nations Commission for India and Pakistan (UNCIP). In the course of his duties, he traveled to both countries, including a two-week visit to the geographically breathtaking and politically heartbreaking land of Kashmir. UNCIP's mission was to mediate a dispute over Kashmir's status arising from the partition of the newly independent India. At the time, Kashmir was a separate princely state, governed by a Hindu maharajah. Rulers in both India and Pakistan coveted the region, and Pakistani tribesmen soon invaded, trying to force the issue. The maharajah did not want to align with either country, but ultimately embraced New Delhi in return for military aid. This prompted protests within Kashmir's majority Muslim population, and the fighting intensified. UNCIP succeeded in brokering a cease-fire, which divided the region along what came to be known as the Line of Control. In 1949, the Security Council called for a plebiscite to determine the province's final status, but such a vote was opposed by India and never taken. Tensions persisted. In a poetic moment, my father lamented, "The once distant home of the fabulous Maharaja, where gay beds of tulips border the flowing fountains of the gardens of Shalimar, has become by the mutations of modern times a grim threat to . . . peace."

That was nearly sixty years ago. My father is long since dead, I am old, and little has changed. Although Kashmir today is rarely the focus of headlines, it is still a key piece in the Pakistani puzzle. As recently as 2000, significant outbreaks of fighting occurred along the Line of Control, while isolated exchanges of gunfire remain routine. For both countries, Kashmir is a symbol of national identity. Pakistan claims that Indian sovereignty over the region's Muslims is illegitimate, while India rejects the relevance of religion. Leaders in New Delhi point to their ongoing dialogue with Pakistan on Kashmir and insist that the international community has no business even discussing the subject. Because the Pakistanis are displeased with the status quo, they have argued the contrary position, that the world should put pressure on India to be more forthcoming. Resentment over Kashmir has long generated support within Pakistani security forces for violent extremist groups. It is in America's interests, and also that of India and Pakistan, that the problem be settled so that it no longer provides a patriotic pretext for Pakistani militants. This is where India could, if it wished, truly fulfill the role of strategic partner. Kashmir may once have been a local issue, but it is now on a short list of grievances fueling a global fire. This does not mean that India is obliged to accept the Pakistani position, but it should go beyond the confidence-building steps taken in recent years (to protect human rights and open bus routes) and search for an equitable way for residents of the region to have the determining voice in their own future.

Rebuffed over Kashmir, Pakistan has also been disappointed in its bilateral relations with the United States. During the cold war, it, unlike India, was a U.S. ally, a member of the Central Treaty Organization. In the 1980s, it served as a staging ground for U.S.-backed efforts to oust the Soviets from Afghanistan. When those efforts triumphed, our two countries should have been able to bask in the satisfaction of a job well done; instead, the senior President Bush imposed sanctions against our ally because of its nuclear weapons program.

Pakistanis were outraged. They felt that Washington had waited until the cold war was over to turn its back. With the Soviets no longer dangerous, we cut off arms sales, stopped economic assistance, and began treating their country as if it were a pariah state. From the U.S. standpoint, these measures were necessary to support the goal of nonproliferation. From Islamabad's point of view, they were an unfair response to the country's effort to protect itself against India. The dispute was exacerbated by America's virtual abandonment of Afghanistan once the Soviets had been driven out. This created a vacuum in which many people had guns but no jobs. For several years, regional warlords battled each other and carved Afghanistan into pieces, causing more than four million refugees to flee. The chaos that followed produced the Taliban, which later played host to Al Qaeda.

This background is brought to the fore every time an American storms into an office in Islamabad and demands action on terrorism. From the Pakistani perspective, they are not to blame, the world is, for Kashmir, the rise of extremism, and terror.

The Pakistani people deserve better leaders than they have had. Since independence, they have either been governed by the military or by civilians, most of whom had reputations for corruption that were well earned. For years, Musharraf got by with his argument that, in a time of grave threats, his country could not afford the risk of having weak and divided leadership. With that excuse, he broke repeated promises to relinquish power, while engaging in a series of increasingly bitter fights with the judiciary, opposition political parties, and the press. The role of money in all this should not be underestimated. The Pakistani military, like that of China and a number of other Asian, African, and Latin American countries, is also a business, deeply invested in the private sector (including bottled water plants, cement factories, and real estate) and with a considerable stake in the awarding of government contracts. A big part of the rivalry between military and civilian leaders in Pakistan can be traced to the competition for control of government favors and jobs.

Ultimately, Musharraf's heavy-handed attempts to monopolize power backfired, causing his popularity to plummet. Pakistanis admire strong leaders, but they also take seriously the constitution. Musharraf's decision, late in 2007, to impose emergency rule produced the remarkable spectacle of well-dressed lawyers being carted away and imprisoned for supporting the law in defiance of a government determined to ignore legal standards.

The resulting political uncertainty is likely to persist for years whether Pakistan's government is nominally civilian or controlled by the military. Civilian politicians, such as Benazir Bhutto, a former prime minister, are not trusted by the armed forces and without military support, no campaign against Al Qaeda strongholds is even possible. Because of Musharraf, the army is both less popular and less confident that it has the answers to Pakistani ills. The United States, meanwhile, has trouble accepting that Musharraf's domestic unpopularity stemmed not from his defiance of our wishes, but from the perception that he was a puppet of Washington.

Pakistan's leaders and the United States remain ensnared in the catch-22 that has bedeviled us since 9/11. The extremists benefit when the government pulls back to preserve its political standing. They also benefit when the military responds to U.S. pressure by attacking terrorists. Bin Laden is relatively popular in Pakistan not because Pakistanis admire him, but because they resent having their government seemingly under orders from a foreign power. Why, they ask, should they help us? What have we done for them? Musharraf was not the first but the fourth Pakistani military dictator the United States has supported. That being the case, how dare we set ourselves up as champions of democracy?

Pakistan has a population roughly half that of the United States. The majority of its people are more interested in plugging into the world economy than in slugging it out on behalf of any political cause. They are, however, as determined as anyone to have their rights and dignity respected. In the past, the United States has failed to take the Pakistani worldview into account. We cannot afford another such failure, even in pursuit of what seem to us to be urgent and overriding goals. If we define our strategic partnership with India in terms that portray Pakistan as a foe, or if we allow India to do so, we will make an enemy we can't afford to have. If we believe the solution to extremism in Pakistan is to make demands and threats, we will be disappointed, as indeed we have been.

We have been allies of Pakistan in the past, when the enemy was the Soviet Union, imperial and godless. It is harder now, when the enemy is actually within Pakistan, and claims to have God on its side. This makes our relationship even more important but also more delicate. Beginning at a low point, you must find ways to build mutual confidence. My suggestions are, first, to admit past mistakes; this will help, especially since you are not the one responsible for those errors. Second, stress what we can do for Pakistan, not what Pakistan can do for us. Focus on public education, on economic issues (especially the allocation of trade preferences for Pakistani textiles), and on the provision of improved services in the frontier regions. Third, encourage interreligious dialogue based on the commitment to peace shared by Hinduism and the three Abrahamic faiths; such initiatives are already under way and are useful, because they address core issues. Fourth, in terms of protocol, treat India and Pakistan with equal respect. When you go to South Asia, spend the same amount of time in each and express similar sentiments. You might think this would annoy India, but a strategic partner should understand the need for balance. Fifth, in public, raise the terrorism issue as a joint problem to be dealt with on a multilateral basis, with Europe, Afghanistan, Iran, India, Saudi Arabia, Russia, and China also represented. Do not portray it as a showdown between Pashtun tribesmen and the United States.

In the short run, you may be tempted to take matters into your own hands by ordering military strikes in the border areas, with minimal advance notice to Pakistani authorities. I would not rule out that possibility, especially if we have timely intelligence with respect to particular high-profile targets. The temptation to launch a broad American military campaign in Pakistan, however, should be resisted. It is highly unlikely that such an initiative would succeed in eliminating the presence of Al Qaeda and the Taliban, while it would almost certainly create thousands of new enemies for the United States. A smarter approach is to step back and ask some basic questions: What do Pakistanis want their country to look like five or ten years from now? What do they see as the obstacles to their aspirations? How can we best help them to achieve their goals, leaving aside for a moment their rivalry with India?

It is not our responsibility to choose Pakistan's leaders. We should be forthright, however, about our desire to see develop in Pakistan a political system that is democratic, accountable, and free from the plagues of cronyism and money politics. In the past five years, we have given Pakistan some $10 billion in aid, of which only about 9 percent has been used for social and economic purposes. That reflects far too narrow a concept of security. We will not gain the loyalty of Pakistan's military by bribing it. We will not gain the support of the Pakistani people by giving aid only to the army. Since 9/11, we have asked Pakistan's government to be our ally in fighting Al Qaeda. As president, you should reiterate that request while underlining America's desire to be a true friend to Pakistan's people. In so doing, you should understand that this is a role we have yet to play. We must educate ourselves about Pakistan's present and past, and give this relationship the extraordinary priority it deserves. If Pakistanis and Americans are to be genuine and effective allies in defeating the forces that threaten us both, we will need an alliance with a whole country, not a temporary pact with a privileged few, or a marriage of convenience with a dictator.

CHAPTER 12

One Iraq Is Enough

H ave you ever seen earthquake damage firsthand? I have, most memorably in Turkey a decade ago. The ground is not where it should be. Houses are torn up, half-demolished vehicles are scattered about, street patterns are obliterated. Even the possibility of reconstruction seems far-fetched. You ask yourself—where to begin?

Now, consider U.S. policy toward the Middle East. Since Henry Kissinger's evenhanded shuttle diplomacy in the early 1970s, America has played straight with both sides in pursuit of Arab-Israeli peace, eventually helping Egypt and Jordan to reconcile with the Jewish state. We brought Israel and the Palestinians into dialogue about each other's needs and nudged Syria toward an agreement, only to see it back away over a disputed strip of seaside land less than half a mile wide. We worked as partners with Arab governments to contain hostile regimes in Libya, Iraq, and Iran. We helped Israel become sufficiently strong to deter aggression while urging that country's leaders to negotiate based on the principle of land for peace. We sought ways to realize the legitimate aspirations of the Palestinian people. Bill Clinton exhausted himself and everyone around him trying to find the formula for a settlement. He did not succeed, but the parties came closer than ever before. No honest person could say during Clinton's presidency that America did not care about people on both sides of the conflict.

George W. Bush thought he had a better approach. Scornful of Palestinian leaders, dissatisfied with merely containing Saddam Hussein, and convinced that American power could create instant democracy, he embarked on a unilateral plan to transform the entire Middle East. In so doing, he reduced an imperfect security structure to rubble.

In the Middle East, the billiard ball effect in international affairs is especially hazardous. The balls don't just smack into one another; struck hard enough, and with the wrong spin, they explode, igniting others. Hence, the invasion of Iraq degenerated into a multisided civil war, heightening tensions between Sunni and Shiite Muslims, increasing the influence of Iran, bringing Turkey to the brink of conflict with Iraqi Kurds, and giving new life to Al Qaeda. Public opinion in many parts of the world turned against the United States, while the leaders who most directly challenged America (and Israel) topped popularity lists among Muslims. Belatedly the Bush administration attempted to undo the damage by parachuting into the Arab-Israeli dispute, only to find that the framework that had once supported the peace process would need to be rebuilt from the ground up.

American prowess in dealing with twentieth-century dangers has rested on two pillars: U.S. leadership and the full participation of alliance partners. We will regain our footing in the Middle East and Persian Gulf only if we are first able to establish an agenda that is supported by our allies and that can be reconciled with the needs of other key countries. Even then we will be at a starting point, for we must reacquire the trust of those in the region. To gain that, we must do a far better job of understanding what people in the Middle East want and why they take the actions they do. We cannot persuade anyone if we fail to comprehend their view of themselves and of us.

If you were to put an Iraqi doctor, a Palestinian school-teacher, an Israeli farmer, a Lebanese businessperson, an Iranian student, and an American GI in the same room, you would likely discover that they see right and wrong differently, but with equal logic given the contrasts in where they live and what they have experienced. To acknowledge this is not to fall into moral relativism—as ideologues might suggest—but rather to take the first step toward a coherent diplomatic approach to the Middle East.

As president, you will find that the struggles in this region, however sacred its land, are not between angels and devils. Nor can you sit back and wait for all the controversy to be settled by a righteous thunderbolt from above; anticipating Armageddon is not a foreign policy. Your task will be down-to-earth: helping people whose ancestors have been killing each other for generations to coexist. This will require leaving many past wrongs uncorrected and a recognition on your part that force, though unavoidable at times, often backfires and rarely settles anything for long. You will find no decisive military solution to any of the current or potential conflicts in the region. The real choice—for you and for other leaders—isn't between permanent victory or defeat, but between a future in which children can play without fear and repeating cycles of violence that leave Arab and Jewish children alike drawing pictures of coffins.

• • •

On the morning of July 18, 1921, Jewish, Christian, and Muslim representatives gathered in the grand rabbi's courtyard in Baghdad to greet their new ruler and hear a speech. These were the most prominent men of the land—political leaders, government ministers, and people of God. They sat in rows, garbed in traditional head coverings and robes, while women and children looked on from surrounding balconies and the open windows of upper rooms. The attention of all was drawn to a man of modest height with a finely trimmed beard and a solemn face. His name was Feisal bin Hussein, descendant of the Prophet Muhammad, confidant of Lawrence of Arabia, and soon to become king. The grand rabbi, a gracious host, presented his guest with a large Torah, which Feisal kissed. He was given next a finely bound edition of the Talmud and a gilded copy of the Ten Commandments. Invited to speak, the Arab told his audience, "There is no meaning in the words Jews, Muslims and Christians in the terminology of patriotism, there is simply a country called Iraq and all are Iraqis. I ask my countrymen to be only Iraqis because we all belong to one stock, the stock of our ancestor Shem (Semites); we all belong to that noble race, and there is no distinction between Muslim, Christian and Jew."

Feisal was crowned king at the invitation not of local leaders but of the British, whose armed forces had liberated the region from its Turkish oppressors. The British were counting on Feisal to generate a spirit of national unity by stitching together an Iraqi quilt out of Sunni, Shiite, Kurdish, Christian, and Jewish swatches. The British planned to "civilize" the Arabs and profit from their oil, but the Iraqis insisted on following their own script, battling each other and rebelling against the dictates of London. Within fourteen months, the British official responsible for Iraq, Winston Churchill, wrote in desperation to Prime Minister David Lloyd George:

> I am deeply concerned about Iraq. The task you have given me is becoming really impossible. . . . There is scarcely a single newspaper—Tory, Liberal or Labour—which is not consistently hostile to our remaining in this country. . . . I think we should now put definitely, not only to Feisal but to the Constituent Assembly, the position that . . . if they are not prepared to urge us to stay and to co-operate in every manner, I would actually clear out. That at any rate would be a solution. . . . At present we are paying eight million dollars a year for the privilege of living on an ungrateful volcano out of which we are in no circumstances to get anything worth having.

More than eight decades later, the idea that Iraqi leaders would gather at the home of a grand rabbi is quaint, and only slightly less so that Christian leaders would be thought relevant. What has not changed is that the West still wants to believe "there is simply a country called Iraq and all are Iraqis," while those in that country continue following a different script. Similar, too, is the awkward relationship between an occupying power that has tired of its mission and local allies who are weary of being hectored but who also fear what will happen if the foreign troops are withdrawn. Winston Churchill's ungrateful volcano is now yours.

•   •   •

In my last book, *The Mighty and the Almighty*, I wrote that "Although we must fervently hope otherwise, the invasion of Iraq—and its aftermath—may eventually rank among the worst foreign policy disasters in U.S. history." In the time since, I have repeated that statement to audiences across America and been stunned by the response: applause. At first, I couldn't understand it. Why were they clapping? I had hoped to be proven wrong. Then it dawned on me that people were applauding because I had said what they had much earlier concluded: the war was a mistake; we need to find the best way out.

I am not among those who have argued for the early withdrawal of all U.S. troops from Iraq. I believe President Bush was right to claim that a precipitous pullback could lead to catastrophe, but wrong to assume that the presence of our troops would somehow prevent catastrophe. In interviews, I am often asked whether America has a moral obligation to people in the region to stay until Iraq is stable. I reply that indeed we do, but that we also have an obligation to our troops. Our military mission, to the extent we retain one, must be restricted to what we can reasonably accomplish. American credibility is important, but credibility is not enhanced by adopting a strategy that has no hope of success and then persisting in it.

As president, you will find that there are no good options in Iraq, whether our troops leave immediately, slowly, or not at all. The reason is that we do not have the leverage to determine the outcome in Iraq; this has been obvious for years. Your responsibility is to limit the damage.

Three nightmares, in particular, may haunt your presidency. First, the Sunni-dominated region of Iraq, lacking legitimate governing institutions, could become a permanent safe haven, training area, and recruiting ground for Al Qaeda. Second, future Iraqi governments may prove subservient to an increasingly powerful Iran, sharing intelligence, cooperating on military matters, threatening Israel. Third, Iraq may become so fractured by conflict that it ignites a region-wide war. If you and your team are lucky and smart, you may be able to avoid each of these nightmares; if not, we could end up with all three.

Luck matters, for the future of Iraq will not be determined by our actions alone. Even when our troop levels were at their peak, we did not control the country because we were unable to establish security, which meant that we were blamed for the resulting disruptions in electricity, economic activity, and public safety. Our sole advantage now is that others have nightmares similar to ours. None of the governments in the region favors Al Qaeda; none, save Iran, wants Iran to dominate Iraq; and none is eager for war.

We must make the most of these assets, because there is no natural stopping point to the violence. Iran, Syria, Saudi Arabia, Jordan, Egypt, and Turkey could all intervene if Iraqis sharing their faith or ethnicity are in danger of being slaughtered. Governments worry as well that mayhem in Iraq will agitate populations with grievances in their own countries—the Sunnis in Syria; the Shiites in Kuwait, Saudi Arabia, and Bahrain; the Kurds in Turkey, Iran, and Syria. In the worst case, we may see an accelerating cycle of murder and sabotage that leads to the redrawing of boundaries, further economic devastation, and the destruction of irreplaceable religious shrines—creating an unquenchable thirst for revenge. As for Al Qaeda, who can doubt it will take advantage of every opportunity?

Already sectarian violence has led to an unconscionable number of civilian deaths and to one of the largest population displacements in the history of the modern Middle East. More than two million Iraqis have abandoned their homes in search of safer neighborhoods or to flee across the border, some to Syria, others to Jordan, many to Iran. This exodus has cost Iraq a core of skilled people whose talents are needed inside the country. Rather than cool conflict, moreover, the displacement of populations tends to prolong fighting as migrants organize to reclaim their homes. Unless tightly supervised, refugee areas can become militia bases and indoctrination camps, where bitter exiles beseech the next generation to fight battles lost by their own. We have seen this with the Palestinians for six decades, and I saw it myself in Central Africa, where refugees from Rwanda triggered round after round of bloodshed.

From your vantage point in the White House, you will point out—as Feisal did—that no one gains from civil war. Iraqis, however, do not look to America to tell them what is in their interest. They make their own judgments and unless more see the value of building a united nation, the central government will remain feeble. As time passes, the Kurds (who already cut their own oil deals and ban display of the Iraqi flag) will surely go their own separate way. The Sunnis, who still believe they are Iraq's rightful rulers, will strive to reclaim their earlier primacy. The Shiites, who are in the majority and determined to consolidate their gains, will try to carve out the largest slice of territory they can, even while quarreling among themselves over who gets to be in charge.

It may be that the only way to keep Iraq together is to allow it to divide—not officially or completely, but enough to create living space for Shiites in the south, Kurds in the north, and the Sunnis in between. This need not be the result of an announced policy, for the Iraqis are well on the way to dividing themselves. Your goal, in partnership with whatever Iraqi leaders are willing, should be to stabilize the process so that it occurs more peacefully and without destroying entirely the concept of a national Iraq. There is no reason, for example, that a person who identifies first with his family and faith cannot maintain some allegiance, as well, to a national identity. Lebanon is not a good model for much, but it survives as a country despite Iraq-like fissures. Baghdad, moreover, must be a place where Sunnis and Shiites (and others) can mix. This means that campaigns of ethnic cleansing, waged by militias on a street-by-street basis, must stop. Iraq's government, whether under new leadership or not, must agree on power and oil-sharing arrangements that are at least marginally acceptable to each of the major factions. The Kurds, landlocked and without many friends, must conclude that autonomy inside a viable Iraq is preferable to independence within a region at war. As we have seen, it is beyond our power to compel military and political solutions in Iraq, but with the active help of each of Iraq's neighbors, it remains conceivable that a fragile equilibrium could be created. The result would be less a normal nation than a trio of fiefdoms, each with its own militia but each also respecting the home turf of the others. For a best-case scenario, this federalized Iraq is poor stuff, but when a country is so badly broken, the wire and duct tape will show.

When I was secretary of state, we were confronted by inter-ethnic strife in the Balkans. What had happened there histori-cally is that each faction inside the region had an ally outside, from which it received arms and political support. We thought the solution might be to get all the countries with an interest in the Balkans to work together, so we created a diplomatic in-strument we called the contact group, with representatives from half a dozen nations, and made sure that our policies were co-ordinated. This approach worked, and I (and many others) said both before and after the second Gulf War that something similar should be tried there. It wasn't. This was a grievous failure. America may have initiated the conflict, but Iraq's neighbors and our allies have an enormous stake in ending it. The administration could have attracted help by admitting mistakes and offering to share decision-making responsibility. Instead, U.S. officials insisted that the coalition could prevail on its own. In May 2003, they even turned down a proposal from Iran for a comprehensive negotiation based on the idea of a democratic and non-theocratic Iraq. Not until 2007 did the United States finally agree to conduct regional diplomacy, and by then, Operation Iraqi Freedom had become more about salvage than freedom.

The Bush administration's failure in Iraq was predictable but not entirely inevitable. The American intervention, however poorly conceived, might have wobbled to a semi-successful conclusion had opposition to it been confined to the Sunni insurgency. We should not forget that millions of Iraqis risked their lives, and thousands died, trying to make democracy work. Through much of the country, people were excited to vote and relished the chance to draft a constitution, form political parties, and engage in self-government. Moreover, for almost three years, Shiite leaders exhibited courageous and commendable restraint in the face of Sunni-initiated violence. The Shiites hoped to build power legitimately through elections, while counting on the United States to defeat the Sunni rebels.

It was only when, in February 2006, terrorists destroyed the sacred Samarra shrine, burial place of two revered ninth-century imams, that the Shiite militias went on the offensive. As the fighting metastasized into civil war, the U.S.-led coalition found itself trying to protect all sides against violence by all sides. Patrolling the streets, an American soldier would not know whom to shoot at until he or she was under fire—an untenable position. The American military advantage is minimized in street-level fighting, where allies and enemies look the same, civilians are all around, and even military gains are often accompanied by political setbacks. It is hard to win battles when you are wearing uniforms and your enemies are not, or to win hearts and minds when you are stopping cars and knocking on doors while waving guns and deploying bomb-sniffing canines in a culture that considers dogs to be unclean.

In addition to complicating the American mission, the Sunni-Shiite rivalry crippled efforts to build an effective national army, professionalize the police, and create a functioning central government. Instead of bringing the various factions together, key Shiite-dominated ministries became active participants in the civil war, using official cover to kill, torture, and imprison their Sunni adversaries. Democracy doesn't work unless the elected majority has enough respect for opponents to entrust them with rights, fair political representation, and a role in providing security. That is one reason trying to create democracy overnight is like trying to run a marathon on the second day of training. You start out fine, but the body isn't ready, so you burn out early and collapse in a heap.

"Iraq is not just one war," observed Philip Zelikow, a former senior advisor to Condoleezza Rice. "It is really five or six different wars in the same country, each with different dynamics and different combatants." Given this reality, it is too much to expect that we can prevent Iraqi factions from tearing each other apart if that is what they choose to do. Our troops should not be asked to try. Our purpose, instead, should be to mitigate the fighting if possible and keep it within Iraq's borders. If there are identifiable Al Qaeda units operating inside Iraq, foreign combatants who are infiltrating, and humanitarian situations where we can help, we should do what we can. Otherwise, our military role must end and diplomacy should occupy center stage.

That diplomacy—your diplomacy—will have to be extremely hardheaded. You do not have the capacity to impose your will. As the embodiment of America, you will be held responsible for the devastation created by our invasion and for any chaos left behind as we depart. It is unclear, moreover, whether those whose help you need will be forthcoming. You should begin by reminding our allies how important their assistance might be, not only to Iraq and to us, but to their own well-being. One doesn't have to be directly under or on top of a bomb to feel its effects.

Much depends on whether Iraq's neighbors are willing to cooperate in limiting arms, quieting internal tensions, and preventing troublemakers from entering the country. Such cooperation hinges on trust, which is scarcer now than desert snow. If your administration is to create a stable security structure in the region, you will have to build bridges to many of those inside and outside Iraq that we have previously identified either as the enemy or as evil: Iran, Syria, Shiite militias, Sunni sheikhs, ex-members of Saddam Hussein's party—it is quite a list. The flexibility, however, is not solely your own, for each of these entities has also identified us—and often one another—as evil. The bad feeling is omnipresent. The business of diplomacy, in this case, is not about doing favors for one another; it is about agreeing that Iraq in flames serves no one's interests except that of everyone's enemy, Al Qaeda. As past initiatives have shown, it is hard to reach out to Sunni and Shiite leaders simultaneously without having your arms ripped off. At this late date, it will require an alchemist's touch to create a multinational, interreligious framework to support stability in a federalized Iraq; it is, however, the right goal to pursue and the best chance you have.

Ordinarily, civil wars end in one of three ways: one side defeats the other; an outside force intervenes to compel peace; or the sides exhaust themselves through violence. The first outcome is unlikely in Iraq; the second hasn't worked; the third could take a decade or more.

Americans have paid a high price for mistakes in Iraq, but we have not paid equally. It is grueling to fight in a military action that is well conceived and successful; far more painful to see one's comrades struck down in a war botched by civilian leaders. The nature of this particular conflict has left us with thousands of freshly dug graves and many thousands of men and women maimed, physically and mentally. Your predecessor felt anguish and prayed with victims and loved ones but was constrained by his own false logic from describing the invasion as what it was: an assault against terror that strengthened terror; a demonstration of American power that exposed the limits of that power; a campaign conducted in the name of democracy that undercut democracy's good name; a blow against extremism that served the agenda of radicals in Iran; above all, a grisly human tragedy.

You must ensure that our returning soldiers receive the best health care and the full package of veterans' benefits. You should also propose two memorials: one in America and one in Iraq, to honor the wounded and dead, military and civilian alike. Arrange for spiritual leaders to offer prayers in English and Arabic. Bring people together in remembrance and mourning. Pray for the wisdom to replace hubris with humility, and pay heed to the

238 Memo to the President Elect

parting advice offered anonymously by one army captain trying
to draw meaning from his tour in Iraq:

> If Iraq is to teach us anything, it must be that a new idea
> cannot be beat into a society. . . . "Extraordinary rendi-
> tion," Guantánamo Bay, and Abu Ghraib have all become
> shorthand for an America (or an American administration)
> that lost faith in the power of its own idea. Their hypocrisy
> seemingly exposed, people who had embraced and were
> gradually working towards that American idea in the
> world's most volatile regions were . . . overwhelmed by a
> new generation of extremists. . . . What gives me some de-
> gree of hope is the ultimate vacuity of this alternative to the
> American idea. But as long as they can point to the *adoo
> baeed*—the external enemy—to deflect the blame from
> their own moral and material bankruptcy, they may stay
> afloat. If we're able to reassert our idea and to hold it up to
> people as a real choice, I know this current setback can be
> overcome. No amount of violence inflicted in the name of
> freedom, however, will be the force to bring it about.

During the election campaign, you concurred with other candidates that, aside from Al Qaeda and the debacle in Iraq, the most
serious threat to American interests is Iran. This assessment is
based largely on the fear that Iran will defy international pressure, violate its commitments to the IAEA, and build nuclear
weapons. A nuclear-armed Iran might engage in diplomatic
blackmail, transfer its technology to a terrorist group, spark a
regional arms race, or try to destroy Israel.

When asked what you intend doing about this, you and your opponents took similar positions: you were clear about the goal, somewhat fuzzy about how to achieve it. You all hoped that a combination of diplomacy and sanctions would cause Iran to back down, but said that a nuclear Iran is not acceptable and that no option is off the table—a transparent code for threatening force.

Since the Iraq invasion, the world has wondered whether Mr. Bush would try to force regime change in Iran or, more likely, dispatch missiles to destroy Iran's nascent nuclear facilities. This possibility has reminded me why Washington should be known as the rumor capital of the world. Over the past year, I have been told in confidence by people who have, in turn, claimed to have been sworn to secrecy, that the decision had already been made to attack Iran. The president would not, I was informed in a whisper, leave office without "taking care" of Iran's nuclear program. Why? The judgment of history.

Benjamin Netanyahu is one among many who have pointed with alarm to the connection between Iran's presumed nuclear ambitions and the fulminations of the country's president, Mahmoud Ahmadinejad, who has questioned both the Holocaust and Israel's right to exist. Declared Netanyahu, "It's 1938 and Iran is Germany. And Iran is racing to arm itself with atomic bombs."

By this logic, Ahmadinejad is another Hitler, and those who fail to do what is necessary to stop him will be damned forever. Moreover, those who suggest that Ahmadinejad can be reasoned with, or doesn't really mean what he says, or will be constrained by his fellow countrymen, are akin to the wishful thinkers who refused to believe the Nazis would act on their professed beliefs. Where Hitler's lust for power was manifested in berserk nation-

alism, racism, and a moral compass gone haywire, Ahmadinejad is said to see himself as a millennial figure chosen by destiny
to lead Iran into an apocalyptic struggle with Israel.

Whether or not you accept this comparison matters because
it will affect your choices. If Iran's leaders are truly analogous to
the Nazis, they must be stopped at any cost. If they are divided,
they may be influenced by the right blend of carrots and sticks.
For perspective, consider how the current stage was set.

America's strategy in the 1950s had been to establish regional
outposts of anticommunist support, particularly in sensitive
locations such as the Persian Gulf. Iran, perched on the Soviet Union's doorstep and rich with oil, seemed ideally suited
to such a role. As in Iraq, however, the local population was
reading from a different script, this one a drama with imperial Britain again playing the part of the villain. Since the early
1900s, the British had counted on the Gulf's hydrocarbons to
fuel its massive fleet; then, at midcentury, Iran rebelled, demanding that the Anglo-Iranian Oil Company be national-
ized. The British were not amused, and turned to America for
help. Truman declined to intervene, but his successor, Dwight
Eisenhower, was more agreeable. Ike authorized the CIA to
overthrow Iran's elected prime minister, installing in his stead
Mohammad Reza Pahlavi, the shah. According to the CIA's
official history, "It was a day that should never have ended.
For it carried with it such a sense of excitement, of satisfaction and of jubilation that it is doubtful whether any other can
come up to it." Pahlavi dutifully agreed to a new oil concession
that benefited both British and American companies, then embarked on a modernization program aimed at making his land

a bulwark of support for the free world—which is not to say that his people were free.

The shah was one of those leaders who equated his own supremacy with the popular good. To inoculate his country against communism, he had to maintain his perch atop the Peacock throne. To guarantee that, he created a brutal intelligence and security network to crush dissent. Betrayed by his own sense of entitlement to rule, he created venomous enemies and few loyal allies. One of those enemies, Ayatollah Ruhollah Khomeini, led a religious movement from exile that first enraged, then rattled, then provoked, then swept the shah and his pro-Western entourage away.

Taking power in 1979, Khomeini was one of those leaders who equated his own vision of truth with absolute good. Secular reformers and liberals who had confronted the shah and welcomed his defeat found no place for themselves in the newly proclaimed Islamic Republic. Khomeini established a government in two parts. The first featured an elected president and parliament with limited power over the budget and public services. The second consisted of an array of religious councils responsible to a supreme leader, who happened to be Khomeini himself. Khomeini, and his successor, Ayatollah Ali Khamenei, have exercised control over Iran's security—both domestic and international—ever since.

Iran's foreign policy under the ayatollahs has been defined by its relentless anti-Americanism. Because we installed and supported the shah, and because of our Middle East policy, we are considered by Iran to be the inheritors of every sin committed by the British, the collaborator in every sin committed by the shah, and the facilitator of every sin committed by Israel. What is more, in the 1980s, the Reagan administration sided with Iraq during its war of aggression against Iran, a conflict that cost more that a million lives. In 1989, while patrolling the Persian Gulf, our navy mistakenly shot down an Iranian commercial airliner, killing all aboard.

When President Ahmadinejad challenges President Bush to a debate, as he periodically does, these are the issues he wants to talk about: the shah, the 1980s war, the shooting down of the airliner, and Israel's treatment of the Palestinians. On the nuclear issue, he argues that his country has a legal right to reprocess nuclear fuel, provided it is for civilian purposes and subject to IAEA inspection. When we object, saying that Iran has cheated in the past and cannot be trusted, he retorts that we are hypocrites, given our own nuclear arsenal and Israel's decision to develop nuclear arms outside the IAEA process. As for who represents evil, Ahmadinejad points out that modern Iran, unlike America and Israel, has never occupied anyone else's land.

The Iranian president was elected because of promises made to the poor and because he had been a popular and competent mayor of Tehran. His penchant for generating international controversy could be a way of distracting attention from his failure to meet the expectations created by his campaign. His hopes for reelection (in June of your first year in office) may depend on his success in portraying himself as a defender of Iran against those who would bully it. His popularity has been harmed by his overzealous campaign to crack down on alleged "propagators of moral decay," such as barbershop owners and female bicyclists. He is aided by the fact that virtually all Iranians believe their country should have the right to build nuclear weapons.

•   •   •

When Iran's people look to their history, they recall most clearly the periods of greatness, whether imperial (under the likes of Cyrus and Darius) or intellectual (the blossoming of Shia Islam). Today, Iran sees itself as a rising power. This view has been bolstered by oil income and by the gift of the Bush administration's invasion of Iraq, which placed Iran's neighbor in the relatively friendly hands of its Shiite majority for the first time in centuries.

Since the 1979 revolution and subsequent hostage crisis, Americans have searched in vain for Iranian leaders with whom we could practice productive diplomacy. I hoped, during my years as secretary of state, that the moment had arrived. In 1997, Iran's voters elected a reformist president, Mohammad Khatami, who startled the world (and surprised us) by advocating dialogue and expressing respect for American traditions and ideals. We had seen false moderates beckon to our country from Iran before, but the mild-mannered Khatami seemed genuine. We felt that he had opened the door to improved ties and was waiting for us to respond.

A president and secretary of state have few opportunities to make history by transforming important relationships for the better. Although I knew that elements of Iran's security establishment were irredeemably hostile, I was intrigued by the possibility of a breakthrough and did not see any objective reason why our countries should be enemies. Indeed, we had several adversaries in common, including Saddam Hussein, the Taliban, and narcotics traffickers (against whom Iranian security forces had launched a determined assault). I admit, as well, a fascination with Iran's culture and people. At the UN, I had regularly walked by the words of a poem by thirteenth-century Persian philosopher Saadi Shirazi. Those words, which were inscribed on a wall near the

Hall of Nations, suggest that pain felt anywhere affects everyone because "Of one Essence is the human race."

Twice, two years apart, I delivered a major speech on Iran. Each address included an offer to Tehran to sit down, without conditions, to discuss all issues. We sent similar messages confidentially via the embassy of a third country. To my disappointment, our invitations were not taken up. If Khatami was sincere, he evidently lacked the clout to lift Iran out of its anti-U.S. rut. Iran's private statement to us still stood: "The United States government has not yet acquired the needed readiness for an official dialogue."

This was an opportunity missed. After leaving office, I was told by intermediaries that at least some Iranian officials regretted not having accepted our offer. The lesson for you is that Iran speaks with more than one voice. Just as Khatami's pronouncements proved of little diplomatic significance, so it is possible that Ahmadinejad speaks mainly for himself. He certainly does not speak for all of Iran, nor does he reflect the sophistication and intelligence of Iran's people.

The highlight of the class I teach at Georgetown is the opportunity for students to assume the roles of senior government officials and consider what they would do in a crisis. The highlight for me is that I assign myself the job of U.S. president. The crisis du jour in recent years has been Iran. I ask students to argue the pros and cons of a military strike under various scenarios, including the sinking of an American gunboat in the Persian Gulf and attacks against Israel or the United States by Iranian-backed terrorists. We discuss whether the better response to Iran's nuclear program is to seek economic sanctions or to launch cruise missiles. The arguments are spirited, with American and Iranian representatives frequently disagreeing among themselves. As the supposed president, I have been impressed by the enormous difference a skilled debater can make. One weekend, the student who portrayed the secretary of defense on Saturday was confident, persuasive, and seemingly had all the answers; a second student in the same role on Sunday was as wishy as he was washy, unwilling to conclude anything from the information at hand. The first student could have led our group anywhere; the second nowhere—but who was closer to being right?

Role-playing is enjoyable because the only damage risked is a bad grade, which in these inflationary days is considered a B. The stakes on the table in the White House Situation Room are literally life and death. Chances are good that using force against Iran will be listed as an option throughout your presidency, especially if Tehran refuses to yield to international pressure and give up its right to enrich uranium.

Regardless of what you said during the campaign, you should be reluctant to turn to military action. So many people are already angry at us or distrust us that the negative consequences of an American strike on Iran would—unless the strike was clearly in self-defense—be substantial.

First, we could forget reconciliation with the Iranian people, many of whom dislike their government and would prefer to have better relations with us. Second, we would have little if any diplomatic support unless we could prove that Iran was actually in the process of building nuclear weapons; because of our well-known intelligence failure in Iraq, the standard of proof would be high. Third, if we attack Iran, we give up on Iraq. Iraqi Shiites would expel our troops and quite possibly our diplomats, as well. Fourth, the projected targets in Iran are numerous and some are in populated areas; military action would likely kill innocent people. Fifth, Iran might well retaliate by orchestrating terrorist attacks against us. Since a military strike on our part would be remembered in the region for centuries, we could expect that acts of revenge might take place throughout the millennium.

Force may in the end prove necessary, nevertheless, and you should keep contingency plans updated. You should also be prepared for the possibility of accidental incidents in the Persian Gulf. The body of water is small, warships are big, tensions are high, and mistakes do happen. If Americans are at fault, you will never convince Iran, and you will have difficulty persuading anyone else, that we did not intend to provoke a fight. If Iran is at fault, you will face enormous domestic pressure to respond harshly, especially if American lives are lost.

Another potential source of tribulation is the apparent rise of the Iranian Revolutionary Guard (IRG) as an independent and assertive force. The IRG was founded shortly after the 1979 revolution to purge opponents of the new regime. Though technically subservient to the supreme leader, the Guard has begun acting more on its own and has shown itself to be ideologically extreme, aggressive to the point of recklessness, and greedy. Like the military in places such as China and Pakistan, the IRG combines its security function with a hunger to monopolize government contracts, a penchant for smuggling contraband, and a willingness to sell weapons to whoever wants them, whether civilian officials approve or not. It has also been accused of training forces to carry out attacks against U.S. troops in Iraq and Afghanistan. If the Guard aligns with Ahmadinejad (a former member) and proceeds to destroy or intimidate rival centers of power, the possibility exists that Iran will drop any pretense of working with the world community. In fact, IRG provocations are at least as likely as Iran's nuclear activities to produce a military confrontation between our two countries.

One way or another, Iran will make you earn your pay. My prediction is that if you are patient and just flexible enough, Iran will not seek a confrontation on your watch. Although Iran is stronger now than it has been, it lacks the resources to be more than a regional power. Oil may generate the majority of Iran's income, but it is a declining resource because burgeoning domestic demand is eating up supplies. Due to a shortage of refining capacity, Iran is already forced to import 40 percent of its gasoline and, under Ahmadinejad, has begun rationing fuel to consumers. The country's need for technical assistance leaves it dependent on the goodwill of others.

There are also social, diplomatic, and military limits on Iran's power. It would take a truly extraordinary set of circumstances for a Persian country to dominate a region that consists of one Jewish state, one Turkish, and the rest Arab. Even Iran's allies in Iraq and Lebanon must take care not to be seen as Tehran's puppets.

These constraints might not matter if, as some believe, Iran is driven by a faith-based mission to destroy Israel and bring human history to a fiery end. Certainly, vigilance is advised, but we should also keep Mr. Ahmadinejad in perspective. He may act as if his country's nuclear program were his number one son, but he had no role in its conception. Iran's commitment to nuclear power dates back to the shah and America's generous Atoms-for-Peace program. Nor does Ahmadinejad have the authority to decide what Iran's nuclear policies will be, a responsibility that belongs to Ayatollah Khamenei, the supreme leader, and his cohort of advisors. Khamenei, who is best described as an extremely cautious extremist, is likely to steer a path between openly giving into outside pressure and sparking a global crisis. The application of international economic sanctions against Iran will not likely make Iran give in, but may make its leaders willing to accept a carefully crafted compromise.

Much depends on whether Iran's collective leadership is intent on protecting the gains it has made or whether—out of ambition, resentment, ideology, or fear—it is determined to pursue a more aggressive strategy. Your administration can clear the air by assuring the government that our intentions are peaceful; we accept that Iran has legitimate interests to protect; and we have no plans to use force to try to change its government. We should also be prepared for diplomatic engagement with Iran's leaders on all topics, ranging from their grievances against us to our alarm about their connections to violence in the Middle East, the activities of the IRG, and the nuclear issue. Ideally, our communications should be frequent, routine, and confidential. Big public set pieces raise expectations too high, and cause both sides to try to score easy points with domestic audiences. In arriving at your strategy, remember that an agreement on the nuclear controversy is more likely if both sides can say they have preserved key positions. Our key position is that Iran must not build nuclear weapons. Provided we secure that goal, an arrangement that permits Iran otherwise to save face should be acceptable.

One tipping point will come if and when Iran ejects IAEA inspectors or is again caught engaging in clandestine nuclear weapons–related activities. Another may arise if Iran is shown to be directing or financing terror attacks against the United States. Under any scenario, our position will be stronger if we have worked with our allies each step of the way and if other major countries understand that we have given Iran every chance to resolve differences without violence. It is vital that the basis for any actions we take be explicitly and truthfully explained—one Iraq is enough. It will help, as well, if we are seen to be active in pursuing a satisfactory end to the most provocative dispute of all—between Arabs and Israelis in the Middle East.

CHAPTER 13

Middle East:
The Power to Choose

O ne of the important things in the Torah is 'do not murder.' Who will give something [so] . . . that all human
beings will live in peace, will not murder and will not
covet the land of one's neighbor and peace will prevail in the
entire world? Who will give to bring this about?"

These questions, recorded in an eighth-grade yearbook
at the Yeshiva of Flatbush in Brooklyn, reflect the profound
and humane yearnings of a child, but with age comes—what?
Twenty years on, the author of those words, Baruch Goldstein,
walked into a mosque in Hebron and machine-gunned twenty-
nine Palestinians as they knelt in prayer. Asked how such an
event could occur, an Israeli general replied that there is no force
in the world able to stop a determined assassin or terrorist given
the close quarters in which Palestinians and Israelis live. No
force in the world.

As you take office, the pursuit of Middle East peace seems
quixotic, reserved for dreamers. When I was in government, we

compared it to a merry-go-round or roller coaster—a machine in constant motion but returning always to where it started. The quest has seemed in recent years more like a child's waterslide, with participants slipping in a single direction (downward), ending in a pool where everyone tries to find someone smaller to dunk but no one knows how to swim.

President Bush cannot be accused of lacking a comprehensive vision for the Middle East. The flaw is that his vision depended on Iraq becoming a model democracy, thus depriving terrorists of support and empowering Arab moderates. In his scenario, tranquility in Jerusalem was to follow naturally from liberation in Baghdad.

Bush was determined not to make the same mistakes he accused Bill Clinton of having made: overestimating Yasser Arafat and pushing Israel to take bargaining positions that the Palestinians might accept. After all, said critics, the Clinton team's strategy had failed, climaxing not in peace but in frustration and disappointment. Arafat had obviously been playing a double game, nattering on about olive branches yet preparing all the while to seek leverage on the streets.

Clinton had intervened, done his best, and fallen short. Bush's plan was to step back and let Israel do whatever it felt it had to do to protect itself. The sticking point in the Middle East is that the opposite of an approach such as Clinton's may be an approach that doesn't work at all. Bush's aloofness was interpreted by Arabs as indifference; his unqualified support for Ariel Sharon, as hostility. Rather than being coerced into moderation, the Palestinians swerved further toward the extreme. American influence declined. It is difficult to see the benefit of this either to us or to Israel.

Midway through its second term, the Bush team switched direction, trying to undo the damage. Secretary Rice spent more time in the Middle East laboriously attempting to impose order on events. The problem is that each time the peace process breaks down, the harder it is to start up again. Diplomacy isn't a light switch that can be turned on and off; it requires a steady current of contacts, discussions, probes, and tests. If interrupted, a dramatic event is necessary to reestablish momentum toward peace; otherwise each party will prepare for a future without peace. For the Israelis, this means using its power to prevent, deter, and punish attacks. For the Palestinians, it means fighting each other for the right to be top gun and then turning that gun on Israel. For Arab leaders, it means catering to the anti-Israeli and anti-American sentiments of their constituencies. For hopes of regional stability, it spells oblivion.

The beginning of wisdom in the Middle East is understanding that even if you do not succeed, how you fail matters. There is a stark difference between a Middle East where the possibility of peace is admitted and one where that hope has been eclipsed. In the former, those who strive for reconciliation are at least looked to with interest; in the latter, warriors alone command center stage.

You do not, of course, have the authority to make decisions for Arab and Israeli leaders. However skilled you turn out to be, chances are good that some level of violence will persist. You do, however, have an opportunity to restore America's reputation as an honest broker and as a country that cares about the lives and well-being of everyone in the region. That is a better position than where we are now.

During your campaign, you made plain your commitment to

Israel's right to exist within secure borders and to defend itself against all threats. You praised Israel as the Middle East's only democracy and referred to it as a strategic ally in the fight against terror. You said that Israel and America share the same values and reminisced about your visits to holy sites in and around Jerusalem. You vowed that America would stand with Israel as long as the Sun shall rise.

All that is fine; I said, and meant, much the same myself. Be aware, however, that every syllable was heard in the Middle East as distinctly as in America. Arab commentators have already dismissed you as just another prisoner of what they refer to as the "Israel lobby." This means you will start out with no reservoir of affection in such key capitals as Cairo and Riyadh, nor have your promises guaranteed you the trust of Israel or its most vocal American backers. You will be watched carefully to see whether you talk differently as a president than you did as a candidate.

To ensure good communication you should maintain a dialogue with leaders in the American Jewish community. You cannot meet separately with each, so be sure to organize a regular conference call every couple of months—or more often if events warrant. Think of this as political insurance. People who have criticized you directly will feel less need to do so indirectly, and those who pick up the phone intent on lecturing you may find themselves so incensed by the comments of their fellow leaders that they lecture each other instead.

Of course, each call to Jewish leaders should be accompanied by one to Arab-American representatives. Neither conversation will lead to the political equivalent of still water and green pastures. The outreach is worthwhile, nevertheless, because it will demonstrate to all your understanding of just how deep the feelings are.

• • •

The pursuit of peace requires both a partner and a plan. Of these the first is more important because, without a partner, a plan is just a piece of paper. Yasser Arafat was hardly an ideal interlocutor, but he could at least represent Palestinian positions. He knew how to rein in factionalism and minimize intra-Palestinian violence. He elevated his national cause to the top of the Arab agenda without relying on religious zealotry. He could have made peace had he dared, but chose not to.

Today, there is no comparable figure with whom to negotiate. Mahmoud Abbas, the Palestinian president, is a brave proponent of reconciliation, but he lacks Arafat's political wizardry. To negotiate on behalf of a people, a leader must have legitimacy and the ability to keep commitments. Although Abbas was duly elected, he cannot speak for Hamas, nor has he shown the ability to control radical factions within his own party. The Palestinian movement has come to resemble a solar system that has lost its star; there is no gravity, just collisions. The religious (Hamas) clash with the secular (Abbas's Fatah). Palestinian exiles have different agendas than people living inside the Palestinian Authority, while Gaza and the West Bank are like tiny separate countries, neither doing very well.

Meanwhile, Arafat's elaborate security apparatus, designed to keep any subordinate from accumulating too much power, has disintegrated as the various factions have battled and miscellaneous armed gangs roam about neighborhoods. Amid the confusion, a subculture that glorifies suicide bombing has developed. Youngsters choose photographs of themselves they hope will one day go up on the wall of martyrs. Some parents talk openly, even excitedly, about sacrificing their children, less often about sacrificing themselves. It is a dismal and depressing spectacle.

For their part, Israelis have all but given up on serious negotiations because they do not believe that those Palestinians who genuinely want peace can outshout or outshoot those who will never agree to terms that Israel can accept. Under Sharon, Israel turned to unilateral measures—withdrawal from Gaza, building a security fence, targeting those responsible for attacks. Sharon's successors, burdened by political weakness, lack any clear sense of direction. Most Israelis still desire peace, see no viable alternative to it, and will support measures to encourage it—but they have lost any gut sense as to how it might be brought about. They are like travelers who, partway to their destination, have come to a river they can't go around and cannot get across. They need someone to arrive in their midst who will part the waters, but there is not, for the moment, anyone in sight.

The war between Israel and Lebanon in the summer of 2006 claimed more than twelve hundred lives, caused billions of dollars in damage, and further deepened Arab anger toward Israel (to the extent that is possible). It also revived memories of an earlier invasion.

In 1982, Israel attacked Lebanon with the audacious purpose of expelling the PLO and of installing a government in Beirut that would sign a peace treaty and, in Ariel Sharon's phrase, "become part of the free world." To this end, the Israelis joined forces with a Christian militia that had been modeled by its founder on Hitler's Nazi Youth. The invasion itself was fierce, killing thousands of Lebanese civilians, wounding and displacing tens of thousands more. After a period of intense fighting, Israel succeeded in ousting the PLO leadership but not in transforming Lebanese politics, which became even more complicated, prompting the deployment of a multinational force including American troops. At one point, President Reagan authorized U.S. battleships to shell Muslim positions in support of Lebanon's impotent national army. The resulting broadcasts to the Arab world showed shells labeled "Made in America" killing Muslims on behalf of a Christian government allied to an invading Israel. During the latter stages of fighting, Israeli soldiers stood guard while a Christian militia slithered into two refugee camps in Beirut and massacred Palestinian and Lebanese civilians.

Proving once again that, in the Middle East, intentions rarely match consequences, the Israelis also created for themselves a new and unneeded enemy on their northern border. The Lebanese Shiites, who generally despised the PLO, were not the intended targets of the Israeli invasion. They were victimized by the violence, nonetheless, because they lived in the invasion's path and lacked the resources to run away. The resulting Shiite anger was exploited by a young political movement—Hezbollah—which created a militia to resist the subsequent Israeli occupation. Devout and disciplined, with close ties to their co-religionists in Iran, Hezbollah organized itself to provide social services and give voice to the Shiites, who had long been stuck on the bottom rung of Lebanese politics and society. When, in 2000, Israeli troops withdrew voluntarily, Hezbollah claimed credit for driving them out.

Lebanon is a land of survivors whose survival is never assured. It is small, roughly the size of Connecticut, with a population divided and then redivided by religion, family, political ideology, and economic status. Christians are split at least three ways, while Muslims include Sunnis, Shia, and the secretive Druze, a thousand-year-old sect that believes in instant reincarnation and reveres as its chief prophet none other than Jethro, the father-in-law of Moses.

As secretary of state, I saw the legacy of Lebanon's civil war, which had shattered the country in the 1970s and '80s; indeed, sections of Beirut were still in ruins when I visited in 1997. Our small motorcade drove through the city streets—with our security people tense, guns ready—to the U.S. embassy, perched on a hill surrounded by checkpoints and an intimidating display of heavy weapons. The civil war had ended because Syrian troops had intervened to end it—and then neglected to leave. Syria's authoritarian leader, Hafez Assad, claimed that Lebanon belonged to his country. Throughout the 1990s, Lebanese politicians were under unyielding pressure to do what Assad demanded. His incessant meddling meant that when I went to my scheduled rendezvous with the Lebanese prime minister, Rafik Hariri, I felt like a girl on a date with a boy of whom my parents disapproved. Hariri and I had to step out of doors to a balcony, beyond the range—we hoped—of Syrian listening devices. I told the prime minister of our support for Lebanese sovereignty and was pleased, not long after, to approve his request to lift the ban on Americans traveling to his country.

The ebullient Hariri was a wealthy businessman who became known as "Mr. Lebanon" because he did not let anyone push him around. In February 2005 he became known as a martyr, killed by a car bomb that may or may not have been planted by Syrian agents. As long as Syria had dominated Lebanon, factional differences within the country had been suppressed. The uproar caused by Hariri's death forced Damascus to withdraw its troops—good news but also the source of new questions, for

Lebanon has yet to find a reliable recipe for social and political stability.

Today, the country is once again perilously fractured. On one side are Hezbollah and its allies; on the other, a coalition that includes the Sunnis, Druze, and most Christians. Outsiders are prone to assume that Lebanon is aligned in ways that correspond to their, the outsiders, sense of right and wrong. It would simplify your life as president, for example, if one side in Lebanon possessed all the virtues. In fact, many of those we associate with political moderation have a reputation for corruption. Hezbollah, which we rightly associate with terrorism, has a reputation for relative honesty. The same split exists among the Palestinians, where Hamas (also terrorist) campaigned on a platform of political reform while Fatah has wasted many of the opportunities it has been given. For too long, Americans have given lip service to good government in the Middle East while funneling money, for political reasons, to those who fail to practice it. If we are not to be considered hypocrites, we must work harder to identify the moderates (and there are some) who care more about helping their citizens than about enriching themselves. We should also cease to engage in the foolish practice, when discussing Arab political groups, of equating "secular" with "moderate." That is a stereotype and, like most, often inaccurate. To a policymaker, it matters less why a person believes something than what they believe. The case for Arab-Israeli reconciliation can be made at least as strongly in religious terms as in political, and the rhetoric of war is as likely to emerge from the mouth of a nationalist as it is from someone whose only acknowledged loyalty is to God.

The 2006 war ended with the deployment of an expanded UN force to keep peace along the border between Israel and Lebanon. The Security Council also called on the Lebanese government to disarm Hezbollah's militia, which it lacks the power to do. Because of the UN presence, the border may be quiet for a time, perhaps for years, but in the absence of political change, the potential for future, even wider, rounds of fighting is considerable. As always in the Middle East, peace seems defined as the lull between wars.

The modern Jewish state has existed for but a brief moment in the region's history—a mere sixty years. Its legitimacy rests on three pillars; the first, religious (the right of Jews to a state in their historic homeland); the second, moral (the Holocaust); the third, legal (UN recognition).

The majority Arab and Iranian view is that God's promises to Abraham do not justify Israel's claim to Arab or Muslim land. The Quran accords as much a place of honor to Abraham's first son, Isma'il (progenitor of the Arabs), as to his second, Isaac, whose descendants became the tribes of Israel. The Muslim holy book also makes repeated references to the episode of the golden calf, which records a failure of Jews to live up to their covenant with God. As for the Holocaust, Arabs have long pointed out that it was perpetrated by European Christians. Where is the justice, they ask, in displacing Arabs to expiate European atrocities? In their view, Israel gained international recognition as a state only because it was favored by the imperial West. Thus, many Arabs do not accept Israel's moral legitimacy, nor do they agree that a fair way can be found for Israelis and Palestinians to live together.* This is an ever-present risk to Israel, even though most Arab groupings, including the PLO, have said they accept—as a legal and practical matter—Israel's right to exist.

---

* In response to a 2007 survey question, "Can a Way Be Found for Israel and Palestinian Rights to Coexist?" only 16 percent of Palestinians, 17 percent of Jordanians, 18 percent of Egyptians, and 21 percent of Kuwaitis answered "yes."

Although Israel is much stronger now than its neighbors, experience warns that such relationships evolve. One troubling possibility is that Arab states will use the specter of a powerful Iran to justify the acquisition of more advanced arms. Even if the United States is careful about what it sells, others (including Russia, China, and even France) may be less discriminating. Further, the number of Palestinians between the Jordan River and the Mediterranean Sea is rising far more rapidly than the number of Jews. If permanent borders are not established, Israel may find itself overwhelmed.

Should Israelis conclude from past disappointments that the dream of peace is indeed dead, they may try even more vigorously to impose their own terms for coexistence. Benjamin Netanyahu, in one of our early meetings when we were both in office, confided that "Israelis know that, without peace, they may have to fight. But they think they will have to fight anyway and would rather fight a weak Palestinian Authority than a stronger internationally recognized Palestinian state." Though his views may have moderated since then, Netanyahu at the time had wildly unrealistic ideas about the kind of arrangements Palestinians might be made to accept. He saw the peace process itself as a trap, because it led to concessions on land and security that would eat away at Israel's military advantage.

This mode of thinking is dangerous to Israel because it leads to the conclusion that security will come only through repeated demonstrations of military, economic, and diplomatic toughness. The theory seems to be that Palestinians can be intimidated into giving up their political objectives. It's not going to happen. If Israelis abandon their hopes for peace, they will find themselves over time with fewer friends and new enemies. That is not the road they want to be on.

The differences between Arab and Israeli positions may

indeed prove impossible to close, but they can be narrowed, and there is little to be lost in trying to do so. The argument that the peace process has weakened Israel is, in fact, balderdash. Would Israel be safer if it still occupied the Sinai or if a state of war still existed with Jordan? Would it be safer if its troops still patrolled Ramallah or if Palestinians had never been offered a peaceful path to statehood? Would it be less safe if, instead of withdrawing unilaterally from Gaza, it had done so as part of a negotiation for which Palestinian moderates received credit?

UN Security Council Resolution 242, adopted in the wake of Israel's triumph in the 1967 war, calls for all states in the region to live in peace within secure and recognized boundaries and for the withdrawal of Israel from territories occupied in the war. This resolution, initially rejected by Arabs, established the principle of land for peace.

Not surprisingly, Israel has since emphasized the language that mentions secure borders; Arabs have focused on the return of land. Israel argues that withdrawal is required from some, not all, the occupied territories. Arabs say the language demands full withdrawal.

The resolution also affirmed the necessity of arriving at "a just settlement of the refugee problem," without specifying what that might be. Palestinians argue that international law gives them the "right of return" to homes lived in prior to the wars of 1948 and 1967. Israelis deny this claim, which, if accepted, would call into question the legitimacy of their past actions and, if implemented, deprive Jews of majority status within Israel.

The opposing perspectives make it tricky, diplomatically, to confine discussions to the future, where the enumeration of shared interests might win out. The past dictates that Israelis not trust in the goodwill of others and that Arabs fight to re-cover what they feel has been taken from them, just as Saladin did in recovering Jerusalem from the Crusaders.

Israelis fear they will return land for the promise of peace only to find themselves still besieged by resistance and terror. As the psalmist warns, "The words of his mouth were smoother than butter, but war was in his heart."

Palestinians—Fatah and Hamas alike—are reluctant to ac-quiesce in Jewish sovereignty over an acre of what they consider to be Arab land or to sign away the right of families to return to their original homes. Not even the prospect of becoming the Palestinian George Washington could persuade Yasser Arafat to take these steps; he feared instead being seen as a traitor like Judas Iscariot and winding up assassinated like Anwar Sadat.

During the final days of the Clinton administration, Israeli and Palestinian negotiators seemingly came close to an agree-ment on all issues, including the division of Jerusalem, border arrangements, and a redefined right of return. Seeming to come close does not mean success is achievable, only that it is possible to come close.

It goes against my habitual optimism to concede it, but con-siderable imagination is required to envision any Palestinian leader agreeing to a deal that offers less than what Arafat turned down—or to envision any Israeli leader accepting a deal that offers more.

Conceivably, the combination of Palestinian chaos, Israeli anxieties, and Arab frustrations will produce such despera-tion that each side will see the merits in compromise and peace will just happen—with no need for nudging and nagging by the United States. It is equally likely that Arafat will return to Earth as Harry Potter. We have learned in the Middle East that

the weak are too afraid to compromise, and the strong see no
need to do so. On all sides, there is a reluctance to agree on a
final settlement that falls short of historic goals. The absence of
an agreement, however painful at present, still allows every faction to dream of a future in which it prevails. Any formula that
purports to establish permanent borders in the Holy Land and
permanent sovereignty in Jerusalem cannot help but extinguish
such dreams—and how many people in the Middle East have
died so that fantasies might live?

My advice to you is to climb on the merry-go-round from the
beginning of your administration. You may or may not be able
to transform it into a vehicle that goes forward, but bystanders
do not make history, and peace efforts, even when unsuccessful,
can nurture hope and save lives. It is argued by some that Bill
Clinton made a mistake by raising peace expectations too high;
that is nonsense, but in any case hardly the problem now. Your
task is to inspire people in the region to resume thinking about
the possibilities of peace and compare that to the realities they
have experienced these past years.

To begin, there is more than one option. The Arab peace initiative, announced by the Saudis in 2002 and reblessed by the
Arab League in 2007, is neither new nor specific nor particularly
forthcoming. It does, however, promise comprehensive Arab
support for real peace and normal relations with Israel. In exchange, Israel is to return to its pre-1967 borders and resolve
the refugee problem in ways that are unclear. As a proposal, the
plan reflects the Arab starting point, but it is one that isolates
Hamas and creates ample opportunity for face-to-face Arab-
Israeli discussions.

A second possibility—one that could be incorporated in the
first—is to reopen negotiations between Israel and Syria. This

is logical because Syria, unlike the Palestinians, has a functioning national government with whom Israel could negotiate. The issues are simpler because they include neither Jerusalem nor the right of return. An Israel-Syria negotiation would also have the advantage of pushing Iran to the sidelines and bringing Syria closer to its fellow Arabs. This could have beneficial consequences in Lebanon, where Hezbollah's militia would lose its reason for being if peace broke out with Israel. There are, however, two weaknesses in this strategy. First, Syria's government must either be held accountable for Hariri's murder or exonerated—a peace deal is not possible until the case is cleared up. Second, Syria is unlikely to sign an agreement until the Palestinians are also ready to sign, not because Syria cares about the Palestinians but because it cares about Arab public opinion.

Whatever your specific approach, you should emphasize the logic of peace. Arabs and Jews have no choice but to dwell side by side. The choice they do have is whether to live in relative peace or perpetual terror. The general terms of peace became evident in 2000 through Bill Clinton's hard work: a Palestinian state, its capital in Jerusalem, encompassing Gaza and most of the West Bank; a compromise on refugees; the return of all or most of the Golan Heights; and Arab acceptance that the conflict is over and that Israel has a right to exist within secure borders. If formal peace along those lines is not possible soon, the choice remains whether it makes sense at least to strive toward reconciliation. The answer is yes. There are steps short of peace, such as indefinite cease-fires, that can create a measure of trust; and just as the process of praying may yield dividends even if prayers are not immediately answered, so the mere process of talking can lead, over time, in welcome directions. We have, in any case, seen the alternative.

I have one suggestion that may be less crazy than it sounds. Almost every essay or book that writes optimistically about the human condition justifies its faith on the transforming power of education. But education is not doing its job today. We have more schools and better information technology, and yet knowledge is losing ground to ignorance. One reason so many adults become fanatics is that, as children, they are taught a history distorted by parochial obsessions. As they grow up among the like-minded, they have no social incentive to question what they have been taught. On the contrary, those most honored are often those most dogmatic in repeating the shibboleths of cultural faith: The land belongs to us. Force is the only language those people understand. We have suffered, so must they. God is on our side.

Narrowness of thought is common in the Arab world but not only there. East or West, we have a tendency to shop for information that confirms rather than tests our assumptions. We look for rhetorical ammunition far more rigorously than we search for objective truth. The problem is larger than your presidency, and yet I think you should make the case for a more critical approach; the Middle East is the obvious laboratory. If Ahmadinejad can sponsor a seminar on falsehoods about the Holocaust, you could at least cosponsor an open-ended dialogue on the dimensions of truth in the Middle East. By this I do not mean a roundtable discussion with idealistic scholars. I envision a forum sponsored by a partnership of Western, Persian, Arab, and Israeli institutions that would display a range of opinion—uncensored and with ample time for questions and rebuttal—that stretches from Israel's most conservative parties to national and spiritual leaders throughout the region to business and professional stakeholders to representatives of the most radical non-terrorist groups, to you.

Why not take a chance? After all, how many of us have really made a sincere effort to understand opposing views—or even different views—about the Middle East? I mentioned earlier the varied perspectives that Iraqis, Palestinians, Israelis, and others bring to ideas of right and wrong in the region. If there is ever to be less divergence, there must first be a determined effort to weed out obvious untruths, challenge stereotypes, and examine the reasons that people think as they do. We may be impressed by what we hear, or appalled, but at a minimum we will be better informed.

So let's use modern information technology to put hate, incompetence, and bigotry under the spotlight. Let's hear Palestinian leaders discuss the kind of country they would like to create and perhaps explain, as well, what in God's name they think they have been doing, given the billions of dollars of assistance they have already received. Let's enable average Palestinians to learn directly from American, European, and Asian businesspeople about the assistance that would be available to create schools, jobs, hospitals, ports, and airports in Gaza as well as the West Bank—once the peace process is back on track and a responsible government is in place. Let's hear the families of those killed by terrorism and other forms of violence give their ideas about how the strife can be stopped. Let's break down the issues so that everyone understands that Israel can't achieve lasting security by killing, jailing, and fencing off its enemies and that Palestinians can't create a viable life for themselves through terrorism—because Palestinians don't give up and Israelis don't scare. Most of all, let us hear from those on all sides who are fed up, and who still believe there is a better way.

Ghazi Hamad, who serves as a spokesman for Hamas, has in the past been imprisoned for his activities both by Israel and the

Palestinian Authority. No friend of the Jewish state, he never-theless says that Palestinians, in assigning blame for their suf-fering, should look beyond Israel to themselves. He has asked why some of his colleagues insist on violating cease-fires and on shelling Israel for no purpose except to provoke counterattacks that kill civilians. He has pointed out that the Palestinians who celebrated Israel's withdrawal from Gaza have squandered the opportunity: "We've all been attacked by the bacteria of stupid-ity. . . . When you walk in the streets of Gaza City, you cannot but close your eyes because of what you see there: unimaginable chaos, careless policemen, young men carrying guns and strut-ting with pride, and families receiving condolences for their dead in the middle of the street." Wrote Hamad, "I do not deny that the occupation committed massacres that cannot be justi-fied. But I support negotiations over what can be fixed."

Consider, as well, the words of David Grossman, an award-winning Israeli author whose twenty-year-old son Uri was killed by an antitank missile during the war with Lebanon:

> The overwhelming majority of Israeli citizens already
> understand—some, admittedly, unenthusiastically so—what
> the solution to the conflict will look like. Most of us under-
> stand, therefore, that the land will be partitioned, that a Pal-
> estinian state will be established. Why, that being the case . . .
> does the political leadership continue to reflect the positions
> of the extremists and not of the majority of the public?
> After all, our situation will be far better if we reach that
> national agreement on our own, before circumstances—
> external pressure, or a new *intifada*, or another war—force
> us to. If we do that, we will spare ourselves years of blood-
> shed and waste. Years of a terrible mistake.

This, then, is the message you should deliver over and over again from the White House: no solution can come to the Middle East without modifying at least some dreams; no force in the world can stop every determined terrorist; but conquest is not the only kind of dream, and determination is not the monopoly of terrorists. Ultimately, violence is a choice, and what people have the power to choose, they have the power to change.

CHAPTER 14

Isolating Al Qaeda

Early each morning for the next four years, the director of National Intelligence (DNI) will enter your office, a document in hand. He will offer you a choice: to read or to listen. Whichever, the news will be unsettling. An informant "of unknown credibility" has come forward, asking for cash, claiming to know of a conspiracy to blow up commercial airliners over the Pacific. A more trusted source reports that an Al Qaeda cell, probably in South Asia, may be planning a spectacular strike in Europe, the United States, or perhaps Africa, sometime in the next three years. U.S. embassies in five countries have received threats signed by five different organizations, none of which—according to the CIA—exists. A longtime prisoner in Pakistan has finally talked, revealing the exact whereabouts of Osama bin Laden . . . on a Monday at 2:00 P.M. four years ago. There are reports that Al Qaeda may have obtained or built chemical weapons, but it could be just a rumor or idle boast. A new Middle East website has been created, dedicated to killing you; it disappeared last night, leaving no information about who put it up. The briefing over, the DNI rises from his seat, smiles slightly, and wishes you good morning. You feel like throwing a brick.

Our intelligence professionals—having been put through the wringer by a bookshelf's worth of 9/11 investigations—now assume that anything they tell the president could end up on the news. This doesn't give them an incentive to be more discriminating in deciding what information to share with you, but simply to shovel along more. Wary of being blamed for understating a danger or ruling out a possibility, they will give you much data about which to worry, but rarely the specific, timely intelligence on which you can act. Despite heroic efforts, they have not pinpointed precisely enough the location of the remaining Al Qaeda leaders, nor do they know for sure how the top terrorists communicate. You will thus be kept constantly on edge, not certain how to prevent a tragedy but knowing that you will be held responsible by the public—and by your own conscience—if the worst happens.

Your predecessor received—and deserved—much criticism. Since the Twin Towers and Pentagon attacks, however, we have not suffered a significant terrorism-related catastrophe on U.S. soil—an impressive achievement. If this record is sustained through Inauguration Day, it will figure prominently among the positive elements of Mr. Bush's legacy. This record also reflects well on the patriotism of the American Muslim community and the diligence of foot soldiers from the intelligence, law enforcement, diplomatic, and homeland defense bureaucracies who have labored to keep us safe.

The responsibility for protecting our people against terrorist attacks will—from the moment you utter "So help me God"—be yours. One handicap you may face is complacency. There are some among us who believe the whole concept of a global confrontation with terror was concocted by Karl Rove to scare voters into supporting his boss. They expect the hullabaloo over terrorism to diminish, and perhaps even to vanish, as soon as the current president begins to pack his bags. We wish. Al Qaeda has exploited the administration's mistakes, but when that group first came together, George W. Bush was running a baseball team. The passions that give life to Al Qaeda were not created by neoconservative Republicans; yet keeping those passions burning is Al Qaeda's urgent need. I worry that our enemies will try, in the initial days of your presidency, to show that they are still relevant and that the fight is still on.

In the early campaign debates, you were asked about your plan to defeat Al Qaeda. You were unsure at first how to wedge all your ideas into the forty-five seconds allotted. You found your stride when you settled on a three-part mantra: "defend the homeland, take the fight to the enemy, and win the battle of ideas." Now the time has come to match actions to words.

Perfect homeland defense is not possible, but imperfect security is better than none. Every attack that is stopped before it can hurt or kill is priceless. You have already prepared measures to increase inspections of container ships, chemical plants, civilian airfields, and medical research facilities. Now you will have to go to Congress in search of the money to pay for these initiatives. Sadly, since 9/11, we have treated homeland defense as just another brand of political pork. Counterterrorism funds are dispersed according to a political formula, scattering dollars to communities in every state—so that security is often tighter at small city airports than at major hubs. We have also established a list of potential terrorist targets that includes a petting zoo, a popcorn factory, a flea market, and an annual parade of mules.

Homeland defense money, whether properly distributed or not, can't defeat Al Qaeda and its allies, nor can our military. Both can slow them, however, and the military can and should cause pain. It can do so by destroying terrorist cells and barring the creation of safe havens where terrorists operate and prepare. Though heavily damaged in the months following 9/11, Al Qaeda has, as we have seen, reestablished itself along the border between Afghanistan and Pakistan. Harnessing outrage caused by the Iraq war, and using the Internet to spread its message, Al Qaeda has organized a loose network of like-minded units. Self-starting imitators could come together almost anywhere, including Europe and the United States. Somalia, parts of North Africa, and the Sunni-dominated regions of Iraq are places where safe havens are most likely to grow.

Al Qaeda has prospered because of its ability to portray itself as a defender of Islam against imperial crusaders and unrepresentative Arab governments. Its limited offensive capabilities are magnified by the willingness of recruits to die and by the ubiquity of potential targets. Tactically, the network is not burdened by the need to conquer or hold territory. It is energized by its own legend—the ability to survive despite years of pressure from the world's mightiest military—and by a propaganda machine that knows how to reach its audience.

Terrorists also benefit from the Iraq war's adverse impact on the coercive power of the U.S. military. Though potential adversaries do not doubt our ability to inflict damage, they have learned to turn our might against us by photographing the destruction and transmitting the resulting images—especially when civilians are among the victims—to the whole wired world. This political tactic, when coupled with suicide attacks, sabotage, and hostage-taking, may not win conventional battles, but it can severely complicate our ability to claim victory in what our defense planners have begun calling the "long war."

That is why the third element in your program, the battle of ideas, should be your centerpiece. If Al Qaeda is exposed and isolated, it will cease to grow. That would reduce the demands on our military and make homeland defense more manageable.

After 9/11, President Bush's message to every country was that "you are either with us or against us." This message would have proven apt if the president's definition of the enemy had remained constant. Uniting most of the world against those who blow up innocent people should have been simple. It was unwise, then, for the president to blur the issue by allowing our focus on Al Qaeda to shift. Soon we were asking far more of people than to stand with us against bin Laden; we were asking them to overlook Abu Ghraib, accept Guantánamo, and endorse both the invasion of Iraq and our view of the Middle East. Simultaneously, Al Qaeda was offering the world its own choice—between suffering Muslims and a bellicose America. This left many people in a quandary. They didn't want to endorse the tactics of Al Qaeda, but they didn't want to stand too close to us either. We had turned allies into spectators.

Religious war, martyrdom, and terror have been part of humanity's lot throughout history. The philosophy that animates Al Qaeda, however, developed over the past half century. It may advertise itself as a return to true Islam, but it is in fact a radical departure from it. Though hostile to the West, it has directed its primary fury at political leaders within the Arab world: Egypt's Nasser and Sadat, Syria's Assad, and the Saudi royal family. Its purpose is to instigate a religious war in which it is seen as the true defender of Islam. It strikes at the West in part to provoke us into lashing out awkwardly and with more might than intellect, so that new "martyrs" are created and new "evidence" generated that Islam is under siege. It gambles that, for every terrorist killed, many others will volunteer, seeking vengeance for freshly shed blood. This is how terror multiplies: when every action we take causes the problem to become worse. This is the arithmetical progression we must stop.

We will not succeed in that by appeasement—backing away from our commitments to Israel, for example, or by suggesting that terrorism can be justified. The idea that America and the West are to blame for terrorism doesn't hold up. Our policies can make a difference, however, by making it easier or harder for terrorists to find new recruits. Terrorism does not, like Darwin's ape, evolve naturally; it is created from the soft clay of circumstances and events.

Al Qaeda gains whenever America acts in ways that can be portrayed as aggressive toward Islam or Muslims. It follows that Al Qaeda will lose if we refrain from such actions. That will not always be possible—because we have to defend ourselves, because much of the world has been conditioned to misinterpret what we do, and because Al Qaeda performs best in the role of accuser. As president, you will likely be appalled at the degree to which your good intentions are distorted. Be patient. Perceptions will change if your policies and words show that you are listening to others.

One of your toughest jobs will be to undo the confusion

President Bush has created about whom and what we are fighting. His administration has tended to treat every angry group of Muslims as part of the same terrorist threat—alike in their beliefs, equally in the wrong, all a danger to us. This may fit well with his conception of a black-and-white world, but the policies of the globe's most powerful nation cannot be based on a fiction. For years, he has acted as if the entire unwholesome crew—Al Qaeda, the Taliban, the followers of Saddam Hussein, the mullahs in Iran, and Hezbollah and Hamas—were coconspirators. It's not so; in many cases, these groups are mortal enemies, with incompatible religious beliefs and clashing interests. In his rush to divide the world into "us" and "them," the president failed to take advantage of the fact that "they" include factions that can be turned against each other. Instead of treating them as one, we should have been doing all we could to keep them at odds.

The president is not, of course, the only one who has been confused. Seven years after 9/11, Americans generally don't agree on what to call the enemy or even on the nature of the struggle in which we are engaged. When I was in government, I was advised by our counterterrorism experts not to cite bin Laden by name, or to link Al Qaeda to Islam, or to refer to our confrontation with terrorists as a war—though "struggle," "fight," and "battle" were deemed acceptable. The idea was that we should avoid playing into bin Laden's hands by building him up as our great enemy, and that we should not give terrorists the satisfaction of being compared to soldiers fighting a war.

I have since been intrigued by President Bush's approach as he has alternately referred to bin Laden as public enemy number one and, at other times, dismissed his importance and gone months without mentioning him. In July 2005, the Defense Department decided that the idea of a "global war" had outlived its usefulness and that we were actually engaged in a "global struggle against violent extremism." At the time, the chairman of the Joint Chiefs of Staff explained that "if you call it a war, then you think of people in uniform as being the solution." The media spent several days analyzing this sophisticated evolution in the administration's thinking—only to have the White House overrule the military and declare that what we were doing was, indeed, fighting a war. The whole episode was a classic case of expertise versus politics—with politics winning.

It is worth remembering that America has had limited success when declaring war against nouns—such as terror, poverty, drugs, disease, or inflation. We use such formulations as a means of mobilizing support, not to be taken literally. If we are serious about defeating Al Qaeda, we must be more precise.

As president, you should be clear that our enemy is neither Islam nor any subset of that faith. We are not endangered by people who merely disagree with us about world politics nor by people who are fighting in their own country for national or sectarian goals. We may not see eye to eye with men who treat women differently than we do in the West, but that does not make them our enemy. The adversaries we must fight are the people who actually attacked us on 9/11 or who have since become active allies of those who attacked us. Our enemy—and you should stress this at every opportunity—is not Islamic terrorism, for terrorism is inherently un-Islamic; our enemy is Islam's enemy, too.

This distinction is important because Al Qaeda has no appeal when separated from its connection to issues that Muslims care about, such as the Palestinian cause, human rights, freedom of political expression, social justice, and respect for their religion— all of which can be pursued far more effectively, and with far less hypocrisy, by opponents of Al Qaeda than by supporters.

Fanatics often hurt themselves by going too far; Al Qaeda has done so repeatedly. Though its goal is to mobilize Muslims, it has condemned almost everyone in a position of authority in the Muslim world, including the governments of Pakistan, Saudi Arabia, Egypt, Iraq, Syria, Iran, and even Hezbollah and Hamas. Al Qaeda has carried out numerous attacks resulting in the death of unarmed Muslim civilians—crimes explicitly prohibited in the Quran and repulsive even to Muslims who fully share Al Qaeda's conservative social views and resentment toward the West. Al Qaeda also lacks an intelligible economic or political agenda. This is in contrast to other militant Islamic groups that provide social services and have joined or tried to join the political process of their respective countries. Bin Laden is admired by some for his brazen assault on the powers that be, but that doesn't mean that many people want to have him running their lives. The bottom line is that we are idiots if we fail to win the public relations war—and ultimately the real war (or struggle, battle, or fight)—against a bunch of murderers whose only tangible promise to supporters is posthumous recognition on a website.

It follows that the smart way to challenge Al Qaeda is to do what President Bush has failed to do consistently enough, and that is to attack the network relentlessly at its most vulnerable point. The 9/11 murders were denounced by every recognized government of a Muslim-majority state, including Iran and also Hezbollah and the PLO. So what is our message? Al Qaeda doesn't defend Muslims; Al Qaeda murders Muslims. It doesn't stand for Islam; it perverts Islam. It desires not to free Muslims from injustice; it desires to imprison Muslims within its own fascist and unorthodox conception of God's will. President Bush has tried to arouse opposition to Al Qaeda based on its expressed desire to re-create a universal Islamic caliphate, but that is not Al Qaeda's weakest point. Al Qaeda's inborn defect is that its means are heretical and its vision so narrow that it would exclude most Muslims, not to mention the rest of us. Al Qaeda isn't offering the world a caliphate; it's offering Hell.

Your job is to re-create a framework for stability in the greater Middle East. The task is pressing but cannot be done quickly, because the foundations are so weak. You will be urged by pundits to apply various simplistic formulas—a temptation you should resist. It is an illusion to believe that the Middle East can be divided neatly into moderates and extremists, with the former representing good and the latter evil. There are more sides to this game than that, and everyone's uniform, including ours, is smudged.

I wrote earlier that military solutions in the region are unrealistic, but it still seems that everyone is preparing to fight. That is why the status quo is unacceptable; the thermostat is set too high. If we allow seventh-century disputes to be settled with twenty-first-century weapons, we will not long survive.

You will begin Middle East diplomacy from a disadvantaged position, with America poorly placed to talk about such basic pillars of security as law, truth-telling, and human rights. You face an emboldened Iran, an increased terrorist threat, and a multiplication of divisions—inside Iraq, among the Palestinians, within Israel, and between Shiite and Sunni Muslims. Because the United States has been either preoccupied or wrong-footed through most of the past eight years, you may find that the chair at the head of the diplomatic table, long reserved for the United States, has been moved. You may also find that the meeting room you have reserved is half empty because the Iranians, Russians, Europeans, Saudis, and Egyptians have all organized their own gatherings at the same time. Don't be put off. We need not fear the efforts of others.

Whoever seizes the reins, the reality will be the same. No one is in a position to dictate the future of the Middle East. Power is too diffuse. The choice, then, is between confrontation and compromise, but people are too stubborn to compromise unless they first accept that they have no alternative. Your contribution will be to ease the principal countries and factions toward that understanding. In so doing, you must recognize that the United States, too, will have to settle for less than it would like. Politically, this will be hazardous for you, but it will be even riskier for Israeli, Arab, Iranian, and other leaders should they back away from maximum goals. Much will depend, therefore, not only on how events unfold but also on how they are presented. Honor, face, and respect are important in every region, but nowhere more so than in the Middle East. As president, your task will be to design agreements sufficiently ambiguous to let most sides claim victory and sufficiently substantive to move toward stability. This may mean living with imperfect solutions and partial justice and putting off some issues for another day.

President Bush conjured up an image of the Middle East as a democratic wonderland where evil had been vanquished and Arabs and Jews alike trooped to the polls with light hearts and empty holsters. I cheer the image but do not expect to witness the reality. In the short term, the Middle East will be molded primarily by power politics set against the backdrop of national interests, ethnic intolerance, and religious ferment. In this environment, the watchword that matters most will not be "freedom" in the sense of democracy, but "freedom" in the sense of independence—the rights of nations and peoples. For diplomatic purposes, the principle that will carry the greatest weight is that old warhorse, sovereignty.

The concept of sovereignty has long served as a basis for international law. Because of globalization, and because sovereignty has so often been abused, the concept is not as strong a foundation for stability as it used to be. It can also be interpreted to mean sectarian sovereignty—the right of a subnational group to be autonomous within its region. It remains, however, a more universally accepted principle than any other.

What does respect for sovereignty mean in today's Middle East?

To Israelis, it means being secure within their borders. To the Palestinians, it means having borders that reflect their historic claims. To the Lebanese, it means protection from Syrian meddling and from Israeli bombardments, especially in major population centers. To the United States, it means an Iran that doesn't send arms to Hezbollah or Hamas, stir up trouble in Iraq, or threaten its neighbors by building nuclear weapons. To Iran, it means a United States that doesn't invade countries in the region, try to dictate nuclear policy, or conspire with Iranian dissidents inside or outside the country. To the Iraqi Kurds, it means the right to live free from threats by Turkey. To Turkey, it means the right to be protected from Kurdish terrorists based in Iraq. To every country, it means protection from the likes of Al Qaeda.

Though these differing perspectives may seem dizzying, they carry within them the glimmerings of opportunity. If respect for sovereignty is the accepted starting point, virtually every party in the region has something it wants and also something it could give up to meet the demands of another. Almost invariably, perceived breaches of sovereignty stem from actions taken under cover of self-defense. In a logical world, both the breaches and the defensive actions could be stopped because each derives from the other. The world is not logical; but a diplomat could do worse than begin with logic as a starting point for discussion.

Consider, for example, the logic of a Middle East four years from now that, in part because of your efforts, looks something like this:

A federalized Iraq, with a figurehead national government and robust regional ones, is limping along. The Iraqi army is similarly divided, with a small central force in Baghdad and three regional components that have absorbed former militias. Oil production is up, with revenues being shared equitably. Despite occasional outbreaks of fighting, most of Iraq is peaceful because Al Qaeda–style groups have passed from fashion and the country's neighbors are working to maintain calm. In Baghdad, regular meetings are held of the diplomatic contact group, which includes representatives from Iraq, Iran, Syria, Jordan, Russia, Saudi Arabia, Turkey, the United States, and the European Union.

Iran, free from UN sanctions, has reiterated its pledge not to build nuclear weapons but continues to enrich a small amount of uranium for use in civilian nuclear power plants, subject to IAEA inspection. It has close relations with the Shiite-dominated parts of Iraq but has not fueled sectarian violence, in part because Iran's Revolutionary Guard has been reined in. While maintaining its ties to Hezbollah, Tehran has reduced arms shipments and not attempted to destabilize Lebanon's still-fragile government, in which Hezbollah remains a troublemaking participant. President Ahmadinejad failed in his bid for reelection because his flawed economic program left voters feeling let down. Iran's leaders—now a pragmatic combination of kleptocrats and theocrats—still call America the Great Satan, but less often.

The Palestinians have a national unity government made up of breakaway elements of Hamas and a new generation of Fatah reformers, some recently released from Israeli jails. After a yearlong campaign of nonviolent resistance, patterned on the teachings of Gandhi and Martin Luther King, Jr., the Palestinians are on the threshold of achieving what decades of terrorism could not: the establishment of an internationally recognized Palestinian state. Negotiations with a more hopeful Israel are ongoing, with both sides seemingly determined to heed Yitzhak Rabin's advice: pursue peace as if there were no terror and fight terror as if there were no negotiations.

A former Syrian intelligence officer has confessed to the murder of Lebanese prime minister Hariri, swearing that he acted entirely on his own. He was found guilty by an international court and sentenced to life in prison. His family, suddenly wealthy, moved to France. The way now clear for talks, Syria and Israel have begun negotiations on the exchange of land for peace, with the understanding that a final agreement is contingent on a settlement also being reached between Israel and the Palestinians. A UN force continues to patrol the Israel-Lebanon border.

Meanwhile, throughout the Arab world, leaders have shifted from a willingness to appease socially regressive and politically rabid clerics to demanding that they either quiet down or get out. Intellectually, a competition is under way to claim rightful ownership of the past. Mainstream leaders from Egypt to Qatar to Qom refer pointedly to the fact that a millennium ago, Islamic culture was the world's most advanced. This golden age, they argue, was characterized by a thirst for knowledge about the whole of God's creation—history, medicine, science, mathematics, astronomy, literature—a quest that is the opposite of bin Ladenism. When terrorists strike in the name of Muhammad, these leaders cite clerical authorities to denounce the terrorists not merely as murderers but as blasphemers and nonbelievers.

This trend is still spotty and remains short of a consensus. Some leaders talk boldly of modernization; others walk on eggshells. Young people are still assaulted by the summons to war, even as they look to find their place in the global economy. The difference between 2012 and let us say, 2004, is direction. Reformers are looking around and beginning to see how many of each other there are. The trend is worldwide, embracing Muslims on every continent, with Indonesia, the world's largest Muslim-majority nation, being especially vocal. The idea has taken hold that forward-thinking is not a betrayal of Islamic doctrine but a return to it. Moreover, the growth of independent media has done much to expose the perverted vanity of the holy warrior mentality. Bad theology is losing ground to the only force that can defeat it: good theology. The Muslim majority is reclaiming its religion from those who tried to steal it.

With a regional peace process under way, America's military presence in the region sharply reduced, Arab reform efforts advancing, and many militant Islamic groups rejecting violence in order to organize politically, Al Qaeda has begun to wither. Just as military action by America and Israel has generated a backlash, so Al Qaeda's attacks in Saudi Arabia, Jordan, Pakistan, Syria, and Egypt have robbed the terrorist organization of its own moral pretensions. The once-impenetrable network has been damaged by a virtual flood of ex-trainees who have agreed to exchange information for immunity. Algeria's most notorious terrorist group, the GSPC, which had changed its name to Al

Qaeda of the Islamic Maghreb on the fifth anniversary of 9/11, has since changed it back. Al Jazeera's decision not to broadcast bin Laden's most recent recorded message because it was "not newsworthy" was, in itself, barely mentioned in the news. Al Qaeda is not dead, and terrorism is very much alive, but the tide has turned—Americans are a bit safer and so is everybody else.

Finally, the enemies of the United States are having a much harder time making their case. Our government is in full compliance with the Geneva Accords; the Guantánamo detention facility has closed; an American special envoy is working full-time for Middle East peace; the Senate has ratified a nuclear test ban; the Pentagon has canceled plans to develop a new generation of nuclear arms; our alliances are reinvigorated; we have taken the lead in addressing global problems on the environment, energy, epidemic disease, and poverty; and the president of the United States, a little tired but popular and respected, seems headed for reelection by a landslide.

PART THREE

CHAPTER 15

Above the Thundering Abyss

The most overused device in American political oratory—and memo-writing—is to suggest that our nation has reached a crossroads and that the next president will face decisions more fateful than any since Valley Forge, Gettysburg, or D-day. It is in our nature to dramatize the present and to purport to see, peering into the future like Frost's traveler in the wood, a choice between two distinct paths. In truth, our times are not so unique and our choices not so distinct. Instead of hiking down a narrow trail, you will find yourself, as have previous presidents, traversing a road with multiple intersections, many of which are poorly marked, and consulting a map seemingly drawn for a much earlier day.

As to direction, you will be hard pressed to define and remain true to a single destination. This is despite the fact that many prominent political and academic figures have attempted to articulate America's twenty-first-century mission. Some have compiled lists of new programs and institutions the United States should propose—such as a reformed UN, a global NATO, a new Marshall Plan, revamped international financial institutions, and a reoriented Radio Free Europe. These attempts to prepare for the future are laudable and may prove helpful to you, but they are, in an odd way, also attempts to recapture the past.

Virtually without fail, when Americans prescribe an architecture for the twenty-first century, we hearken back to the middle portion of the century just gone by. We yearn to restore the world as it was when America was riding its highest—having won the war, demonstrated unparalleled economic and military prowess, and commenced building new institutions to promote prosperity and preserve peace.

It is understandable why such a memory might appeal to us; it should be equally evident why it does not appeal to anyone else. If we went back to 1947, we would see a Japan and Germany under occupation, West Europe in ruins, East Europe dominated by the Soviet Union, China in the midst of civil war, and most of Africa, much of Asia, and many Arabs still chafing under colonial rule. We might wish to return to the era of Truman and Eisenhower; the world has other dreams.

The reason we admire America's postwar generation is precisely because its leaders were not nostalgic; unlike the inward- and backward-looking men who guided our country after World War I, they acknowledged that the globe had changed and that these changes should be reflected in the policies of our country. They did not try to re-create an America that had begun to fade, nor did they expect others to stand still. They knew that their way of life had been transformed by the destruction of war, the shock of Holocaust, the birth of the nuclear era, the rising specter of communism, and the spread of contagious ideas about independence and freedom. They saw that the old order had to give way to something new. But did they have a clear sense of where they were headed? Absolutely not.

According to Dean Acheson, this was a period of great obscurity to those who lived through it:

> Not only was the future clouded, a common enough situation, but the present was equally clouded. We all had far more than the familiar difficulty of determining the capabilities and intentions of those who inhabit this planet with us. The significance of events was shrouded in ambiguity. We groped after interpretations of them, sometimes reversed lines of action based on earlier views, and hesitated long before grasping what now seems obvious.

Truman is remembered fondly not because he had a particular gift for envisioning the future but because he brought certain valuable traits to his job as chief executive, qualities that most good presidents have possessed in varying degrees: optimism, resilience, a capacity to adjust to new information, a willingness to accept responsibility, wisdom in judging people, the patience to listen, and the ability to inspire cooperation among Americans and between our country and the world.

Many of the challenges you will face as president cannot be prepared for by launching new institutions or by deciding in advance to allocate more dollars to one cause or another. Catastrophes, whether caused by humans or by nature, will surely occur, but where and when? The measure of your presidency will be found in how well you and your team prepare for the unexpected, how patient you are, and whether you keep learning while in office.

I mentioned earlier that the desire to match the celebrity of

Henry Kissinger has been the bane of some national security advisors; the yearning of a president to get his face on a mountainside or the ten-dollar bill can be equally damaging. It was said of FDR that although he was supremely self-confident, he never "felt himself heaven-sent to accomplish a divine mission. He simply felt that he had been given a 'grand opportunity' to do something about the problems that beset the nation."

It is a truism that no one comes to the presidency fully qualified. You may not want to hear it, but your victories are less likely to be final than fleeting and more likely to be incremental than spectacular. You may be thought by some to be endowed with superhuman powers, but your miracles, if any, will be of the type that grow from organic sources. In this sense, a president can be compared to a gardener, nurturing and watering, trimming and weeding, fighting off pests, doing a thousand tiny chores with a larger goal in mind. You can observe, guide, and make inventive use of the gardener's tools, but you cannot create something that is not already there.

You will assume power at a moment when America has lost influence while others have gained it. For the first time in history, our leadership is needed in the world but in many places not wanted. Any efforts you might make to lay out a plan for organizing the globe will meet resistance—and understandably so. Given the events of the past eight years, we can hardly dictate to others what they should think, feel, and fear; we should suppress our impulse to scold; your first responsibility is closer to home—to heed what we do and stand for, and what norms we set for ourselves.

Democracy's inherent advantage is its capacity to correct its own failings. Unless democratic processes are short-circuited, voters, legislators, the media, and the courts have a way of leaning in the opposite direction when the executive goes too far. This counterbalancing can also go too far, but with time, good sense, and kind fortune, it usually settles in the right place.

If you are to fulfill your promise to refurbish America's reputation, you would do well to begin with an elementary proposition: success comes from uniting friends and dividing enemies. That goal requires continual consultation with our historic partners, respect for rising powers, a sense of how to approach unfamiliar cultures, precision in identifying both who we are against and what we are for, and a determination to join with others in addressing global problems. Like JFK, you will need to master the art of reaching audiences of every description, exhibiting sympathy without pandering, showing the way forward, and inviting listeners to come along. While never beating your chest, you must still recognize that our role in global affairs is a dynamic one; we will not be respected if we are always holding doors and saying, "after you." Leadership, though, need not be overbearing or shrill; better to be quietly persuasive, firmly in the right, and fair.

As president, I urge you to have confidence so that you may give us confidence. We do not doubt that fear has its place. Prior to World War II, the world did not fear Hitler enough. In our time, the dangers of terrorism, genocide, proliferation, desperation, pollution, and disease are real, and they demand our vigilance. Al Qaeda and its offshoots warrant the most scrutiny, because when people say they want to kill us, we would be fools not to take them at their word. Still, we have had an overdose of fear in recent years. We have been told to be afraid so that we might be less protective of the Constitution, less mindful of international law, less respectful toward allies, less discerning in our search for facts, and less rigorous in questioning what our leaders tell us; all this to avoid being accused of aiding our enemies. That is not what Franklin Roosevelt had to say about fear.

I hope that when you stand for the first time behind the presidential seal, you will have uppermost in mind the need to restore our faith in each other. Speak to us as adults—share with us your thinking, tell us your doubts, make it easier for us to see how one action leads to others. Beyond that, let us know what we can do to help. Challenge us. We aren't afraid of the truth, and we are more willing to make sacrifices than we ordinarily let on. We don't think it fair to have soldiers die while nothing more is asked of us than to stand in line at the airport. We don't believe we were put on Earth just to drive SUVs, putt, watch TV, and eat Happy Meals. We want to be proud of our country and would like to do our part.

Remember the theme associated with Peter the Great? "Fear not change; strive that tomorrow be better than today." This banal instinct for self-improvement is at the root of all human gains. It is banal because it has been translated into everything from the language of Weight Watchers to the pep talks given to Boy Scouts, but in a world held hostage by the cycles of nature, nothing is more revolutionary than the idea that we have it within our power as humans to lift lives in ways that matter, that our power to choose has meaning. That is the conviction that brought the *Susan Constant, Godspeed,* and *Discovery* to Jamestown in 1607; it is the promise that was tested at Bunker Hill in 1775; and it is the faith that brought Americans of every description to polling places from Key West to Ashtabula and Anchorage to vote for you this very Election Day morning.

The language of liberty has taken a beating in recent years.

American leaders have exalted themselves, equating their own work with God's plan, yielding catastrophic results. Perhaps you will help us to find again the right balance. Perhaps you can remind us that military action cannot advance the cause of freedom unless minds have already been changed to acknowledge that one person's dignity is dependent on every other. Remind us as well that America does not have a calling, sacred or otherwise, to extend democracy across the globe, but that we do have an obligation to safeguard our own democratic system and to extend a hand to those who seek our help in building the brand of democracy that digs deep and lasts. In 1861, speaking in Philadelphia on the occasion of George Washington's birthday, Abraham Lincoln said that the Declaration of Independence did more than bestow liberty on America; it gave hope to the world "that in due time the weights should be lifted from the shoulders of all men and that all should have an equal chance." Rather than surrender that principle, said Lincoln, he would choose to be assassinated on the spot.

Our sixteenth and greatest president did not suffer from lack of advice. Since he was thought by so many to be unfit for the office, he was lectured at—in print, at public meetings, even ridiculed to his face. Everyone, it seemed, knew better than he how to win the war, reunite the nation, and handle the question of slavery. The story is told that after one especially condescending harangue, delivered with fault-finding zeal by a delegation of New England clergymen, Lincoln asked quietly: "Gentlemen, do you remember that a few years ago a man named Blondin walked across a tightrope stretched over the falls of Niagara?" The men nodded their heads, so Lincoln continued:

Suppose that all the material values in this great country
of ours, from the Atlantic to the Pacific—its wealth, its
prosperity, its achievements in the present and its hopes
for the future—could all have been concentrated and
given to Blondin to carry over that awful crossing and that
their preservation should have depended on his ability to
somehow get them across to the other side—and suppose
that everything you yourself held dearest in the world, the
safety of your family, and the security of your home, also
depended upon his crossing?

And suppose you had been on the shore when he was
going over, as he was carefully feeling his way along
and balancing his pole with all his skill, proceeding with
slow, cautious steady steps over the thundering abyss.
What would you have done? Would you have begun to
shake the cable and shout at him, "Blondin! stand up a
little straighter! Blondin! stoop a little more; go a little
faster; lean more to the south! Now lean a little more
to the north!" Or would you have stood there speech-
less and held your breath and prayed to the Almighty to
guide and help him safely through the trial?

We all need reminding of what you among all others will soon
so clearly understand: the president carries not only the hopes of
party leaders for political advantage, and not only his own personal aspirations for lasting glory, but also the hopes of an entire
nation and of many beyond our borders as well. During the
next four years, you will be required to bear your burden and
maintain your balance while being shoved at ceaselessly from
every direction. What is more, you will be expected not only to

reach the far side safely but also to choose the right jumping-off point among many possibilities, some seemingly secure but with ground that crumbles the moment weight is applied.

So, God bless you, Mr. President, and keep you, and guide you, and help you. Know that I will be praying for you each day to stand a little straighter, go a little faster, lean a little more to the center . . . and bring us all safely home.

Notes

ONE: A MANDATE TO LEAD

12   *"splendid misery"* Thomas Jefferson, quoted in *The American President*, Philip K. Kunhardt, Jr., Philip B. Kunhardt III, and Peter W. Kunhardt, New York: Riverhead Books, 1999, 270.

12   *"the personal embodiment"* William H. Taft, quoted in *The American Presidency*, Clinton Rossiter, New York: New American Library, 1956, 14.

13   *"a remarkable time"* Republican Party platform, Republican National Convention, Philadelphia, Pa., July 31, 2000.

13   *"We will need to work well together"* Colin Powell, testimony before the Committee on Foreign Relations, United States Senate, Washington, D.C., January 17, 2001.

14   *"the last best hope"* Abraham Lincoln, annual message to Congress, Washington, D.C., December 1, 1862.

14   *"provokes more conflicts"* World poll, British Broadcasting Corporation, "World View of US Role Goes from Bad to Worse," January 23, 2007.

15   *"Our national consciousness"* George F. Kennan, *American Diplomacy 1900–1950*, Chicago: Mentor Book, New American Library, University of Chicago Press, 1951, 9.

15   *"We are living in an age of disorder,"* Walter Lippmann, *Essential*

Lippmann: A Political Philosophy for Liberal Democracy, Clinton Rossiter and James Lare (eds.), Cambridge, Mass.: Harvard University Press, 1982, 30–31.

16   *"Only the most stubborn and obtuse"* John H. Hallowell, *Main Currents in Modern Political Thought*, New York: Henry Holt and Company, 1953, 618, 622.

16   *"The superiority of our way of life"* Hans J. Morgenthau, *The Purpose of American Politics*, New York: Alfred A. Knopf, 1960, 326.

17   *"pay any price"* John F. Kennedy, inaugural address, Washington, D.C., January 20, 1961.

17   *"to those old allies"* Ibid.

18   *"genuine peace"* John F. Kennedy, American University, Washington, D.C., June 10, 1963.

18   *"the man who accompanied"* John F. Kennedy, quoted in "State Visits Abroad," selections from John F. Kennedy Library and Museum, www.fieldmuseum.org.

18   *"to lift your eyes"* John F. Kennedy, remarks in the Rudolph Wilde Platz, Berlin, Germany, June 26, 1963.

23   *"mind its own business internationally"* Pew Research Center, Washington, D.C., statement released February 3, 2006.

24   *The same polls that show a decline in our popularity* Pew Global Attitudes Project, "Global Unease with Major World Powers," Pew Research Center, Washington, D.C., June 27, 2007.

TWO: WHAT KIND OF PRESIDENT?

27   *"A president knows"* Theodore Sorensen, quoted in *Bureaucratic Politics and Foreign Policy*, Morton Halperin, Washington, D.C.: Brookings Institution, 1974, 82.

27   *you will one day be described by your biographer* Reference to biography of Washington by Mason Locke Weems, cited by Paul F. Boller, Jr., *Presidential Anecdotes*, New York: Oxford University Press, 1996, 3.

29   *"He kept us out of war"* Woodrow Wilson, 1916 Presidential Campaign Slogans, CB Presidential Research Services, www.presidentsusa.net/1916slogan.html.

29   *"Your boys are not going to be sent"* Franklin Roosevelt, cited in "The Foreign Policy of Franklin Roosevelt to the Entry Into World War II,

by Henry J. Brajkovic, Yale-New Haven Teacher's Institute, www.yale.edu/ynhti/curriculum/units/1978/3/78.03.05.x.html.

29   *"We are not about to send American boys"* Lyndon Johnson, cited in "The President's Choices in Iraq," ABC News opinion by Casimir Yost, November 29, 2006.

30   *U.S. Representative John Marshall* Marshall quoted in *The American Presidency*, Clinton Rossiter, New York: New American Library, 1956, 14.

31   *"The 'little touch of Harry'"* Dean Acheson, *Present at the Creation: My Years in the State Department*, New York: W.W. Norton & Company, 1969, 730.

32   *"it is easier to remove tyrants"* Harry S Truman, address to closing session of the founding conference of the United Nations, San Francisco, California, June 26, 1945.

32   *"Reagan's was an astonishing performance"* Henry Kissinger, *Diplomacy*, New York: Simon and Schuster, 1994, 764–65.

32   *"the CIA and [its director]"* George Shultz, *Turmoil and Triumph: My Years as Secretary of State,* New York: Charles Scribner's Sons, 1993, 84.

33   *George W. Bush reportedly told John McCain* Bob Woodward, *State of Denial*, New York: Simon and Schuster, 2007, 419.

33   *A June 2005 survey* See the Discovery channel website, dsc.discovery.com/convergence/greatestamerican/top100.html.

33   *"crisis of spirit"* Jimmy Carter, televised address, July 15, 1979.

33   *"too great for small dreams"* Ronald Reagan, quoted in *The American President*, Philip K. Kunhardt, Jr., Philip B. Kunhardt III, and Peter W. Kunhardt, New York: Riverhead Books, 1999, 299.

33   *"Mr. Gorbachev, tear down this wall"* Ronald Reagan, speech, Berlin, Germany, June 12, 1987.

34   *"Insist on yourself"* Ralph Waldo Emerson, "Self-Reliance," in *Ralph Waldo Emerson: Selected Prose and Poetry,* Reginald L. Cook (ed.), New York: Holt, Rinehart and Winston, 1950, 187.

34   *"experienced politicians of extraordinary temperament"* Richard E. Neustadt, *Presidential Power and the Modern Presidents*, New York: The Free Press, 1991, 207.

34   *"unselfconscious rootedness"* Ibid., 208.

35   *"I can understand the theory"* Gerald R. Ford, quoted in "Ford Disagreed with Bush About Invading Iraq," by Bob Woodward, *Washington Post,* December 28, 2006.

35   *"Why has Jesus Christ"* Woodrow Wilson, quoted in *The Presidential Character*, James David Barber, Englewood Cliffs, N.J.: Prentice Hall, 1972, 36.

36   *"There is coming a time"* Woodrow Wilson, statement, October 19, 1916.

36   *"no other nation has rested its claim"* Henry Kissinger, op. cit., 46.

37   *"We have about 50 percent of the world's wealth"* George F. Kennan, Policy Planning Study 23, *Foreign Relations of the United States*, Washington, D.C., U.S. Government Printing Office, 1948.

37   *"calling from beyond the stars"* George W. Bush, speech to the Republican National Convention, New York, September 1, 2004.

38   *"a new world order"* George H. W. Bush, address to joint session of Congress, September 11, 1990.

38   *"Morally, a failure to respond"* George H. W. Bush, remarks at Texas A&M University, College Station, Texas, December 15, 1992.

39   *"forward strategy for freedom"* George W. Bush, address to the National Endowment for Democracy, Washington, D.C., November 6, 2003.

THREE: THY STAFF SHALL COMFORT THEE

41   *"The choice of a prince's ministers"* Niccolò Machiavelli, *The Prince and the Discourses,* New York: Modern Library, 1950, 85.

41   *"priority attention be given immediately"* Transition Plan for President Elect Michael S. Dukakis, 1988, 78.

42   *As president elect, he was warned* Paul F. Boller, Jr., *Presidential Anecdotes*, New York: Oxford University Press, 1996, 135.

43   *"Every time I make an appointment"* William H. Taft, quoted in *Transition Plan for President Elect Michael S. Dukakis*, 154.

44   *"too many of State's upper-level career personnel"* Franklin D. Roosevelt, quoted in *FDR: My Boss*, Grace Tully, Chicago: Peoples Book Club, 1949, 175.

44   *"sprawling Washington and worldwide bureaucracy,"* Jimmy Carter, quoted in *Running the World,* David Rothkopf, New York: Public Affairs, 2005, 194.

44   *Henry Kissinger dismissed it as a backwater* Ibid., 118.

44   *Newt Gingrich referred to it scathingly* "Gingrich Urges Overhaul of State Department," Eric Schmitt, *New York Times,* June 18, 2003.

45   *"We're heading hell bent"* George Ball, quoted in Rothkopf, op. cit., 98.

46   *"No secretary of state is really important"* Richard Nixon, quoted in Roderick MacFarquhar, "Mission to Mao," *New York Review of Books,* June 28, 2007.

46   *The NSC's official purpose* Study prepared by Ferdinand Eberstadt, cited in a handwritten memo entitled "History of the NSC," prepared by Robert Gates during the Carter administration (1977–1981).

48   *"Bud always gave me the impression"* George Shultz, *Turmoil and Triumph: My Years as Secretary of State,* New York: Charles Scribner's Sons, 1993, 815.

49   *I found in my basement a handwritten assessment* Handwritten memo entitled "History of the NSC," prepared by Robert Gates during the Carter administration (1977–1981).

55   *"The chief embarrassment"* Woodrow Wilson, quoted in *The American Presidency,* Clinton Rossiter, New York: New American Library, 1956, 102.

55   *"isn't a crime exactly"* Finley Peter Dunne, *Mr. Dooley: Now and Forever,* Stanford, Calif.: Academic Reprints, 1954, 207–10.

FOUR: THE ART OF PERSUASION

62   *"It's true hard work never killed"* Ronald Reagan, quoted in *The American President,* Philip K. Kunhardt, Jr., Philip B. Kunhardt III, and Peter W. Kunhardt, New York: Riverhead Books, 1999, 300.

68   *She may adopt the tactful approach* Assessment of Franklin's diplomacy, contained in letter of Thomas Jefferson to Thomas Jefferson Randolph, November 24, 1808.

70   *"No man can tame a tiger"* Franklin Roosevelt, radio address, Washington, D.C., December 29, 1940.

71   *As he told Americans* Philip K. Kunhardt, Jr., op.cit., 195.

72   *"If you have a mother-in-law"* Lyndon Johnson, quoted in *Great Presidential Wit,* Bob Dole (ed.), New York: Simon and Schuster, 2002, 100.

73   *Andrei Gromyko, the longtime Soviet foreign minister* Over the years, this story about Gromyko has been told and re-told in Washington circles. I expect the incident occurred, but was not there and so can't prove it. The story was first told to me by Zbigniew Brzezinski.

75   *"America, in this young century"* George W. Bush, second inaugural address, Washington, D.C., January 20, 2005.

75   *Even Peggy Noonan* "Way Too Much God," Peggy Noonan, *Wall Street Journal,* January 21, 2005.

76   *Truman announced a broader initiative* Harry S Truman, inaugural address, Washington, D.C., January 20, 1949.

77   *According to Donald Rumsfeld* Donald Rumsfeld, "The World According to Rummy," *Washington Post,* October 8, 2006.

FIVE: FIFTY LADY SHARPSHOOTERS

81   *"I for one feel confident"* Letter signed Phoebe Ann Moses, *Dear Mr. President: Letters to the Oval Office from the Files of the National Archives,* text by Dwight Young, Washington, D.C.: National Geographic, 2005, 34–35.

81   *Herbert Hoover, quoting his Quaker uncle* Philip K. Kunhardt, Jr., Philip B. Kunhardt III, and Peter W. Kunhardt, *The American President,* New York: Riverhead Books, 1999, 283.

83   *"Only when our arms are sufficient"* John F. Kennedy, inaugural address, Washington, D.C., January 20, 1961.

83   *"Beware the twelve-division strategy,"* Gen. Eric Shinseki, cited in *In the Company of Soldiers,* Rick Atkinson, New York: Henry Holt & Company, 2005, 302.

85   *"The greatest contribution Vietnam is making"* Robert S. McNamara, quoted in *On Strategy: A Critical Analysis of the Vietnam War,* Harry G. Summers, Jr., New York: Dell, 1982, 42.

85   *"As military professionals we must speak out"* Fred Weyand, quoted in ibid., 68–69.

87   *"Given the goals of rogue states"* National Security Council, *National Security Strategy of the United States of America*, Washington, D.C., September 2002, 15.

87   *"We have to deal with this new type of threat"* Richard Cheney, quoted in *The One Percent Doctrine: Deep Inside America's Pursuit of Its Enemies Since 9/11*, Ron Suskind, New York: Simon and Schuster Paperbacks, 2006, 62.

87   *"Saddam Hussein was dangerous with weapons"* George W. Bush, *Meet the Press*, NBC News, February 8, 2004.

89   *In a speech at West Point in 1993* George H. W. Bush, West Point, N.Y., January 5, 1993.

91   *It was observed of James Cagney* Otis Ferguson, "Cagney: Great Guy," in *American Movie Critics: An Anthology from the Silents Until Now*, Phillip Lopate (ed.), New York: Library of America, 2006, 122.

SIX: BE SURE YOU'RE RIGHT; THEN GO AHEAD

99   *"Somewhere there must be a book"* Warren G. Harding, quoted in Paul F. Boller, Jr., *Presidential Anecdotes*, New York: Oxford University Press, 1996, 230.

101   *"frantic . . . white-water canoeist"* David Broder, *Washington Post*, February 2, 1977.

102   *"If you see ten troubles"* Calvin Coolidge, quoted in *The American President*, Philip K. Kunhardt, Jr., Philip B. Kunhardt III, and Peter W. Kunhardt, New York: Riverhead Books, 1999, 278.

103   *"The personal command post"* Richard E. Neustadt, *Presidential Power and the Modern Presidents*, New York: The Free Press, 1991, 172.

109   *"What if the Sicilians in terror combine against us"* Thucydides, *The Peloponnesian Wars*, New York: Washington Square Press, 1963, 199.

109   *"although some disapproved"* Euripides, cited in ibid., 200.

110   *"we come not to enslave you"* Ibid., 235.

110   *"Though we are supposed to be the besiegers"* Ibid., 256.

110   *"When [the Athenians] recognized the truth"* Ibid., 308.

SEVEN: THE LION AND THE LION-TAMERS

114   *"Half of a president's suggestions"* Jonathan Daniels, quoted in *The Purpose of American Politics*, Hans J. Morgenthau, New York: Alfred A. Knopf, 1960, 314.

114   *"The Treasury is so large"* Franklin Roosevelt, quoted in *Presidential Power and the Modern Presidents*, Richard E. Neustadt, New York: The Free Press, 1991, 37.

115   *During the Cuban missile crisis* Morton Halperin, *Bureaucratic Politics and Foreign Policy*, Washington, D.C.: Brookings Institution, 1974, 280.

115   *"If the president knows what he wants"* Harry S Truman, quoted in *Diplomacy*, Henry Kissinger, New York: Simon and Schuster, 1994, 425.

119   *"The country has come to feel"* Quotations from Will Rogers, www. quotationspage.com

122   *"our Printers were more discreet"* George Washington, quoted in *Decision-making in the White House*, Theodore C. Sorensen, New York: Columbia University Press, 1963, 55.

122   *"The man who reads nothing at all"* Thomas Jefferson, quoted in *Great Presidential Wit*, Bob Dole (ed.), New York: Simon and Schuster, 2002, 150.

122   *"a sort of assassin"* John Quincy Adams, quoted in ibid., 198.

122   *"Why is it that they have such an itching"* Martin van Buren, quoted in *Presidential Anecdotes*, Paul F. Boller, Jr., New York: Oxford University Press, 1996, 88.

122   *"villainous journalists"* Abraham Lincoln, quoted in *The Gettysburg Gospel,* Gabor Boritt, New York: Simon and Schuster, 2006, 57.

122   *In Pennsylvania, he procured kind coverage* Ibid., 60.

123   *The task of preserving an official record* Grace Tully, *FDR: My Boss*, Chicago: Peoples Book Club, 1949, 91.

123   *"If you give me a week"* Dwight D. Eisenhower, press conference, Washington, D.C., August 24, 1960.

124   *"We make it our business,"* Walter Lippmann, "The Job of the Washington Correspondent," *Atlantic Monthly*, January, 1960, 47–49.

124   *As soon as this directive became public* James Baker, *Work Hard, Study . . . and Keep Out of Politics*, New York: G.P. Putnam's Sons, 2006, 193–95.

126   *"Nothing has changed"* Caspar Weinberger, statement received third prize in National Council of Teachers' doublespeak competition for 1984, cited in www.csd.uwo.ca/staff/magi/personal/humour/General_Audience/Doublespeak.html.

127   *Political scientist Clinton Rossiter* Clinton Rossiter, *The American Presidency,* New York: New American Library, 1956, 53.

EIGHT: NEW FOUNDATIONS

131   *"There is something astonishing in American courage"* Paul Tillich, *The Courage to Be*, New Haven, Conn.: Yale University Press, 1952, 107–8.

132   *"The greatest asset of the Americans"* Victor Vinde, excerpted in *America in Perspective*, Henry Steele Commager (ed.), Chicago: Mentor Books, 1947, 328.

135   *the combination of mobility and fecundity*, "UN Predicts Population Explosion," Celia Dugger, *New York Times*, June 28, 2007.

140   *"the act, process or policy"* Webster's II, *New Riverside University Dictionary*, Boston: Riverside Publishing Company, 1984, 534.

140   *"No two countries"* Thomas Friedman, *The World Is Flat: A Brief History of the Twenty-first Century*, updated and expanded edition, New York: Farrar, Straus and Giroux, 2006, 522.

140   *"Contrary to popular belief,"* Kevin H. O'Rourke, research paper, "Europe and the Causes of Globalization," Dublin, Trinity College, 2.

141   *"It is impossible that old prejudices"* review of *The Victorian Internet: The Remarkable Story of the Telegraph and the Nineteenth Century's Online Pioneers*, author Tom Standage, Berkeley Publishing Group (1998), review is by Kimberly Patch, technology Research News, TRN Bookshelf, http://www.trnmag.com/Bookshelf/The%20Victorian%20Internet.html

142   *"Observers in the tail of our ship"* William T. Laurence, "Nagasaki, 9 August 1945," in John Carey (ed.), *Eyewitness to History*, New York: Avon Books, 1987, 637–38.

142   *"Within a few seconds"* Marcel Junod, "Visiting Hiroshima," in ibid., 639.

143   *"determination to help solve"* Dwight D. Eisenhower, "Atoms for Peace," address to the United Nations General Assembly, New York, N.Y., December 8, 1953.

143 *"suits me fine"* Ronald Reagan, quoted in *Reagan and Gorbachev*, Strobe Talbott and Michael Mandelbaum, Council on Foreign Relations book, New York: Vintage Books, 1987, 174.

144 *"have this cynical environment"* Mohamed ElBaradei, quoted in op-ed by Joseph Cirincione, *Los Angeles Times*, October 17, 2006.

146 *"I can't believe"* Ronald Reagan, quoted in *Diplomacy*, Henry Kissinger, New York: Simon and Schuster, 1994, 781.

148 *In Nigeria . . . satisfaction with democracy* Lydia Polgreen, "Africa's Crisis of Democracy," *New York Times*, April 22, 2007.

149 *"If we fail, then the whole world"* Winston Churchill, radio broadcast, London, June 18, 1940.

150 *Roosevelt, of course, rose from his wheelchair* This image is derived from a line in Mario Cuomo's address to the 1984 Democratic Convention: "Ever since Franklin Roosevelt lifted himself from his wheelchair to lift this nation from its knees." San Francisco, California, July 16, 1984.

150 *"no vision of a distant millennium"* Franklin Roosevelt, third inaugural address, Washington, D.C., January 20, 1941.

NINE: HOOPS OF IRON

153 *"the other great nations"* Tony Blair, speech to joint session of the United States Congress, Washington, D.C., July 17, 2003.

155 *"The crimes of the United States"* Harold Pinter, by video, from London to audience in Stockholm, December 7, 2005, quoted in "Art of the Impossible," *The Economist*, October 26, 2006.

157 *"missed an opportunity to shut up"* Jacques Chirac, quoted in "France Looks Ahead, and It Doesn't Look Good," Tony Judt, *New York Times*, April 22, 2007.

159 *a smaller percentage of Americans now think* Pew Global Attitudes Project, "Global Opinion Trends 2002–2007: A Rising Tide Lifts Mood in the Developing World," Pew Research Center, Washington, D.C., July 24, 2007.

161 *In 2000, almost eight out of every ten* Pew Global Attitudes Project, "Global Unease with Major World Powers," Pew Research Center, Washington, D.C., June 27, 2007, 13.

161 *"punish France, ignore Germany"* Condoleezza Rice, quoted in "Three Miscreants," Jim Hoagland, *Washington Post*, April 13, 2003.

165   *according to reputable studies* Livestock, Environment and Development Initiative, Food and Agriculture Organization of the United Nations, "Livestock's Long Shadow," Rome 2006.

168   *economic growth has been uneven* Joy Olson, executive director of the Washington Office on Latin America, testimony before the Committee on Foreign Affairs, Subcommittee on the Western Hemisphere, United States House of Representatives, Washington, D.C., March 28, 2007.

170   *"the devil that represents capitalism"* Hugo Chávez, quoted in "For Venezuela, as Distaste for U.S. Grows, So Does Trade," Simon Romero, *New York Times*, August 16, 2007.

173   *"According to a recent poll"* Jay Leno, quoted in Week in Review, *New York Times*, March 18, 2007.

174   *The offending candidate's name?* "County G.O.P. Asks Candidate to Withdraw Over Letter Threat," Cindy Chang, *Washington Post*, October 20, 2006.

TEN: AMERICA'S PLACE IN THE ASIAN CENTURY

178   *one U.S. diplomat complained* George Shultz, *Turmoil and Triumph: My Years as Secretary of State,* New York: Charles Scribner's Sons, 1993, 183.

181   *"all our clothes were given to us"* Ban Ki-moon, quoted in "For New UN Chief, a Past Misstep Leads to Opportunity," Warren Hoge, *New York Times*, December 9, 2006.

181   *U.S. efforts to open Korea to trade* Thomas Bender, *A Nation Among Nations: America's Place in World History*, New York: Hill and Wang, 2006, 200–206.

182   *"I don't have any anti-American sentiment"* Roh Moo-hyun, quoted in "A Turning Point: Democratic Consolidation in the ROK and Strategic Readjustment in the US-ROK Alliance," Alexandre Y. Mansourov (ed.), Asia-Pacific Center for Security Studies, Honolulu, Hawaii, 2005, 209.

187   *"praying for the souls"* Kim Il-sung, quoted in *Under the Loving Care of the Fatherly Leader: North Korea and the Kim Dynasty,* Bradley K. Martin, New York: Thomas Dunne Books, 2004, 27.

187   *the correlation cannot be accidental* Ibid., 261.

188   *"study history only to find the faults"* No Yong-Park, excerpted in *America in Perspective*, Henry Steele Commager (ed.), Chicago: Mentor Books, 1947, 292.

188   *In 2007, a survey reported* Pew Global Attitudes Project, "Global Opinion Trends 2002–2007: A Rising Tide Lifts Mood in the Developing World," Pew Research Center, Washington, D.C., July 24, 2007.

191   *Now, more people in more countries* Pew Global Attitudes Project, "Global Unease with Major World Powers," Pew Research Center, June 27, 2007, 9, 35.

195   *Reportedly, Chinese leaders backed away* Susan L. Shirk, *China: Fragile Superpower,* New York: Oxford University Press, 2007, 193.

196   *"Keeping U.S. forces deployed"* Ibid., 263.

ELEVEN: PRIDE AND PREJUDICE IN
RUSSIA AND SOUTH ASIA

202   *"a more democratic, open, transparent Russia"* John Edwards and Jack Kemp, "Russia's Wrong Direction," Task Force Report No. 57, Council on Foreign Relations, New York, March 2006.

202   *The czar is credited* B. H. Sumner, *Peter the Great and the Emergence of Russia*, London: English Universities Press Ltd., 1951, 31.

207   *"an almost uncontained hyper use of force"* Vladimir Putin, address to Forty-third Munich Conference on Security Policy, Munich, Germany, February 10, 2007.

210   *"Give them time"* George F. Kennan, *American Diplomacy* 1900–1950, Chicago: Mentor Books, New American Library, University of Chicago, 1951, 112.

213   *A recent survey of Indians* Pew Global Attitudes Project, "Global Unease with Major World Powers," Pew Research Center, Washington, D.C., June 27, 2007, 3.

215   *In his memoir* Pervez Musharraf, *In the Line of Fire: A Memoir*, New York: The Free Press, 2006.

217   *the chief minister of the North-West Frontier Province told me* Meeting between the author and Akram Khan Durrani, chief minister of Pakistan's North-West Frontier Province, Washington, D.C., July 15, 2005.

218   *"The once distant home"* Josef Korbel, *Danger in Kashmir* (rev. ed.), Princeton, N.J.: Princeton University Press, 1954, 304.

223   *In the past five years, we have given Pakistan some $10 billion* Article, "For Every Martyr Who Died, 2,000 Were Born," *FT.com Financial Times*, September 15, 2007.

TWELVE: ONE IRAQ IS ENOUGH

228   *"There is no meaning"* Feisal bin Hussein, quoted in *Desert Queen,* Janet Wallach, New York: Anchor Books, 1999, 314.

229   *"I am deeply concerned"* Letter from Winston S. Churchill to David Lloyd George, September 1, 1922, included in *Winston S. Churchill,* IV, Companion Volume Part 3, London: Heineman, 1977, 1973–74.

230   *In my last book* Madeleine Albright, *The Mighty and the Almighty: Reflections on America, God and World Affairs,* New York: HarperCollins, 2006, 172.

235   *"Iraq is not just one war,"* Philip Zelikow, "Plan Delta: Leveraging Power to Protect American Interests in Revolutionary Iraq," private paper quoted with permission, July 17, 2007.

238   *"If Iraq is to teach us anything"* Tom Ricks's Inbox, *Washington Post*, October 8, 2006.

239   *"It's 1938 and Iran is Germany"* Benjamin Netanyahu, quoted in "The Next Act," by Seymour Hersh, *The New Yorker*, November 11, 2006.

240   *"It was a day that should never"* CIA's secret history of the coup in Iran, cited in "How a Plot Convulsed Iran in 1953," James Risen, *New York Times*, April 16, 2000.

244   *"Of one Essence"* The translation from Saadi Shirazi's poem is credited to Iraj Bashiri.

THIRTEEN: MIDDLE EAST: THE POWER TO CHOOSE

251   *"One of the important things,"* Baruch Goldstein, quoted in "Goldstein's Effect on History Not How It Was Meant to Be." Aaron D. Maslow, *Seattle Post-Intelligencer*, March 10, 1994.

256   *"become part of the free world,"* Ariel Sharon, quoted in *Lebanon: Death of a Nation*, Sandra Mackey, New York: Anchor Books, Doubleday, 1989, 174.

256   *modeled by its founder on Hitler's Nazi Youth* Gemayel family, Encyclopedia Britannica Online, 2007, http://www.britannica.com/eb/article-9036339.

260   *In response to a 2007 survey question* Pew Global Attitudes Project, "Global Unease with Major World Powers," Pew Research Center, Washington, D.C., June 27, 2007, 56.

263   *As the psalmist warns* Psalm 55, verse 21.

268   *"We've all been attacked by the bacteria of stupidity"* Ghazi Hamad, quoted in "From Hamas Figure, an Unusual Self-Criticism," Steven Erlanger, *New York Times,* August 28, 2006.

268   *"The overwhelming majority of Israeli citizens"* David Grossman, address at peace rally in Tel Aviv, reprinted in *Yedioth Ahronoth,* November 3, 2006.

FOURTEEN: ISOLATING AL QAEDA

274   *We have also established a list* "Safeguarding Amish County Popcorn," *Indianapolis Star,* July 15, 2006.

278   *"if you call it a war"* Richard Myers, quoted in "Washington Recasts Terror War as 'Struggle,'" by Eric Schmitt and Thom Shanker, *New York Times,* July 27, 2005.

FIFTEEN: ABOVE THE THUNDERING ABYSS

291   *of great obscurity to those who lived through it* Dean Acheson, *Present at the Creation: My Years in the State Department,* New York: W.W. Norton and Company, 1969, 3–4.

292   *It was said of FDR* Grace Tully, *FDR: My Boss,* Chicago: People's Book Club, 1949, 65.

295   *"that in due time"* Abraham Lincoln, speech in Independence Hall, Philadelphia, Pa.., February 22, 1861.

295   *"Gentlemen, do you remember"* Abraham Lincoln, composite derived from citations in *Great Presidential Wit,* by Bob Dole (ed.), New York: Simon and Schuster, 2001, 35–36; and in "Abraham Lincoln's Classroom: Abraham Lincoln and Public Opinion, The Lincoln Institute, www.abrahamlincolnsclassroom.org/Library/newsletter.asp?ID=124&CRLI=172.

Acknowledgments

I like to travel and don't find it wearing, so I was taken aback recently when a middle-aged woman came up to me at an airport and exclaimed, "You look great! Just like my grandmother. She's one hundred and six and fit and sharp as she can be."

There are times when saying "thanks" doesn't quite seem to be enough.

Presidents rely on teamwork; so do authors. This is my third book since the end of my tenure as secretary of state. Once again, I am grateful to have had the benefit of a first-rate cabinet, especially two people who are friends and with whom I have worked for decades: Bill Woodward, whose brilliant writing and research is matched only by a truly distinctive temperament and variation on the concept of charm; and Elaine Shocas, who has superb judgment and continues to help me decide what to say and, more important, what not to say. I have learned to have supreme confidence in my legal counselors Bob Barnett,

Deneen Howell, and Jacqueline Davies, who—unlike some attorneys general I could name—always steer me in the right direction. Ever reliable, too, is Richard Cohen, my multitalented editor whose keen intelligence improved the text immensely and whose probing questions caused me to recall experiences I had forgotten (or repressed). Special thanks are also due to the sharp-eyed, quick-witted, and seemingly inexhaustible Raj Salooja, who worked long hours to assist with research and reconcile conflicting information.

I was delighted once more to have the support of the highly skilled and uniformly gracious members of the HarperCollins family—including Jane Friedman, Michael Morrison, Jonathan Burnham, Kathy Schneider, Tina Andreadis, Archie Ferguson, Sandy Hodgman, Campbell Wharton, Allison Lorentzen, and Tara Cook—each of whom contributed to this project. I worked most closely with executive editor Tim Duggan, who encouraged me at every stage while also helping to iron out rough spots in the draft. Photographer Timothy Greenfield Sanders and his team have, once more, demonstrated exactly the right touch in creating a picture that conveys a mood, making it easier to tell my story.

I could not be more grateful to friends who kindly took the time to read and provide helpful comments on all or parts of the draft: Carol Browner, Les Campbell, Jean Dunn, Lee Feinstein, Jen Friedman, Wini Shore Freund, Suzy George, Evelyn Lieberman, Jim O'Brien, John Podesta, Steve Richetti, Lula Rodriguez, Susan Shirk, Wendy Sherman, Jamie Smith, Ken Wollack, and Fariba Yassaee. Authors, again like presidents, benefit from the wise counsel of their families, and I am eternally in debt to mine for their help, advice, and, on occasion, permission to cast them in quasi-embarrassing anecdotes. I thank my daughters, Alice, Anne, and Katie, my brother John Korbel, and especially my sister, Kathy Silva, who came through as she always does, reviewing the text, making suggestions, providing a fresh perspective. I am grateful, as well, to our friend Carl Cortese, who did the same. I also want to express appreciation to my colleagues Anna Cronin-Scott, Kristin Cullison, Margo Morris, Natalie Orpett, and Elizabeth Raulston for their invaluable encouragement and assistance on a daily basis.

Finally, I am obliged to all the former foreign ministers, students, friends, acquaintances, and total strangers whom I asked, "What advice would you give to the next president?" You know who you are; thank you for your patience and for the benefit of your thoughts, passion, and ideas.

Index